CONTENTS

ACKNOWLEDGMENTS

The editors would like to acknowledge the following manuscript reviewers: Therese Bigelow, Virgil Blake, Roberta Brody, Joan Durrance, Raya Fidel, Kwong Bor Ng, and Nancy P. Thomas.

INTRODUCTION

Mary K. Chelton and Colleen Cool

The study of youth information-seeking behavior transcends several different areas of scholarly and practical concern, spanning multiple scholarly disciplines over several decades. It includes work on human information behavior, which originated within information science; studies within the school library media context, which examined information technology implementation and use within school settings; information literacy instruction and learning; and the design of technology for instruction within the field of instructional design. All of these disciplines are represented in this collection.

The essays throughout this volume represent a variety of approaches to understanding how children and young adults seek, process, and use information in its variety of forms in order to satisfy some goal. Although the terms "youth" and "children" are often interchangeable, our concern in this book is not with the prelinguistic child. Although this area of concern is indeed fascinating and increasingly important, we have limited our focus to the active information-seeking behaviors of young people who have developed beyond the picture book stage.

For the most part, the material in this book is organized in chronological order, in order to demonstrate the development of the literature. However, a thematic organizational structure is superimposed. The final chapter is a selected, ongoing bibliography on this topic, provided to help those who want to pursue further scholarly research in this area.

First, we provide a lengthy historical background to the study of how children and youth have used electronic information systems over the course of information-seeking episodes and experiences. This period of scholarship roughly covers 1980–1990. During this early period, attention to children's use of electronic databases did not develop out of a well-formed theoretical framework. Instead, research reflected the pragmatic concerns of librarians and educators who saw a need to train students in the effective use of these new information resources. With the growing awareness that information technologies were shaping both the role of information in society and the nature of information retrieval, the development of information skills was given a high priority and was formulated within the context of teaching library skills. This attention came primarily from those working within the school systems.

The development of "information literacy" became a priority, and with the appearance of electronic information sources in school, there was a strongly felt need to teach children skills in the use of these systems. Computer literacy and information literacy were treated as related goals. Teaching information skills was cast within the larger framework of developing skills for lifelong learning. Those who called for the development of information literacy were not always clear what this development involved in a concrete sense or how the evaluation of the effectiveness of such an effort might be determined. Such a lack of specificity has led to an unclear picture of which techniques have been successful and which have not. Answers to this question require specifying the meaning of "success" in the acquisition of information literacy.

Researchers during this period asked questions about the ability of students to use electronic information systems effectively and to a lesser extent about the effect of these retrieval services on students' information-seeking capabilities. The focus was very much technology driven and performance based. There was little attention to questions about the "information needs" of children and how these needs might be served by new technologies. An underlying assumption was that one of the child's most important information needs was to learn to use these new information services. For the most part, questions were not asked about the ways in which children search for information in general or about the cognitive processes involved in information retrieval.

The early stages of research in this area did not focus on studying the information-seeking behaviors of children with the goal of determining whether electronic database retrieval could function in support of these behaviors. Research was developed after the technology was already in place, leading to a focus on the effectiveness of new technologies. This narrow focus has limited our ability to develop a more general understanding of youth information-seeking behavior, in and out of the school environment, with and without the use of electronic information retrieval systems.

The development of more general models of the information-seeking process among youth began in the early 1990s and extended to the present. A central concern is the importance of processes of cognitive development and how they impact information behaviors and learning. The period following 1990 can be characterized as less "practically oriented" and more "theoretically concerned." Thus, the beginning of this decade brought the rise of researchers who endeavored to develop a more general understanding of the information-seeking process among youth, across different contexts, and with a variety of information resources, electronic and online. The emphasis here was to better understand how children and young adults sought information in response to tasks, problems, and goals. Perhaps the major contribution of this early research was the discovery that information seeking is inherently process oriented, that it takes place over time, and that any single point in the process represents only a partial snapshot of the entire information-seeking episode.

The very well known name of Carol Collier Kuhlthau must be mentioned as one of the formative figures in the development of this stage-based approach to understanding youth information-seeking behavior. Kuhlthau's research (chapter 2) with high school students and their information-seeking behaviors over the course of completing a term project led to the development of a model she labels the information search process (ISP), which consists of seven stages covering topic initiation through task completion. The major contribution of Kuhlthau's ISP model is the insight that information seeking over the course of a specific task or goal is an iterative, rather than a linear, process, and that each stage in the process may be associated with affective, or emotional, states that can impede or perhaps facilitate movement in the process. In further development of this model, she has recommended "zones of intervention" for overcoming problematic stages in the ISP, which are based on Zygotsky's *Thought and Language* (1986) "zones of proximal learning."

Delia Neuman, whose doctorate is in instructional design, gives us insight into the field of youth information-seeking research during its second decade when she examined the use of electronic information resources as venues for the mastery of higher-order thinking skills in the school context. Her research review reprinted in chapter 3 summarizes insights that can be extended to learning and digital libraries, while distinguishing between digital and traditional print environments. She documented the conceptual naiveté that stymied novice student searchers in their information seeking and documented the chasm that existed between the rather basic needs of the students and the complexity of the resources they were using. She points out that "it is also important to make room in the digital library for information that is conceptually accessible to, and useful for, a student audience whose interests, needs, abilities, and goals make them a truly unique user group."

This period also saw initial attention to the ethics of information seeking, represented in chapter 4 by Joy McGregor and Denise Streitenberger's classic study on student writing and information seeking for research papers and plagiarism, culminating in the social responsibility standards of *Information Power.* Diane Nahl and Violet Harada, in chapter 5, examine variables influencing student self-confidence in an experiment that tests their abilities to interpret and construct search statements in a presearch activity. In chapter 6, Jinx Stapleton Watson suggests that researchers should use naturalistic inquiry methods to study how children construct meaning from their searching experiences. In an attempt to understand children's information seeking and use, Linda Cooper (chapter 7) has studied the ways in which children intuitively organize materials they believe fit into a library, in ways that match their own cognitive classification systems rather than formal library structures such as the Library of Congress or Dewey Decimal systems. The crux of her argument is that children simply think differently from adults, and these differences are related directly to developmental stages that children grow through. In other words, they ultimately "learn" how to be library users in order to conform to the ways in which adults have constructed the organization of materials they wish to access. Learning to become a library user is a socialization process, and those who do not become socialized into the proper ways of using the library are blocked from access to it.

Looking specifically at the nature of children's questions posed to librarians and other information providers, Melissa Gross (chapter 8) has developed a model that dichotomizes their questions into the "imposed query," where the question or information need has been given to the child by someone else, and the "self-generated query," which reflects an information problem that arises from the child's own interests. The classic example of the imposed query is the term paper assignment typically assigned in school; however, other examples can also be given, such as the topics imposed on teachers themselves through curricular goals. Gross's contention is that information providers need to recognize the differences between these types of queries in order to understand users' attitudes toward the information sought and to provide effective assistance. In chapter 9, Sandra Hirsch revisits her earlier work on children's search behavior in conjunction with the development of the Science Library Catalog, concluding that the opportunity to use multiple search options enabled most children to use the system effectively, but differences in success rates were evident based on level of domain knowledge.

The next section of this book focuses explicitly on the ways in which children and young adults use the World Wide Web for information-seeking purposes, an area of tremendous concern and research activity at this time. Two very prolific writers in this area—Dania Bilal and Andrew Large—provide comprehensive background literature on this topic. In chapter 10, Bilal provides a thorough overview of the variety of ways in which researchers have approached the problems of understanding how children retrieve, use, and evaluate information on the Web. She takes a more specific look at some of the difficulties children have in effectively exploiting the resources of the Web, even though they and their teachers appreciate the wealth of information resources to be found there.

A running theme throughout most of the literature dealing with children's use of the Web focuses on the inherent problems that arise when an information resource such as the Web appears to be easy to use but is in fact far more difficult to use appropriately and effectively. In chapter 11, Large points out that the continued presence of the Web constitutes a rich, global information resource for students, including those in elementary schools, to be exploited in support of their class projects. At the same time, these students appear to be encountering considerable difficulties in exploiting the Web's full potential, and he suggests what might be done to improve this situation.

The final section of the book addresses personal, as opposed to school-based, information seeking and suggests future issues and concerns in this area. In chapter 13, Ross Todd and Susan Edwards deal directly with the very real and important issues of how adolescents seek and utilize information related to drugs. Drawing heavily on earlier frameworks developed by Elfreda Chapman (1996), Todd takes a holistic perspective on drug information-seeking behavior that locates drug use and information seeking about drugs within a larger social matrix, which includes friends, locally developed social norms about appropriate and inappropriate drug use, and perceptions about risks and benefits of using drugs, relative to information about it. This study is especially interesting because it combines multiple methods of investigation, including interviews with the adolescents themselves.

Somewhat related to the approach taken by Todd, Heidi Julien (chapter 12) studied the information-seeking behaviors that went into adolescents' decision making about careers, an increasingly important topic, which has received little research attention thus far. Julien draws upon sense-making theory, Kuhlthau's ISP, and decision-making theory to investigate career-making decisions made by adolescents. One of her findings was that although the decision-making process was not a linear process, Kuhlthau's ISP model did not fit this particular situation. Other factors, such as the type of decision faced and the degree of formality of information consulted, were more important predictors of information-seeking behavior about career decisions.

It is our hope that by putting as much of this research as possible in one place we will enable students and researchers to learn about and expand upon what has been done, even though much remains to be accomplished.

ONE

Information-Seeking Behaviors of Children Using Electronic Information Services during the Early Years: 1980–1990

Colleen Cool

The decade of 1980–1990 witnessed an explosion of computer-based information systems. It is not an exaggeration to say that electronic information systems of all varieties have changed the way we live and think. Although this information is typically discussed in terms of the adult world, people are increasingly exposed to these information systems at ever-earlier ages. How children and young adults come to understand and utilize electronic information systems in the pre-Web and in the current Web environment will be a critical area for information scientists, instructional designers, and educators to explore.

This chapter reviews the early literature on youth information-seeking behavior, published between 1980–1990, in order to contextualize the research that follows. It raises questions about the theoretical frameworks and issues within which this body of research developed, the nature of the research questions that were addressed, and the methods used. Taken with the rest of the essays in this book, this chapter contributes to our understanding of youth information-seeking behavior over a two-decade span—before and after the World Wide Web. In reviewing the body of scientific research that has developed in this area, we can trace an evolution from a focus on technology-driven questions about effectiveness and performance to a more integrative perspective that incorporates recent theoretical developments in the field of information science. Overall, we see a shift from a systems-oriented approach to a more user-oriented focus in this work, which parallels changes in the thinking that has occurred in the study of human information behavior in general, as discussed more fully in the next chapter.

THE IMPORTANCE OF STUDYING CHILDREN'S USE OF ELECTRONIC DATABASES: EARLY FRAMEWORKS

Early attention to the study of children's use of electronic databases did not develop out of a well-formed theoretical framework. Instead, this attention reflected the pragmatic concerns of librarians and educators who saw a need to train students in the effective use of these new information resources. With the growing awareness that information technologies were shaping both the role of information in the society and the nature of information retrieval, the development of information skills was made a high priority and was formulated within the context of teaching library skills. This attention came primarily from those working within the school systems. The development of information literacy became a priority, and with the appearance of electronic information sources in school, there was a strongly felt need to teach children skills in the use of these systems. Computer literacy and information literacy were treated as related goals (Kuhlthau, 1987). Teaching information skills was cast within the larger framework of developing skills for lifelong learning (Cleaver, 1987).

Those who called for the development of information literacy were not always clear what this development was to involve in a concrete sense, or how the evaluation of the effectiveness of such an effort might be determined. Such a lack of specificity led to an unclear picture of which techniques have been successful. Answers to this question require specifying the meaning of success in the acquisition of information literacy.

Addressing the rationale for teaching students to use online databases, Mancall and Desking (1984) stressed the value of preparing students for the world of tomorrow. They presented a set of guidelines to help school media specialists design appropriate curricula for instruction in online retrieval. Aversa (1985) also reviewed methods for teaching online searching skills to students. Borrowing from Borgman et al. (1984), they suggested a distinction between the teaching of "system independent" skills, related to processes of information retrieval itself, and "system dependent" skills, related to the effective operating of the specific database.

In later writing, Aversa (1988) developed a framework that suggested the advantages and disadvantages of online searching for high school students, with goals for teaching online searching to students. Among the believed advantages of online searching were the ability to access information outside of the school library and the ability to retrieve more current references than is possible with print sources. The disadvantages of online searching were the frustration caused by retrieving citations to references not immediately available, system technical difficulties, and the possible inappropriateness of a single-concept approach to the searching strategies of all students. Among her suggested goals for teaching online skills were training students to become knowledgeable information searchers and assisting them to refine their information searches. She urged that students be taught broader information searching skills that go beyond the learning of specific system commands.

Writing from a similar perspective, Montgomery (1987) argued that the development of library media literacy, which involved the effective use of all available information sources, had to include not only the mechanics of how to work the system, but also the development of cognitive processes of categorization, concept formation, and symbol manipulation. She further indicated some of the ways in which the development of information literacy parallels the development of reading, and suggested that teachers adopt similar strategies in their teaching of both sets of skills.

Ward-Callaghan (1987) discussed new information technologies related to children's library services and suggested a future role for librarians as "instructors in strategy," rather than as information providers as they had been in the past. She saw these new technologies leading to different roles between children and librarians in public libraries, with children becoming increasingly closer to "independent learners."

In a departure from the uncritical acceptance of new technology, Hooten (1989) questioned the extent to which online catalogs would effectively improve children's ability to access materials. She discussed the different skills needed to retrieve material online versus manual searching. Card catalogs required users to have the ability to understand alphabetical ordering, to know the filing structure, and to recognize specific information elements, such as call letters, on the card. Online catalogs with touch screen terminals require similar skills in alphabetizing and filing. However, Hooten suggested that these catalogs might be harder than card catalogs for children to use. Touch screens were less concrete than card catalogs. Using the card catalog, children could see the physical distance between two entries and estimate where a third might fall in between them. The touch screen online catalog required users to make the same kind of distance judgments, but without the concrete context clues.

The skills required in keyboard terminals were different altogether. Instead of browsing and "recognizing," the user had to "recall" keyword terms. Accuracy of spelling and punctuation became important here, along with the ability to associate the keyword with the right category on the screen.

Hooten's point, as well as those cited above by Aversa and Montgomery, was that although new information technologies had great potential to improve the information literacy of students, it should not be assumed that the development of this literacy or ability would follow a steady course. All three researchers cautioned that there may be variables that haven't been considered that influence whether a young person has success with the system.

These writings, coming primarily from those working in school library settings, reflect concerns about the child's ability to use new information systems. At the same time, a large literature base documented the appearance and use of online retrieval sources in schools. The purpose of these general usage surveys was to profile "who was using what" and to provide some descriptive information about the perceived benefits of new information systems to students, along with observations about the ways in which new information technologies can be implemented and integrated into the curriculum. These general surveys, although they discussed children's behaviors with information retrieval systems, were not designed to test any ideas about children's information-seeking behavior but to provide a descriptive picture of the use of these systems in the school.

Profiles of Use and the User

A number of articles catalog the extent to which electronic information services were adopted in school libraries. Many of these articles provide anecdotal accounts of the benefits derived from these information sources along with descriptions of the way students use them.

A special issue of *Online* (May 1987) presented a series of user reports from high schools that used online retrieval services (Aversa and Mancall, 1987; Dowling and Pruitt, 1987; Epler, 1987; Fiebert, 1987; Lodish, 1987; Lynch, 1987). According to these articles, online services were most frequently found in high school libraries and only rarely in elementary school environments. The most frequently used service at the time was *Dialog*, reported in use by over 50 percent of the high schools responding to the survey. Overall, the most frequently searched databases tended to be broad, general sources such as *Magazine Index*, not specialized databases in scientific or technological areas. The profiles presented in the articles tended to stress the success, rather than the problems, that high schools had had in adopting online services. One of the biggest benefits, as reported there, was the access to a wider network of materials.

Tenopir (1986) provided another overall survey of the use of online retrieval services in high schools. One of the benefits she highlighted was that students developed logical thinking and problem-solving skills in their use of these databases. Pruitt and Dowling (1985) report that after two years of availability, student users in twenty-two area high schools that used *Dialog* tended to use the retrieval service most often for projects in social sciences and current affairs. The authors noted that before online retrieval became available, students had difficulty researching "hot" contemporary topics, because the first person to the library usually exhausted all of the sources. Furthermore, print indexes did not have up-to-the-minute information and, in addition, the subject headings did not reflect contemporary usages—for example, "teen suicide" did not appear as a heading in the early days of interest in this topic. The authors mentioned briefly that the students were able to acquire the skills necessary for searching *Dialog*, and they offered examples of how to search the system.

In a 1990 article on the use of online services in a South Brunswick, New Jersey, school, Kuhlthau and Sherman (1990) described the use of *Dow Jones/News Retrieval* in an elementary school. This menu-driven system required only the most basic keyboard skills of the user, and the stated benefits were developments in critical thinking and increased motivation to search for information.

Clyde and Kirk (1989) further report on a survey of the growing use of online information systems in Australian schools. They found online systems used in a variety of curriculum areas, along with recreational uses, in elementary as well as high schools. The primary benefit reported by the schools was faster access to information and access to more current information than had been available to them previously. Other profiles of Australian school use of electronic databases can be found in Hancock (1989) and Oley (1989).

The underlying model guiding the descriptive surveys reviewed to this point is one in which electronic information retrieval systems were expected to have a positive effect on children's information retrieval abilities. Questions were not asked in this model about the ways in which children searched for information in general, or about the conditions under which electronic "traditional" information sources facilitated these cognitive behaviors.

The literature cited above also gives an idea of the framework within which research on children's use of electronic databases has developed. Early research in this area developed in an environment in which questions were asked about the ability of students to effectively use electronic information systems and, to a lesser extent, about the effect of these retrieval services on students' information-seeking capabilities. An underlying assumption was that one of the child's most important information needs was to learn to use these new information services. For the most part, questions were not asked about the ways in which children search for information in general, or about the cognitive processes involved in information retrieval. The early stages of research in this area did not pay much attention to studying the information-seeking behaviors of children with the goal of determining whether or not electronic database retrieval could function in support of these behaviors. Research was developed after the technology was already in place, leading to a focus on questions about the effectiveness of new technologies. This narrow focus limited the ability to develop a more general understanding of the information-seeking behavior of youth, in and out of the school environment, with or without the use of electronic information retrieval systems.

In one of the few examples of research focusing on youth's actual information-seeking behaviors, Kuhlthau (1988) studied the information search process (ISP) of high school students over the course of their research for a term paper topic. From her findings, she developed a model of the ISP, which attempts to identify the psychological states associated with different stages in the model. The beginning stages of the ISP are characterized by feelings of uncertainty, gradually changing to feelings of confidence and optimism as the topic is formulated and the search for information is begun. It appears as if a next step in this line of research will be to identify the specific information retrieval behaviors that correspond to the stages in her model and to evaluate where and to what extent electronic retrieval services fit in.

In another example of research in the area of youth information-seeking behaviors, Shoham and Getz (1988) studied the bibliographic searching behaviors of two hundred Israeli high school students, looking for patterns in the search process and for correlations between these patterns and characteristics of the searcher. They argued for more "user-oriented" research in the area of children's information searching and attempted to close the gap. Students were given a self-administered questionnaire that asked them to reconstruct their bibliographic searching behaviors during the course of researching a final paper. Three patterns were identified in the study: "simple," characterized by reliance on informal channels of communication and use of few information sources; "intermediate," in which informal channels were also relied on, along with a wider range of information sources and use of more complicated reference tools; and "sophisticated" patterns, which are characterized by the use of the many different information sources. The authors found a correlation between search pattern, treated as a continuum from simple to sophisticated, and receiving instruction about the project from an advisor. No correlation between search pattern type and parents' education was found. This study could have made a contribution along the lines envisioned by the authors if it had provided more detail about the behaviors involved in the searching itself. It is also unclear how reliable the retrospective method of data collection is in this study, especially when it was the only method employed.

The studies by Kuhlthau and by Shoham and Getz attempted to understand something about the information search process among adolescents. There are few older studies with this orientation. The empirical work that has been done in the area of youth information seeking with electronic databases falls into two broad approaches: system-oriented studies, which attempt to evaluate the child's performance with the system, and the user-oriented studies, which attempt to understand some of the cognitive processes involved in information seeking and searching with electronic retrieval systems-searching behavior.

SYSTEM-ORIENTED STUDIES

System-oriented studies, which dominated early research in this area, attempted to systematically evaluate the ability of young users to effectively retrieve information from electronic information systems. Some of this work also pays attention to the effects of the system itself on system or user variables. For the most part, this research is an extension of the thinking discussed above.

Bibliographic Retrieval Using Online Services

One of the areas quickest to develop in response to the calls for evaluation of online retrieval sources was the study of children's use of online catalogs. Other studies of general bibliographic searching online soon followed. There are two general types of studies in this area. The first primarily focuses on the effectiveness of online versus manual retrieval. The second analyzes materials retrieved online compared to those retrieved manually, along with the study of the relevance judgments made by children in their decisions to use or not use materials retrieved through online bibliographic sources.

Effectiveness of OPACs versus Manual Methods

An early example of research on the effectiveness of online catalogs was the study conducted by the Alberta Department of Education (1983). The goals of this research were to see if students in grades 1–6 could effectively use the automated card catalog and to test the relationship between use of the online public access catalog (OPAC) and development of computer literacy in general. Although no sample sizes are provided, students in grades 2 and 5 were selected to participate in the study. Tests of computer literacy were administered before and after several months' use of the online catalog. Interviews were also administered to the same students to determine their overall evaluation of the OPAC, their problems in using it, and the benefits they derived from using it. An additional "sampling" of impressionistic interviews was conducted with students in grades 1, 3, 4, and 6. In addition to the interview data, circulation records were examined and librarians were questioned about their impressions.

Results of this study indicate no difference in pre- and post-test measures of computer literacy based on exposure to the OPAC. Based on the interview data, the researchers discovered that the online catalog was associated with increased use and greater overall interest in the library than was the case before automation. However, circulation figures indicate no increase in the number of materials being checked out. We don't know from this data if the children merely *thought* they were visiting the library more, or if in fact the online catalog stimulated greater frequency of visits.

The authors also report that students across all grade levels, except grade 1, had little difficulty using the automated card catalog. Students reportedly found the online catalog easier to use because it overcame the difficulties of alphabetical ordering. On the negative side, students reported frustration in having to wait in line at the school library to use the OPAC and frustration with the keyboard layout.

An interesting finding of this study concerns the nature of the role relationships between student and librarian. After the implementation of the OPAC, the amount of time spent between student and librarian was the same, but the nature of their interaction was different. Librarians reported that they were spending more time assisting students in finding materials that had already been retrieved from the OPAC, and less time answering questions about either the card catalog or what materials might solve the students' questions.

Another evaluation of the effectiveness of OPAC, this one conducted with children using public libraries, is reported by Edmonds, Moore, and Balcom (1989). The purpose of this research was to assess the ability of children in grades 4, 6, and 8 to use online and card catalogs. The researchers began with questions about the developmental abilities of children and the skills necessary to conduct online searches. The Illinois public library where the study was done had both online and card catalogs available, with the online system accessed by a touch screen terminal. The researchers used both observations and interviews to study the ability of students to successfully complete a title, author, or subject search on either the online or card catalog. Data were gathered on the techniques used by the students in their searches along with their final success in locating the call number of the assigned search item.

A sample of 207 students took part in the study as part of a school visit. A general skills test was given to the children before the search to determine their ability to alphabetize and file appropriately. Results of the study show that students had higher success rates with, and stronger preference for, the card catalog. Success with both the card and online catalogs increased with age, but the difference between the age groups was more dramatic for the OPAC. Only 4 percent of the fourth graders versus 51 percent of the eighth graders found the item in the online catalog. Using the card catalog, 31 percent of fourth graders and 68 percent of eighth graders were successful.

The authors made some interesting observations about the searching behaviors of the children. In using the card catalog, fourth graders were more likely to search card by card, ignoring the guides that appeared in the drawer. Older children looked first for the labels on the drawers, then looked at the guides within, and finally went for the right card. In using the touch screen, younger children had fewer touches per search on average, reflecting their tendency to give up early on in the search. All students made fewer mistakes and corrected more of them when they used the card catalog.

The authors concluded that the online catalog has too many steps for children who are familiar with the simple search routine involved in using the card catalog. Fourth graders are believed to be "developmentally unready" for the type of searching involved in manipulation of the OPAC. The touch screens offered eleven items to read and eleven choices to make. Also, the entry screen was too difficult for many to read, because it contained too much information and too high a percentage of print to screen.

This study is interesting because it discussed children's information searching behavior within a larger context of developmental differences. The authors argued that the reasons for the differences between fourth and eighth graders is that developmentally, the younger group is at the stage of what Piaget has termed "concrete operations," in which trial and error problem-solving skills are commonly used. This is reflected in their approaches to the card catalog. By sixth, seventh, or eighth grade, children have moved into the stage of "formal operations" in which they have developed the ability to use logic and apply rule-based decision making.

One might question why the study conducted by Alberta Department of Education shows that children had no difficulty using the online catalog, and the study by Edmonds et al. found otherwise. The measure of "success" with the system may have been different. Edmonds et al. used very specific criteria—retrieval of a specific piece of information—while the Alberta study relied on the students' impressions of their own difficulty with the system. Also, there may have been differences between the touch screen and keyword access methods, but we can't really evaluate these differences from the data provided in these reports.

Effectiveness of Other Online Bibliographic Services

Craver (1985) reports on the effectiveness of a program designed to teach online searching behaviors to high school seniors who had had experience with OPACs. As part of research for a debate project, students were given instruction in the basics of online searching terminology, knowledge of available databases, and knowledge of thesauri. This study did not attempt to examine the ways in which students formulate their own searches. Its approach was to present the children with a model of the ideal search and then to evaluate how well they adopted it.

Four classes of high school students were involved in the project where they were told to formulate an appropriate search for an assigned topic. Students designed the search strategy, selected a database, and looked at its thesaurus. The school librarian conducted the actual search. According to the author, the results of this study demonstrate the effectiveness of the teaching approach used. Students' scores on a test of knowledge about online searching were high. During the actual search, students were involved in the decision-making process to pursue a sequence of steps or to abort the search. Unfortunately, this aspect of the data was not developed more fully in this study, and nothing was conveyed about how the children made these decisions, or even about the nature of the decisions that were made. This study also missed an opportunity to study the nature of the interaction between students and the intermediary searchers.

One of the weaknesses of the "effectiveness" studies of this era is that they did not apply uniform criteria to the measurement of "performance" with the system, nor did any of them apply stringent performance criteria. "Ability to use," in the sense of retrieving the material or in terms of believing that the system was useful, was how many of these studies defined effective performance. Very little can be known from this research about the nature of the decision making that was involved in searching for materials electronically versus manually.

Analysis of Materials Retrieved

In one of the earliest reported studies of online bibliographic searching among children, Wozny (1982) studied the materials used by ninth-grade students using online and card catalogs in their research for an assigned paper topic. After receiving basic instruction in online bibliographic searching, students were told to use print indexes to narrow their topic, to formulate a searchable query, and then to perform their search with the assistance of the media specialist. The focus of this research was on the materials retrieved and, from these, the materials used in the final report.

Wozny based her analysis on an examination of the students' bibliographies; results of interviews with students, teachers, and library media specialists; as well as printouts from the online searches. Comparing the materials cited in these bibliographies with earlier research conducted without online searching, Wozny found a wider variety of materials used and less reliance on books. Looking at the online printouts and comparing them to the bibliographies, Wozny found that a majority (81 percent) of the students did not cite any of the materials that were retrieved from online sources. Less than 5 percent of all references in the bibliographies were from online sources.

One of the goals of the research assignment was to develop searching abilities among the students. Not having database thesauri available to them, the students relied on their own natural language keyword terms in formulating their searches. These were developed as they worked their way through the print indexes. Wozny found that students sometimes reformulated their search terms after examining the online descriptors. Little detail is provided about the nature of the children's success or failure in developing good search terms in the absence of a thesaurus. This study also did not ask questions about the reasons for accepting or rejecting materials that were retrieved online or about the relevance judgments made by the children.

In a similar study, Mancall and Desking (1984) analyzed the bibliographies of 132 high school students who had used online searching in the course of researching a self-selected term paper topic. In this project, librarians conducted the searches, which had been prepared by the students. The study looked at the relationship between references retrieved and references used, as evidenced in the bibliographies. Bibliographies were analyzed for the number of references and the date of materials in them, and then compared these same variables in the online search printouts.

The authors found that few of the online references were incorporated into students' bibliographies; 84 percent of the students used none of the online sources. Most of the online materials that were used referred to materials in the past five years. Interviews with the young adults indicated that the main reasons for rejecting many of the references were that they were hard to locate or that they seemed too hard to understand.

In a related study, Callison and colleagues (1986) looked at the ability of high school students to retrieve information using the online Wilsearch system. Students were in the process of researching a self-selected topic. All were trained in how to use Wilsearch, and encouraged but not required to use it. The researchers analyzed the bibliographies produced by students who had not had online searching available to them one year prior. Questionnaires were also administered to the students to evaluate their impressions of the usefulness of Wilsearch.

Findings of this study showed that thirty-six of the forty-one students used Wilsearch at least once. Comparing the bibliographies of the online searchers with those who had searched manually a year earlier, they found that those who used Wilsearch had a wider variety of journals and publications, fewer books, and a greater number of journals. Similar to the results of Wozny (1982) and Mancall and Desking (1984), the authors found that many of the materials retrieved through Wilsearch were not used in the final bibliographies.

USER-ORIENTED STUDIES

The research of user-oriented studies began with questions about the young user of electronic information sources, not with questions about the system. Efforts were made to understand the information-searching behaviors of the young person and how these behaviors or strategies are enhanced or impeded by electronic information sources. This research looked at the cognitive processes of information seeking and how these processes interacted with electronic information systems. The general model within which this work developed is one that starts with the information user and looks at his or her information goals or needs and the strategies or searching behaviors that are involved in the accomplishment of these goals. It asks questions about the thinking that goes on in searching for information, the mental strategies used by children as they approach information retrieval systems, and the search techniques they actually employ. This broader model was developed from current thinking in the field of information science, which has itself moved from a system-oriented to a more user-oriented focus (Bates, 1981; Borgman, 1986).

Within this more cognitively oriented approach to the study of children's use of electronic databases, two different approaches are discernible. There is a body of research that studies the information behaviors of children in an effort to design better systems. These behaviors may be viewed in terms of "mental models," or information strategies, or combinations of both. This line of research, evidenced, for example, in the work of Marchionini, Borgman, and their colleagues (Barlow, Karnes, and Marchionini, 1987; Borgman, Chignell, and Valdez, 1989a, 1989b; Borgman, Krieger, Gallagher, and Bower, 1990b; Borgman, Gallagher, Krieger, and Bower, 1990a; Liebscher and Marchionini, 1988; Marchionini, 1989a, 1989b; Marchionini and Teague, 1987), contains both system-level application and theoretical connections to the field of information science.

Another body of research that is also cognitively oriented has developed in tandem, but it has as its goal the empowerment of children with information-seeking abilities, not primarily the design of good systems. This work is represented in early research from the United Kingdom (Carter, 1989; Davison, 1984; Galpin, 1989; Spavold, 1990), where the use of electronic databases in classrooms was accompanied by ongoing qualitative research to track users' experiences with the system. The underlying philosophical difference between this approach and that represented in work in the United States is reflected in their different end goals. Research in the United States, represented in this volume in chapter 7 by Linda Cooper, is being conducted in an attempt to design better "user- and cognitively oriented" systems, while in the United Kingdom the goals of the research have been to develop better searching children. It is unfortunate that there has been no cross-citation between these two bodies of research.

Cognitive Approaches to the Study of Children's Use of Electronic Databases—Research in the United Kingdom

Spavold (1990) presents the most comprehensive description to date of the research on children's use of electronic databases in the united Kingdom. She reported on a yearlong study conducted in two schools, one urban and one rural, with children nine to eleven years old. Children in this study were involved in the creation of a database, using the 1981 census data, which they then interrogated through the use of INFORM, a double front-end system with both menu and command sets. Students became both information providers, contributing to the database, as well as information searchers. The jointly compiled database was used as a history project, and the information in it became a shared resource.

The underlying assumption of this research is that if children are involved in the creation of the database, they will have a better understanding of how it works, and this will be reflected in better queries. As noted by Spavold, when children have no experience in the compilation of the system, they tend to regard its operations as "magic" and have trouble developing search procedures. Other hypotheses tested in this study involved an expected change in the nature of the student-teacher and student-student relationships because of the cooperative nature of the project and a predicted preference for menus over commands. No specific hypotheses were formed, but general questions were asked about the nature of the images formed by children to understand the database.

The study used observational research methods, with researchers unobtrusively taking notes on the children's experiences with data entry and interrogation. Study results showed that children had difficulty with the command set because the command language was different from anything they experienced before. Attempts to translate natural language into appropriate queries met with frustration among the children. This study is rich in detail about the feelings of "getting lost in the system" that were expressed by many of the children. Some of the behavioral responses to this fear involved finding a partner who had mastery over the system and working closely with this person. Consequently, leaders were defined in one of the schools based on competence with the database system.

In looking at some of the ways children navigate through the system, Spavold found that only after gaining experience with the database did children attempted to "explore" through the system, venturing beyond single condition searches to more complicated inquiries.

Looking at the experiences of the children in terms of their "problem-solving" strategies, Spavold found a big difference between the number of problem-solving activities engaged in by children and those used by adults. Very few of the children applied hypothesis testing in their approach to interrogation, reflecting the inability of these children to engage in abstract thought. The suggestion here is that at the age of "concrete operation," to use Piaget's phrase, younger children approach information searching with different capabilities than children who are older. Spavold stresses the importance of the "mental maps" formed by the children in their use of the database. Although they had been given a conceptual model of the database system early in the year, the children rejected this model as irrelevant and developed their own mental models of the system. Three mental models were observed. One model treated encoded data as a "secret code"; another model involved "turn taking," which facilitated the tedious procedure of data entry. A third model integrated the format of a television game show, in which the person formulating the query was somewhat like a contestant whose questions were either correct or incorrect.

The importance of the mental maps Spavold discussed is in their ability to provide a relevant cognitive framework for the experience of database searching. This view of mental models is not the same as those described by Marchionini and others, where models of the information system itself, rather than models of the situation of information searching in electronic databases, are used. Spavold's data do not provide statements about the precise ways in which the mental mapping played a role in children's performance; but her observations indicate that it made the experience more real for them.

Other studies that have been conducted in the United Kingdom reflected a similar qualitative, primarily observational, approach pursued throughout the course of the school year. Although these studies contain a wealth of qualitative data on children's experiences with electronic information retrieval systems, it is difficult to evaluate the research on methodological grounds because of the nature of the results that have been reported. Apart from Spavold's research, much of this data is presented in descriptive, almost anecdotal, form.

Carter (1989) discusses the results of a two-year study of the uses of online services in primary and secondary schools in the United Kingdom. In order to prepare students for searching with Boolean operators, instruction was given in the concepts of AND/OR categorization, using solid colored blocks to illustrate examples of these conditions. The methods used in this study involved observations of teachers and students, taped interviews with the children, analyses of the search routines, staff diaries, and a videotape of the students involved in preparatory exercises with the colored blocks.

Results of this study indicated that the concrete approach to teaching Boolean searching was effective. Looking at the children's information-searching behaviors with the "Profile" database, it was found that even though this debate is a full-text system, students tend to use it as an index service by merely taking the citation and turning to the printed copy. Although not discussed by the author, this suggests something about the ability of the students to read and process information on screen versus the printed format. Additionally, some of the students in this study experienced frustration in having to read the entire (possibly irrelevant) record to find their search term.

In another related study, Davison (1984) describes a project that was designed to teach information-retrieval skills to high school students in the United Kingdom. Students were involved in the creation of a data file, with an emphasis on the instruction in keyword categorization. After participating in this exercise, students were given textual and graphic information and asked to identify keywords in it. A 60 percent success rate was achieved, and the researchers noted that the children tended to translate the terms into their own language. For example, "wireless" became "radio," and so on. They concluded that information systems need to contain index terms that relate not only to the curriculum but to students' own language as well.

Galpin (1989) reported on another UK project involving primary school children in the creation of an expert system shell. Small groups worked together to develop a system that would advise police and other emergency services how to respond to emergency calls. Although Galpin provided only scant details of his research methods, his summary report suggests that the ability to use the expert system is correlated not entirely with age, but also with cognitive ability. The ability to reason abstractly is the most important variable here. The author makes another observation that when children become involved in the use of new information technologies, it is important that the teacher have a thorough working knowledge of the system because the nature of the relationship between teacher and student changes dramatically if the student outlearns the teacher.

Overall, the early research from the United Kingdom holds promise for a better understanding of the in-depth experiences of young users. This research, conducted over long periods of time in naturalistic settings, provides insights that cannot be obtained from more isolated observations, taken in quasi-experimental settings. Although it appears as if ongoing research-based systems of evaluation are in place, the ability of this research to contribute to any larger body of thinking on the subject will depend on the extent to which the researchers involved in these projects attempt to communicate their observations to a larger community, with a more detailed explication of the research methods employed.

Cognitive Approaches to the Study of Children's Use of Electronic Databases—Early Research in the United States

Cognitively oriented studies of children's information seeking in electronic databases appeared primarily near the end of the 1980s. Marchionini and his colleagues (Barlow et al., 1987; Marchionini, 1989a; Marchionini, 1989b; Marchionini, 1991) conducted a number of studies on children's use of electronic encyclopedias, looking at some of the cognitive processes involved in information retrieval system. Questions addressed in this research concerned which seeking strategies or mental models children employ as they search for information and how their behaviors work with the information-retrieval system.

Marchionini and Teague (1987) looked at elementary school children's use of an online encyclopedia, comparing the behaviors of children in grades 2 and 3 with those in 4 and 6. They began with questions about the developmental ability of children who are in the stage of "concrete operations" to use the menu system. The children in this study worked in pairs researching self-selected topics. The topics selected by the students were primarily for concrete items rather than for topics that addressed relationships among concepts. The authors found that children were able to use the menu system effectively for simple selections, but that they sometimes lost their sense of position within the larger system of menus. At these times, "menu floundering" tended to occur.

The search patterns observed in this study showed a pattern of children following a single path through to exhaustion, looking up articles one after another. Overall, the study demonstrated the feasibility of using menu-based electronic systems with elementary children, although some of the problems encountered with the online transmission, such as disconnections, proved to be annoying to children.

In an early study of young-adult use of CD-ROM encyclopedias, Barlow et al. (1987) found that high school students were able to retrieve information in the electronic encyclopedia if they used the "browsing" mode, but that almost all of them had difficulty using Boolean operators in the "word search" mode. All students had been given a ten-minute demonstration of how to search in both of these modes. Apparently, this was not as effective as the development of the underlying skills required to understand the concepts of Boolean searching described by Spavold (1990). This study found that reading problems hindered students' ability to search the system, because reading on screen is normally slower than for print copy.

Later, Liebscher and Marchionini (1988) developed some of these findings further in a study of high school students' use of a full-text CD-ROM encyclopedia. They used an experimental design in which students were assigned to either an "analytical" (Boolean) search strategy group or a "browse" group. Questions were asked about which search strategy would be most effective in terms of information-retrieval performance. Performance was measured by an examination of the search terms used, the number of queries formulated, the number of articles viewed, recall of relevant documents, and precision. It was hypothesized that analytical strategies, although more difficult to learn, would result in better searches. This hypothesis was not supported. Both groups performed equally well on recall, but the analytical groups had higher precision. The authors conclude that the analytical training might be insufficient and suggest that both methods be taught to students, so they can adapt their own strategy to fit their needs.

The theoretical framework that Marchionini et al. used here and in subsequent research is a cognitive model in which an individual's "mental model" or preexisting mental framework is believed to shape the nature of one's interaction with the information system. The mental model is an image of the information system that the individual holds. In adopting the mental model perspective, Marchionini and his colleagues did not attempt to test a theory of mental models. In his early studies, Marchionini does not attempt to test the effectiveness of one mental model over another or the differences between having or not having a mental model of the information system. Rather, he embraced the concept of mental models and uses this concept to explain the results he has found.

In another study of information seeking in electronic encyclopedias, Marchionini (1989a) looked at the search strategies employed by children in grades 3–6. Children were given two assigned searches, one open-ended and the other closed. Observational methods were used to determine strategies used by the children, as evidenced by the keystroke records. This study found that older children were more successful than younger ones in finding the required information at all, and also that they took less time retrieving it. Younger children in this study used fewer system features, such as proximity selection, and when they did use some of these features, they were more likely to be unsuccessful.

All of the children approached their queries using natural language terms, and the younger children went so far as to use actual sentences. Marchionini concluded that the younger children, who believed the system to be far more intelligent than it was, had poor mental models. This study raised questions about the difference between electronic and print-based mental models that are subsequently addressed by Marchionini in his most recent (1989b, 1991) work.

Marchionini (1989b) looked at the mental models held by high school students of the information-search process itself. He examined the breadth of knowledge held by students about information sources available to them and the usefulness of these sources. He also looked at print-based mental models and how students would go about searching for information in a print encyclopedia as indicated by the terms they would use and whether the strategy involved going to the index or directly to the article. Finally, he examined electronic mental models, which parallel the procedures for print.

These mental models were elicited verbally by the investigators. The goal of the research was to evaluate the ways in which print-based mental models are applied or misapplied to electronic encyclopedias. Sixteen students took part in the study, which involved three searches. The first was a mental search, talking about the sources students would consult and what they expected to find in them. The next searches involved the use of print and electronic encyclopedias. In each simulated search condition, questions were asked to elicit students' mental models of the information system. Marchionini found that students perceived the electronic source to be faster, easier to use, and to contain more information than the print version. However, the electronic searches, in fact, took longer, were more difficult, and the electronic encyclopedia contained the same amount of information as the print version.

Overall, students employed global-search strategies that minimized cognitive load. They made little use of some of the sophisticated system features. Marchionini found different levels of adaptation of print-based mental models to the electronic encyclopedia. Marchionini (1991) provided case study illustrations of three types of adaptation: First, successful electronic searches without any adaptation of the print-based mental model, made possible because the electronic encyclopedia supports both browsing and analytical search capabilities. Second, successful adaptation of existing mental models to the electronic encyclopedia. Finally, exacerbation of poor existing mental models with the use of the electronic encyclopedia.

Marchionini (1991) also attempted to explain these adaptations of mental models in terms of developmental abilities in reading skills, vocabulary knowledge, and ability to translate topics into keywords. He noted that the importance of making relevance judgments is greater with the electronic encyclopedia than it is with print because in the print source a student either finds an article or does not, while in the electronic encyclopedia many potential articles are retrieved.

In another study of students' use of electronic encyclopedias, Edyburn (1988) looked at the ability of junior high school students to retrieve specific factual information from a print encyclopedia with a menu interface and an electronic encyclopedia using command sets. Thirty students participated in this study, fifteen of whom had learning disabilities. Two groups of students—learning impaired and normal—were randomly assigned to one of the encyclopedias and given four information-retrieval tasks, two of which involved assigned questions and two student-selected questions.

Results of this study indicate that among both learning impaired and normal students the percentage of tasks completed successfully was the same for print and electronic sources. All students were more successful with the menu-driven system than with using commands. Both groups of students had greater success with the assigned tasks than they did with the self-generated questions. They also were more successful with simple rather than complex retrieval tasks.

Another body of research on children's use of electronic databases was developed by Borgman and her associates (Borgman et al., 1989a, 1989b, 1990a, 1990b) in their work on Project SEED, an interactive science simulation catalog. In a series of reports on successive developments in this project, Borgman and her associates have described some of the research in the development of Project SEED and some of the evaluations they have undertaken.

Prior to developing the HyperCard interface, which was designed to enable students to search the science database, Borgman et al. (1989a, 1989b) investigated children's ability to categorize science concepts with the goal of designing the interface around their knowledge. Theoretically, this should result in a system that is more effective than an "externally driven model." They conducted several experiments with elementary school children to see if they were able to categorize the concepts in the Project SEED simulation. Two experiments were carried out with children in grades 3–6, who were asked to sort concept cards with plant and animal names on them into categories. The goal here was to understand the children's cognitive structures, including their level of concept knowledge and their classification of like terms, before designing the interface. They found lower levels of knowledge and category consistency in the area of plant classification than they had expected. The interesting questions raised here concerned whether the information should have been designed around the faulty knowledge children hold or to correct the children.

SUMMARY AND CONCLUSIONS

The research conducted on the use of electronic databases by children and young adults during the decade of 1980 to 1990 was developed from a collection of somewhat anecdotal descriptions of user behaviors and utilization, ranging from more systematic studies of the effectiveness of information systems, to a more recent approach that locates the subject within the larger concerns of the field of information science, applying a cognitive psychological orientation.

A fully developed model of the nature of the relationship between children, their information-seeking behaviors, and electronic databases ended the decade while still in the formative stages. From this research some of the directions taken during the 1990s are represented in the chapters in this book. The body of research discussed above leaves many questions unanswered and suggests several future directions, touching upon the concerns outlined in the following sections.

Developmental Aspects of Child Users 1980–1990

The study of children's use of electronic information resources contained few systematic attempts to discuss the role of developmental characteristics of children in their information-processing capabilities and their overall stage of cognitive development. Results from some of these studies have indicated that developmental abilities, such as the ability to alphabetize and file properly, figure into the ability of children to retrieve information with both manual and electronic systems. Valdez and Sollie (1990) cautioned that simple skills such as keyboarding should not be assumed to be uniformly possessed by children. Several studies cited above have pointed to reading ability as a strong factor in the child's ability to retrieve information on screen versus in a printed source.

There has also been a suggestion (Spavold, 1990) that adult models of problem solving may not be applicable to children. That is, children may go through different steps in this process than adults. The ability to advance knowledge here depends on the extent to which child-based models are developed, not merely imported, from research on the information-seeking behaviors of adults. Attention to the developmental processes involved can ensure that information systems are sensitive to children's particular information abilities and needs. For example, many of the studies found age differences in children's ability to use Boolean operators effectively and to search in a command mode, a subject taken up in more detail by Nahl and Harade in chapter 5 with her experiment with different kinds of presearch-user instruction. It is thought that this represents the differences in stages of cognitive development; that as a child progresses from the stage of concrete operations to the more abstract reasoning of adolescence, more complex searching becomes possible. We might also look at the difficulty children have been found to have with keyword searching in terms of psycholinguistic variables and then focus attention on the nature of the structure and development of language capabilities of the young user and how these play a role in information searching behavior.

The focus on ability should not lead us down the path of trying to develop the perfect system that is easiest for children to use, or the system that ultimately has the least "cognitive load." As Spavold (1990) learned and Nahl reiterates in this book, young people develop a sense of confidence as they master the information system, and this development can be important in their overall development of information skills. Bates (1990) extends this line of reasoning, arguing that in general, people enjoy overcoming a challenge and like to solve some of the problems involved in navigating through the information system. It may be a mistake to think in terms of designing systems that will be "easiest to use."

Mental Models

Further study of mental models and the role they play in information-seeking behaviors was also warranted. The UK studies indicated that the whole notion of mental models needs to be expanded beyond the narrow conceptualization of an individual's cognitive model of the information system itself to include the broader context or situation of use. Beyond just expanding conceptualizations of mental models, subsequent research, such as that produced by Pitts (1995), attempted to specify the ways in which different mental models, or the absence of mental models, shape information-seeking behaviors with electronic-retrieval systems.

There is also little known from the research thus far about the nature of the decision making that children apply, or the relevance judgments they make in their decisions to use or not use materials retrieved through electronic versus print retrieval sources.

Methodological Approaches

Most of the empirical research cited employs multiple measurement techniques, such as observations combined with interviews and printouts of query entries. However, a limitation of much of the research is that quasi-experimental research designs have been conducted, representing only one point in time. Although this approach offers the benefits of experimental control over the variables under study, much is lost in the somewhat artificial snapshot that is captured. Spavold and other researchers in the United Kingdom offer another model, one that is more qualitative in design and is conducted over long periods of time, in more naturalistic settings. If the goal is to more fully understand the child's information-seeking behavior experiences, then this longitudinal, more qualitative approach might be productive.

Importance of Indexing

A common thread throughout the many 1980–1990 studies cited here is the need for user-oriented indexing, or better thesauri. Borgman's work in the development of Project SEED is a good example of research being used to develop concept terms that parallel the knowledge structure of the children for whom the system is designed. Other studies have stressed the ways in which children approach electronic searching with natural language terms.

Human-Computer Interaction

One of the most neglected aspects of the early study of children's use of electronic databases is the examination of the nature of the role relationships that are created when these systems become implemented in institutional environment. Galpin (1989) and the Alberta Department of Education (Edmonton Public Schools, 1983) have found subtle differences in student-teacher and student-librarian relationships after children became proficient in the use of new information systems. Spavold (1990) and Epler (1987) describe how the introduction of electronic information systems in the classroom can actually create new roles and relationships among the children. However, most of what is known here is secondhand, from incidental observations made in these studies, rather than from systematic exploration of these computer-facilitated interactions.

Unknowns

Because of the restriction of this body of research to the institutional context of the classroom, there is virtually no knowledge of the precursors to information-seeking behavior among youth. Chapters 12 and 13 in this volume, which focus explicitly on information seeking from a variety of human and nonhuman sources during the course of important life decision-making processes, such as risk-taking behavior and career-making decisions, are a welcome addition to this much-needed area of investigation. There should be further work in this direction. Researchers have for too long worked within a model that assumes that the school entirely defines the parameters of children's and young adults' information needs. Overcoming this neglect to consider the desire of youth to find out about their world, apart from specific classroom assignments, is necessary in order to develop more general models of youth information-seeking behavior. Research on the effectiveness of education indicates that family factors play as important or a more important role than school factors. There is good reason to think that these same factors will influence the development of children's information behaviors and skills, as well as the mental models they form about information systems. An additional topic for future exploration involves the specification of how factors such as gender, race, ethnicity, and social class influence information-seeking and information-searching behaviors among children. Most previous studies have either involved homogenous groups of users, stratified only by age, or neglected to explore whether children of varying characteristics display different levels and styles of information need, information behaviors, and different mental models.

REFERENCES

Aversa, E. S. (1985). "Teaching online searching: A review of recent research and some recommendations for school media specialists." *School Library Media Quarterly* (Summer): 215–219.

Aversa, E. S. (1988). *Online information services for secondary school students: A current assessment*. ERIC ED 303 175.

Aversa, E. S., and Mancall, J. C. (1987). "Online users in schools: a status report." *Online* (May): 15–18.

Barlow, D., Karnes, K., and Marchionini, G. (1987). "CD-ROM in a high school library media center: A research project." *School Library Journal* 34 (November): 66–68.

Bates, M. J. (1981). "Search Techniques." In M. Williams, ed., *Annual review of information science and technology* (pp. 139–169). White Plains, N.Y.: Knowledge Industry Publications.

Bates, M. J. (1990). "Where should the person stop and the information search interface start?" *Information Processing and Management* 26: 575–591.

Borgman, C. L. (1986). "Why are online catalogs hard to use: Lessons learned from information retrieval studies." *Journal of the American Society for Information Science* 37 (6): 387–400.

Borgman, C. L., Chignell, M. C., and Valdez, F. (1989a). "Designing an information retrieval interface based on children's categorization of knowledge: a pilot study." In J. Katzer and G. Newby, eds., *Proceed-*

ings of the American Society for Information Science annual meeting. Washington, D.C., October 29–November 2.

Borgman, C. L., Gallagher, A. L., Krieger, D., and Bower, J. (1990a). "Children's use of an interactive catalog of science materials." In D. Henderson, ed., *Proceedings of 53rd American Society for Information science meeting.* Toronto, Ontario, November 4–8.

Borgman, C. L., Krieger, D., Gallagher, A. L., and Bower, J. (1990b). "Children's use science library: Exploratory research." *School Library Media Quarterly* (Winter): 108–111.

Borgman, C., Moghdam, D., and Corbett, P. (1984). Effective Online Searching. New York: Dekker, pp. 176–77.

Callison, D., Daniels, A., Estell, D., and Gunderson, H. (1986). *Using Wilsearch with high school students: A pilot study.* ERIC ED 275 343.

Carter, C. (1989). "From John the Baptiste to knee replacements: The use of online systems in school." *Education Libraries Journal* 32 (3): 35–44.

Cleaver, B. P. (1987). "Thinking about information: Skills for lifelong learning." *School Library Media Quarterly* (Fall): 29–31.

Clyde, L. A., and Kirk, J. (1989). "The use of electronic information systems in Australian schools: A preliminary survey." *School Library Media Quarterly* (Summer): 193–199.

Craver, K. W. (1985). "Teaching online bibliographic searching to high school students." *Top of the News* 41 (2).

Davison, S. G. (1984). "Data file creation—a case study: The pupil created data file project at Milne's High School, Grampian Region." *Education Libraries Journal* 27 (3): 52–58.

Dowling, K., and Pruitt, E. (1987). "From bulletin boards to Boolean using online to teach online." *Online* (May): 31–33.

Edmonds, L., Moore, P., and Balcom, K. M. (1989). *An investigation into the effectiveness of providing bibliographic access to children in a public library setting.* ERIC ED 311 921.

Edmonton Public Schools. (1983). *Utilization of a micro computer in an elementary school learning resource center.* ERIC ED 239–601.

Edyburn, D. L. (1988). "Examining the successful retrieval of information by online databases." *School Library Media Quarterly* (Summer): 256–260.

Epler, D. M. (1987). "Lin-tel in Pennsylvania the BRS connection." *Online* (May): 24–26.

Fiebert, E. E. (1987). "Online at Radnor High: a pattern of change." *Online* (May): 19–21.

Galpin, B. (1989). "Using information technology in primary school topic work." *Education Libraries Journal* 32 (3): 46–50.

Giacquinta, J. B., and Lane, P. A. (1990). "Fifty-one families with computers: A study of children's academic uses of microcomputers at home." *Educational Technology Research and Development* 38 (2): 27–37.

Hancock, J. (1989). "Learning with databases." *Journal of Reading* 32 (7): 582–589.

Hooten, P. A. (1989). "Online catalogs: Will they improve children's access?" *Journal of Youth Services in Libraries* 2 (3): 267–272.

Kuhlthau, C. C. (1987). *Information skills for an information society: A review of research*. ERIC ED 13244-2340.

Kuhlthau, C. C. (1988). "Developing a model of the library search process." *Reference Quarterly* (Winter): 232–242.

Kuhlthau, C. C., and Sherman, J. C. (1990). "On-line computer databases in school library media centers." In C. Wargner, ed., *Technology in today's schools* (pp. 51–56). Association for Supervision and Curriculum Development.

Liebscher, P., and Marchionini, G. (1988). "Browse and analytical search strategies in a full text CD-ROM encyclopedia." *School Library Media Quarterly* (Summer): 223–233.

Lodish, E. K. (1987). "Classmate to 2100: dialog at Montgomery Blair." *Online* (May): 27–31.

Lynch, E. A. (1987). "Online at East Lyme (CT): Dow Jones gets high marks. *Online*, May 1987, 21–23.

Mancall, J., and Desking, D. (1984). *Teaching online bibliographic skills to high school students.* ERIC ED 252 823.

Marchionini, G. (1989a). "Information-seeking strategies of novices using a full-text electronic encyclopedia." *Journal of the American Society for Information Science* 40 (1): 52–66.

Marchionini, G. (1989b). "Making the transition from print to electronic adaptation of mental models." *International Journal of Man-Machine Studies* 30: 591–618.

Marchionini, G. (in press). "Information seeking in electronic encyclopedias." *Journal of Machine-Mediated Learning*.

Marchionini, G., and Teague, J. (1987). "Elementary students' use of electronic information services: An exploratory study." *Journal of Research on Computing in Education* (Winter): 139–144.

Montgomery, P. (1987). "Library media literacy: Making the library media and reading connection." *School Library Media Quarterly* (Fall): 32–35.

Olney, E. (1989). "Information retrieval in the classroom." *Journal of Reading* 32 (7): 590–596.

Piaget, J. and Inhelder, B. *Psychology of the Child*. New York: Basic Books, 1969.

Pitts, J. M. (1995). "Mental models of information: The 1993–94 AASL/Highsmith Research Study Award." J. H. McGregor and B. K. Stripling, eds., *School Library Media Quarterly*, 177–184.

Pruitt, E., and Dowling, K. (1985). "Searching for current information online . . . how high school library media centers in Montgomery County, Maryland, are solving an information problem using Dialog." *Online* (March): 46–60.

Shoham, S., and Getz, I. (1988). "Patterns of bibliographic searching among Israeli high school students." *Library and Information Science* 10 (1): 57–75.

Spavold, J. (1990). "The child as naïve user: A study of database use with young children." *International Journal of Man-Machine Studies* 32: 603–625.

Tenopir, C. (1986). "Online searching in school." *Library Journal* (February 1): 60–61.

Ward-Callaghan, L. (1987). "The effect of emerging technologies on children's library service." *Library Trends* (Winter): 427–447.

Wozny, L. A. (1982). "Online bibliographic searching and student use of information: An innovative teaching approach." *School Library Media Quarterly* (Fall): 35–42.

Valdez, G., and Sollie, S. (1990). "Keyboarding: A necessary transitional skill." In C. Wargner, ed., *Technology in Today's Schools* (pp. 158–72). Alexandria, Va.: Association for Supervision and Curriculum Development.

Two

Student Learning in the Library: What Library Power Librarians Say

Carol Collier Kuhlthau

Library Power sought to improve student learning opportunities Over the course of the initiative, librarians in Library Power schools were asked to describe meaningful learning experiences for a student or students in their libraries and to explain what made them good learning experiences. The librarians' responses were analyzed for the quality of the learning experience described and for the kinds of indicators cited as evidence of learning. Focused case studies observed how the school library media centers in selected schools provided improved learning opportunities for students.

The National Library Power Program, funded by the DeWitt-Wallace Reader's Digest Fund, sought to improve opportunities for student learning by providing funding for library resources in elementary and middle schools in 19 communities across the United States. Although contributions to all of the schools were similar, some schools had more success than others in providing student learning opportunities. Although improved resources made an important contribution in all of the schools, other factors were at work that affected student learning in the libraries. Where Library Power seems to have had the most significant influence on student learning is in those schools where it has been tied to other reform efforts that were moving the climate in the school to a more constructivist approach to learning, centering on inquiry in the research process.

AN INQUIRY APPROACH TO LEARNING

The Library Power Program was more effective where there was a commitment to an inquiry approach to learning shared by the librarian, teachers, and administrators. An inquiry approach involves students in the process of learning from a variety of sources of information that begins with students developing their own questions (Harste, 1994). Students are guided through inquiry by asking: What questions do I have? How do I find out? What did I learn? Inquiry learning takes students out of the predigested format of the textbook into the use of a variety of resources for constructing their own understandings. They learn to think through issues that do not have prescribed responses or preset solutions. Through a process of construction, each student actively builds on what he or she already knows to come to a new understanding of the subject under study.

Collaboration Based on Inquiry

Where an inquiry approach to learning is in place, the library is an integral part of the learning process. The inquiry approach requires more than just activities that involve the library. Collaboration between teachers and librarians is a fundamental component of an instructional program based on inquiry. Extensive planning and direction by the teacher is needed to guide students in the learning process with instruction given at the "teachable moment." Through collaborative planning and teaching, opportunities are provided for students to use library resources for constructing a depth of understanding in the content areas of the curriculum. Teachers and librarians are drawn together in a close partnership for developing inquiry as a way to meet the instructional goals of the school (Harste, Callison, and Jurewicz, 1994).

Inquiry is not a new idea for school librarians. Learning through a variety of resources has been the basic concept of library programs since the 1960s, with roots of the idea going back to the founding of libraries in schools. In an article on inquiry in libraries, Callison (1986) described how an inquiry approach changes the librarian's role from that of reacting to immediate information demands to that of interacting with teachers and students in the development of learning through the use of the media center resources. Over the past decade, while researchers in education have been building a strong case for an inquiry approach to learning, there has been a parallel stream of research in school libraries on the information search process. This research has contributed significantly to our understanding of learning through the process of inquiry. The Library Power Evaluation Project revealed that findings from these two streams of research are coming together in many schools to provide enabling learning environments for students. Taken together, this research offers a strong empirical base for building collaborative library programs that are designed for learning in the information age.

Learning Through the Inquiry Process

In school libraries, the process of inquiry has been intensively studied and modeled as the information search process (ISP). Research has centered on investigating the student's perspective on the process. From the perspective of the student, strategies were developed to be implemented by librarians to improve student learning. My research in this area was initiated in the mid-1980s with a qualitative study of one class of high school students revealing a sequence of stages in the ISP. Since then, the stages of the ISP have been verified in series of studies applying both qualitative and quantitative methods and incorporating longitudinal and large-scale design. Full descriptions of the studies and of the model of the stages in the ISP have been given in prior publications (Kuhlthau, 1993, 1994). In brief, the ISP may be thought of as occurring in seven stages: initiation, selection, exploration, formulation, collection, presentation, and assessment. These stages are named for the primary task to be accomplished at each point in the process. The model describes the thoughts, actions, and feelings commonly experienced by students in each stage of the process. When students are engaged in an extensive inquiry project, their thoughts evolve from vague and unclear to focused and personalized; their actions change from general and exploratory to specific and comprehensive; and their feelings emerge from uncertain and hesitant to interested and directed. The critical component of the ISP is the student's own formulation of a focus that involves gaining a personal perspective of the subject or problem while using a variety of sources of information. In other words, they are constructing knowledge through inquiry.

STUDY OF OPPORTUNITIES FOR STUDENT LEARNING

In 1994, the National Library Power evaluation project directors Dianne McAfee Hopkins and Douglas Zweizig called on me to study opportunities for student learning in the Library Power schools. The key question addressed was, has Library Power influenced student learning opportunities? Two methods were developed for investigating student learning in Library Power schools: an analysis of responses to an open-ended survey question eliciting the librarians' description of learning in each of the schools and theme case studies in three selected schools. This article discusses evidence of improved opportunities for student learning in Library Power schools through these two primary sources of data.

In the first phase of the study, the librarians in the Library Power schools were asked to give examples of student learning in their libraries. One of the questions on the Library Power annual survey was designed to elicit examples of student learning and was administered to the librarians in 1995, 1996, and 1997. The librarians' responses to the survey question provided a crucial clue that was considered to typify in some way what first comes to mind when the librarian is asked to describe a student learning experience. These initial responses or reactions were treated as an indication of what the librarian judged to be important to emphasize when asked to describe a situation of learning in the library. In each of the three years that the survey was administered, the librarians were asked to respond to the following prompt. "Think back over your Library Power project to when a student or students had a meaningful learning experience in the library. How did you know something new was learned? What stands out in your mind that made it a good learning experience?" The examples of learning given by the librarians were then coded as to what the librarians had emphasized as indicators of learning. A comparison was made of changes in the aggregate responses over the three-year period.

Scale for Coding Examples of Learning

A coding scale was designed to classify the critical incidents by what was emphasized in each librarian's response. The coding scale identified the librarian's perception of learning as an indication of the vision and objectives of the library program at that time. Was the librarian emphasizing more materials and technology, increased library use, improvement in attitude, better library and information skills, or use of resources for content learning? Although this analysis did not directly measure student learning, it revealed the underlying perspective on learning in the library of the person responsible for developing a library program.

In the spring of 1995, through content analysis of a sample of thirty responses, a 5-point coding scale was developed, which was intended to represent levels of opportunities for student learning, with 1 representing the lowest level and 5 the highest, as shown in figure 2.1. It should be noted that all of the levels represented evidence of the implementation of library services. However, at each level, the librarian emphasized a different element of the library program to indicate evidence of student learning. Responses identified as level 1 emphasized what the librarian did and not what the student did, such as adding to the collection or describing a lesson taught. Level 1 responses were coded as "input." Responses identified as level 2 emphasized quantitative measures of student

Level 1: *Input*
Emphasis on what librarian did, not on students, i.e., adding to collection, adding new technology, describing lesson or unit plan.

Level 2: *Output*
Emphasis on quantitative measure of student use, i.e., more visits, more use of materials and technology.

Level 3: *Attitude*
Emphasis on change in student attitude, i.e., increased interest and enthusiasm.

Level 4: *Skills*
Emphasis on location of resource and use of technology, i.e., locating books, using CD ROM encyclopedia.

Level 5: *Utilization*
Emphasis on content learning, i.e., using resources to learn through inquiry in content areas of the curriculum.

0 no response or response does not answer question.

Figure 2.1. Coding Scale For Librarians' Descriptions of Student Learning

use, such as a greater number of materials circulated, more class visits, or increase in technology use. Level 2 responses were coded as "output." Responses identified as level 3 emphasized change in student attitude, such as increased interest and enthusiasm. Level 3 responses were coded as "attitude." Responses identified as level 4 emphasized library and information skills, such as ability to locate materials through a catalog or ability to use an encyclopedia on CD-ROM. Level 4 responses were coded as "skills." Responses identified as level 5 emphasized content learning, such as using resources to learn about a subject. Level 5 responses were coded as "utilization." Level 5 identifies opportunities for student learning that apply inquiry integrated into curriculum areas. At this level, information literacy is not taught as isolated skills, but is embedded in the inquiry process. Both process and content learning are emphasized at level 5. Surveys with no response or a response that did not answer the question were coded 0.

The responses from the librarians were coded by two coders from the School of Communication, Information and Library Studies at Rutgers University, myself and Mary Jane McNally, library media specialist and doctoral candidate. All of the responses were read and coded separately by each coder. The coders discussed each response on which they were in disagreement and came to a consensus. This coding and analysis was independent of the analysis of the responses to the survey as a whole and has not been correlated with other questions on the survey. The same two coders were used each of the three years, applying the same method of coding.

LIBRARIANS' DESCRIPTIONS OF LEARNING

Analysis of the coding revealed patterns in the librarians' responses in each of the three years of their involvement with Library Power. Results are reported in frequencies and percentages of the aggregate responses in each level category. These findings reveal what the librarians emphasized when asked to give an example of student learning.

In 1995, the first year of the study, 331 responses were received to the survey question regarding student learning. The highest number of responses, 105 or 31.7 percent, were coded at level 3, emphasizing a change in attitude toward the library and its resources. Approximately a third of the librarians noted that they saw a positive change in attitude in their students as a result of the Library Power initiative. The second highest number of responses, 95 or 28.7 percent, were coded at level 4, emphasizing library and information skills. These responses gave examples of students using library skills to locate materials or some of the new technology. The third highest number of responses, 89 or 26.9 percent, were coded at level 5, emphasizing utilization of library resources for content learning. These responses gave examples of students using resources to learn about some topic or question that they were either studying in connection with a subject in the curriculum or something they were curious about that related to a personal interest. Taken together, the three levels represented 86 percent of the responses.

In 1996, the second year of the study, 405 responses were received to the survey question. The highest number of responses, 155 or 38 percent, were coded at level 4, emphasizing library and information skills. The librarians noted that they saw evidence of influence of Library Power on students' ability to use the library resources and technology. The second highest number of responses, 97 or 24 percent, were coded at level 3, emphasizing a change in attitude of the students. Change in attitude continued to be a strong indicator of student learning in the librarians' responses. The third highest number of responses, 94 or 23 percent, were coded at level 5, emphasizing students' utilization of resources for learning in connection with a subject in the curriculum or related to a personal interest. Taken together, these three levels represented 85 percent of the responses of the librarians.

In 1997, the last year of the study, 495 responses were received to the survey question. The highest number of responses, 185 or 37.4 percent were coded at level 5, emphasizing utilization of library resources for learning. Librarians' responses gave examples of students learning through research in collaborative units throughout the curriculum. The second highest number of responses, 122 or 24.6 percent, were coded at level 4, emphasizing library and information skills. The third highest number of responses, 113 or 22.8 percent, were coded at level 3, emphasizing a change in attitude regarding the library and its resources. Taken together, these three levels represented 83 percent of the responses.

In summary, results of the survey showed that in each of the three years, the combined levels of attitude, skills, and utilization represented approximately 85 percent of what the librarians emphasized in their responses. Only 15 percent of the responses in each of the three years were at the input and output levels combined. However, there was actually a slight rise in the input level during the last two years when librarians were being introduced to collaborative planning. Many responses at the input level were examples of lessons taught, in other words, what the librarian did, not what students learned. During these years many of the librarians were developing instructional units through collaborative planning. There may have been some confusion about the subtle, but important, distinction between the lesson planned and the learning achieved.

CHANGE IN LIBRARIANS' RESPONSES DURING INVOLVEMENT IN LIBRARY POWER

A comparison of the librarians' responses in 1995, 1996, and 1997 showed an important change over the years of involvement in the

Library Power project as shown in table 2.1. In 1995, the highest number of responses emphasized change in attitude. In 1996, the highest number of responses emphasized increased competence in library and information skills. And in 1997, the highest number of responses emphasized utilization of resources for learning. This would indicate that, over the course of the Library Power initiative, many librarians were changing their perceptions of student learning. Early in the initiative they noted a change in attitude about the library. Midway in the initiative, they stressed competence in locating resources and using technology. In the third year, however, many had turned their attention to learning in the content areas. This progression suggests an increasing awareness on the part of many librarians of inquiry as a way of learning. This important finding indicates that the sustained effort of the Library Power initiative was a critical component in changes that influenced student learning opportunities. The nature of this effort was further investigated in the case study section of this study.

INDICATORS OF LEARNING IDENTIFIED BY SCHOOL LIBRARIANS

In 1996, while analyzing the librarians' responses to the survey question, the coders noted that many responses identified specific

Table 2.1 Changes in Librarians' Descriptions of Learning

	1995 n = *331*		*1996* n = *405*		*1997* n = *495*	
	freq.	*%*	*freq.*	*%*	*freq.*	*%*
Non-response/uncoded	12	3.6	27	6.7	44	8.9
Input	10	3.0	16	4.0	20	4.0
Output	20	6.0	16	4.0	11	2.2
Attitude	105	31.7	97	24.0	113	22.8
Skills	95	28.7	155	38.0	122	24.6
Utilization	89	26.9	94	23.0	185	37.4

indicators that some librarians were using to describe learning. In order to capture these "indicators of learning," all of the responses were reviewed a second time to identify phrases that were used to explain how the librarian had determined that learning was taking place. Indicators of learning were identified in 251 of the 405 responses. These were coded into ten separate categories as described in table 2.2.

The most frequently mentioned indicator was "independence in applying skills" with fifty responses in this category. Examples of responses in the independence (I) category were: uses computer independently; able to use information skills in another assignment; skills reapplied in similar but varying projects. The second most frequently mentioned indicator was "returning to the library on a consistent basis and reluctance to leave when there" included in thirty-seven responses. Examples of responses in the comes back (B) category were: asked if we'll be doing it again; did not want to stop; came back after lunch. The next two most frequently mentioned indicators were "comments made by students to the librarian" included in thirty-two responses and "facial expressions of students" included in thirty responses. Examples of responses

Table 2.2 Coding Scale for Indicators of Learning Identified By Librarians

	Categories	*Frequency*	*Percentage*
I	Independence in applying skills	50	19.9%
B	comes Back, is reluctant to leave, or wants to do activity again	37	14.7%
C	Comments to librarian	32	12.7%
F	expression on Face	30	12.0%
H	Helps and teaches other students	23	9.2%
S	Shares ideas with others	20	8.0%
Q	Questions asked and/or connections made	20	8.0%
P	final Products	17	6.8%
R	Recalls at a later time (content)	16	6.4%
T	Test results	6	2.4%

in the comments (C) category were: calling me over to show what they had discovered; discussed books with me; explain in their own words. Examples of responses in the facial expression (F) category were: face lit up indicating mental connection; expression on their faces; evident in their faces. These four categories accounted for 60 percent of the indicators of learning identified by the librarians.

The next three most frequently mentioned indicators, accounting for 25 percent, were "helps and teaches other students how to locate materials and use technology," "shares ideas about content learning with other students," and "questions students asked and connections they made while using resources for content learning." Examples of responses in the helps (H) category were: helping younger student locate materials; students teaching other students; taught to others. Examples of responses in the shares (S) category were: immediate need to share new information; able to share knowledge with each other; shares learning with class. Examples of responses in the questions and comments (Q) category were: students asked pertinent questions; good questions evolved; makes connections.

The last three, "final products," "recalls content at a later time," and "test results," accounted for 15 percent of the indicators of learning identified by the librarians. Examples of responses in the products (P) category were: seen in final products; new ideas in oral and written reports; student plays were performed. Examples of responses in the recalls (R) category were: commented on months later; remembered so much from their research; able to tell about it three weeks later. Examples of responses in the test (T) category were: test; test results; answers on quiz bowl.

The results of this analysis identified ten indicators of learning that ranged from intuitive observation to documentable evidence. The more traditional ways of assessing learning in libraries is to observe students while they are using the library, with heavy emphasis on library and information skills, typical of the first four most frequently mentioned categories. The second tier of responses represent more interaction and involvement on the part of students, with more emphasis on content learning and information literacy. The fact that the more interactive, documentable indicators were mentioned in 25 percent of the responses suggests an awareness on the part of some librarians of more authentic approaches to assessment. Documenting substantial effects of learning mentioned in the third tier of indicators represented a relatively small number of responses by the librarians.

These findings reveal that the librarians were grappling with the task of identifying and assessing learning related to the use of library resources. The Library Power initiative called for librarians to play a significant role in student learning by collaborative planning and teaching throughout the curriculum. In order to assume this role, they needed to have an understanding of indicators of learning and be able to assess student learning. Although many librarians were aware of this task, this study suggests further expertise was needed for assessing, evaluating, and documenting the learning related to libraries.

Case Study Phase of the Study

The second phase of the study was to take a closer look at selected schools to gain a better sense of the factors influencing opportunities for students to learn. Three theme case study schools were selected from those coded in the librarians' survey on the utilization level and identified by the project directors as places where a high level of learning was likely to be taking place.

The theme case studies were analyzed using a 5-point scale that was based on the same scheme developed to code the examples of learning given in the librarians' survey. The scale was adapted as five levels of evaluation to gain a fuller picture of what was taking place in individual schools and to analyze how the Library Power initiative was affecting opportunities for student learning in each setting. The scale provided a framework for identifying differences in library programs and for analyzing why some schools were having more success than others in providing opportunities for student learning.

FRAMEWORK FOR EVALUATING OPPORTUNITIES FOR LEARNING IN LIBRARY POWER SCHOOLS

A framework for evaluating quality learning opportunities in these three school libraries was developed on five levels as shown in figure 2.2. Level 1, input, investigated the contributions to the library that provided opportunities for student learning. Contributions of Library Power were identified in ten areas: funding, collection, renovation, technology, staffing, administrative support, flexible scheduling, professional development, collaborative planning, and other reform efforts. Basic contributions were funds for books to improve collections. However, as the Library Power project progressed, matching funds and grants were solicited for renovation of facilities and introduction of technology. The basic requirements of participation in Library Power were a full-time librarian,

Level 1: *Input*
Contributions of LP in each school.
Level 2: *Output*
Evidence of quantitative impact of LP.
Level 3: *Attitude*
Evidence of increased interest.
Level 4: *Skills*
Evidence of increased information skills.
Level 5: *Utilization*
Evidence of student learning using LP resources.

Figure 2.2. Framework for Evaluating Libraries Provision for Student Learning

flexible scheduling, and administrative support. In addition, Library Power provided professional development for implementing collaborative planning between librarians and teachers in the participating schools. Taken together, these contributions of Library Power made significant changes in these schools. Other reform efforts were in place in many of the schools as well. These contributions were identified as level 1 input in this study of student learning opportunities.

Level 2, output, investigated the quantitative evidence of increased opportunity for student learning. Quantitative measures of the impact of Library Power were identified, such as increased circulation of books and increased use of the library. Level 3, attitude, investigated the attitudinal changes related to the Library Power initiative. Evidence of changes in attitude were identified, such as increased interest and enthusiasm. Level 4, skills, investigated development of skills in locating materials and using technology that were related to the Library Power initiative. This level was limited to identifying improvement in library and information skills and did not include skill development in curriculum areas and in the learning process in general.

Level 5, utilization, investigated evidence of use of resources for learning through inquiry. This level incorporated student learning in the content areas of the curriculum and the skills for using resources associated with information literacy. This level addresses the deeper questions related to the impact of Library Power on student learning. Are students having a different experience as a result of Library Power? Are students engaging in more independent research? Are students approaching topics in a new way? Are students conducting high-quality research? Are students acquiring an in-depth understanding of topics? Are students performing tasks that may be associated with constructivist learning? The utilization level involves the process of constructing knowledge through the use of a wide range of resources. The criteria for judging student learning at this level were based on a constructivist approach to learning through inquiry as described in the ISP.

In summary, input identified contributions of Library Power including the more intangible inputs of professional development, collaborative planning, and the presence of other reform efforts. Output identified evidence of the amount of use of the library resources and the facility, indicating how the initiative was being received in the school. Attitude was another measure of how the initiative was being received. Skills identified evidence of emphasis of the program on location of materials and information as isolated skills. Utilization was considered the optimal level, where students were learning both information skills and content knowledge through the inquiry process in collaborative units.

A COMPARISON OF OPPORTUNITIES FOR STUDENT LEARNING IN THREE CASE STUDY SCHOOLS

The evaluation scale was used to analyze opportunities for students to learn in three case study schools. The survey section of this study revealed that Library Power clearly has influenced student learning opportunities in each of the participating schools. However, there were important differences in the opportunities for learning in individual schools that were difficult to explain from the survey data. This part of the study examined three library programs to investigate factors underlying the librarian's role in providing opportunities for learning throughout the curriculum. What was the difference in the role of the librarian from one school to another in providing opportunities for student learning? And was that role related to the perception of learning pervasive in the school? The case study section of the study sought to use more qualitative methods to uncover some of the factors underlying these differences. A comparison of the three case study schools, referred to as School 1, School 2, and School 3, highlighted some important factors about these differences.

Input Related to the Library Power Initiative

Important elements influencing opportunities for student learning were a combination of funding, full-time librarian with appropriate support staff, flexible scheduling, and professional development in collaborative planning and teaching strategies. However, an important underlying element revealed in these schools was the presence of an inquiry approach to learning and a commitment to making this type of learning happen. Each of these schools was in a somewhat different position regarding this key element related to the influence of Library Power on student learning.

A major contribution of Library Power was funding for library collections. In each of the schools, new library resources greatly improved library collections, and Library Power funding prompted other sources of funding for renovation, technology, and additional materials. A highly competent librarian was employed full time in each of the schools with support staff in School 1 and School 3. Flexible scheduling was also in place in each of the schools.

Although Library Power had resulted in similar input in all three schools, there were substantial differences in the professional development programs offered and in prior reform efforts that laid the groundwork for the Library Power initiative. School 1 had intensive on-site professional development in place related to a major reform effort based on an inquiry approach that had been under way for six years. A team of professional trainers had been guiding teachers in revising instruction and teaching strategies to provide inquiry learning across the curriculum. Inquiry as a way of learning was well accepted and established before Library Power came into the building. Finding that the inquiry approach was compatible with the objectives of Library Power, the trainers from both efforts joined forces to provide a comprehensive professional development program.

School 2 was also involved in prior reform efforts that were compatible with the Library Power initiative, but were in earlier stages of acceptance and implementation. An ongoing program of professional development was in place, although not as intensively as in School 1. The faculty was open to an inquiry approach and had identified the research process as an area they needed to learn more about through future professional development. In School 3, no consistent reform effort was in place that stressed inquiry or a constructivist approach to learning. Although there were numerous opportunities for professional development, emphasis had not been on inquiry or any other compatible concept. Professional development was more of the awareness variety, sampling an array of different programs without concentration on a consistent underlying philosophy of learning.

Output Related to Library Power

Increased use of the library and its resources, considered output in this study, also revealed evidence of a difference in opportunities for student learning in the case study schools. At School 1, there was a steady stream of classes coming in for research as well as high use of the library by individuals. At School 2, circulation and class use had increased considerably, although more teachers in primary grades were using the library for collaborative research projects than those teaching the fourth and fifth grades. At School 3, circulation and library use initially had increased, but later had gone down mainly as a result of a decrease in student population due to the opening of a new school. However, even considering the smaller student body, it seemed a warning that sustaining the Library Power effort in this school may be difficult over the long term.

Attitude Related to Library Power

Improved attitude toward the library as a place for learning as a result of the Library Power initiative was evident in each of the schools. At School 1, where an inquiry approach was well established, children were excited and interested in what they were learning. At School 2, teachers reported seeing a marked improvement in their students' attitude toward learning through research, particularly in classes where use of the library for curriculum-related projects had increased. At School 3, teachers' and students' enthusiasm mainly centered on the renovated facility and improved collections. However, interest and enthusiasm in learning through research was uneven. Some students expressed concern with collaborative projects where they felt rushed and had received conflicting instructions from the teachers involved.

Library and Information Skills Related to Library Power

At School 1 and School 2, library and information skills were integrated into content learning. Each of these schools had developed a research process model similar to the ISP for guiding students. In both schools, students who used the library for research were found to have the ability to apply their library skills for locating information and resources in other situations and in other libraries. The principal of School 1 noted that the public librarians had reported to him that students knew how to retrieve the information they needed when they used the public library. The librarian at School 2 reported that test scores relating to research skills went up appreciably for students in those classes that had extensive library use. Only at School 3 were isolated library and information skills lessons mentioned in the case study. The librarian was described as orienting students in preparation for future research projects.

Utilization of Resources for Learning Related to Library Power

Use of library resources for learning was the most pertinent level of evaluation for addressing the question of impact on student learning. The other four levels—input, output, attitude, and skills—provided the background for interpreting the differences in utilization of resources for learning in the three schools. All three schools had been identified as places that were likely to have a high level of student learning. And indeed each was found to be providing opportunities for students to learn through the use of a wide range of resources.

The difference between the schools at the utilization level was in an understanding of the inquiry process and how to facilitate the construction of knowledge in the process in areas of the curriculum. The teachers and librarian at School 1 were most advanced in their understanding of inquiry and were providing numerous opportunities for students to learn through the research process. At School 2, the teachers and the librarian had reached a point in their provision of research opportunities for students where they had become aware of a need to know more about the research process and ways to guide student inquiry. They had requested workshops to gain this expertise. Although the librarian and some of the teachers at School 3 had gotten off to a good start with problem-initiated research projects, their understanding of the underlying process of learning through inquiry was not sufficient to sustain their efforts through changes in personnel at the school. When use and interest began to drop, they had difficulty identifying what was going wrong and how to remedy the situation.

At School 1, the instructional program was based on an inquiry approach to learning. Using library resources for learning throughout the curriculum was not an additional, occasional activity, but at the very center of the instructional program. Inquiry was a way to learn, and the resources in the library and the research process were essential components in the learning process. The contributions of Library Power provided funding for essential resources and program elements to support the inquiry approach, which pervaded the school and resulted in increased use of the library and its resources. Collaborative planning and flexible scheduling were well established, as was an ongoing program of professional development. Intensive professional development incorporated technology, philosophy, and strategies in a cohesive whole. The inquiry approach was viewed as the way to achieve the objectives of the school. The case study revealed no doubt in the continuation of the program by the faculty. The program was well established and accepted as the usual way of functioning in the school. Opportunities for student learning at the utilization level were everyday occurrences. The school had been selected as a model to demonstrate a well-functioning program to other schools.

School 2 had made good use of the resources provided by Library Power and had come a long way toward improving opportunities for student learning. Support of administrators provided incentive for the faculty to develop learning through research. Use of the library and resources was increasing. The librarian was open to change and developing a new perspective on her role in the school and new skills for collaborating with teachers on inquiry units. Teachers in the primary grades were responsive to collaborative planning and teaching and had made considerable progress in extending student learning opportunities. Some teachers in the intermediate grades were beginning to develop collaborative plans, but teachers saw that more progress was needed in this area. Substantial progress had been made, but as they became more involved in developing an inquiry-based program, they realized that the research process as a central element needed to be better understood by the teachers and librarian in order for student learning to be guided in meaningful ways. They were not ready to rest on their accomplishments but saw a need for improvement, particularly in expertise in the research process and technology. Professional development efforts for the future were planned in these areas. Some teachers indicated a concern for sustaining the initiative, but most felt assured that the program had shown a degree of merit that supported future development.

At School 3, the teachers had been involved in several collaborative planning workshops related to the Library Power initiative where they developed interdisciplinary units with the librarian. Before Library Power, little collaboration existed at the school. After participation in the workshops, many of the teachers viewed the collaborative opportunities as having a positive influence on student learning. However, the librarian reported that although about 50 percent of the teachers did some kind of collaboration as a result of the workshops, for some it just meant telling her what they planned to do in the library. She estimated that between 10 and 20 percent were truly engaged in collaborative planning and teaching. However, there did not seem to be any set mechanism to ensure that collaboration took place. Through memorandums and announcements at faculty meetings, the librarian had invited teachers to continue to plan with her. But she noted, "Getting people to collaborate with me is hard because everyone is so busy. Time is really a big factor." A change in personnel had resulted in a serious reduction in collaboration and learning through research. The librarian seemed somewhat discouraged at the prospects for sustaining collaboration over the long term.

Summary of Comparison of Student Learning in Library Power Schools

Student learning opportunities related to the Library Power initiative varied in these schools according to the presence of an inquiry approach to learning. School 1 had an established model of learning through inquiry on which the Library Power initiative could build. School 2 had changed considerably with Library Power contributions and was on a good track for establishing an inquiry approach. School 3, however, seemed to be foundering because no set mechanism was in place to sustain collaborative teaching of an inquiry approach.

The philosophy of learning in each school directly affected the role that the librarian assumed in the learning process. At School 1, the librarian was a full partner with teachers in learning through research. School 2 was well on the way toward a fully collaborative program in the primary grades. At School 3, the librarian, although highly regarded, was mainly considered a resource provider and teacher of library skills rather than full collaborator in the learning process, even after faculty had participated in workshops on collaborative planning.

A predisposition to a constructivist approach to learning through research was revealed as essential for establishing a consistent collaborative library program. School 1 had a research process model similar to the ISP in place prior to the Library Power initiative. There they integrated reading and writing process strategies with the research process to create a way of learning through inquiry. School 2, although not as developed as School 1, had a research process approach in the primary grades where learning through inquiry had taken hold, but had not yet established the approach in grades 4 and 5. The difference in the impact on learning between primary and upper-grade students was noted in the case study. School 3 had relied primarily on a model of collaboration without the foundation of other reform efforts to connect learning through research across the curriculum. Without this foundation, the librarian had difficulty breaking out of the traditional role of resource provider to move into a more central role as coplanner and teacher and difficulty sustaining the role of collaborator in the learning process.

In response to the key question in this study, the answer would be a qualified yes that Library Power has influenced student learning opportunities. But the degree to which Library Power influenced opportunities for students to learn varied in these schools as a result of the basic underlying philosophy of learning prevalent in the schools. Where teachers, librarians, and administrators were committed to learning through inquiry, the library was a integral part of the learning process.

CONCLUSION AND IMPLICATIONS OF THE STUDY ON OPPORTUNITIES FOR STUDENT LEARNING

The impact of libraries on student learning is a key issue for librarians and school administrators. How do we determine the impact of the library on opportunities for students to learn? What evidence do we have that students are learning in libraries? What is the librarian's role in providing opportunities for student learning? This study addressed these questions in the Library Power initiative, first, by asking the librarians to describe incidents of learning in their school libraries, and, second, by taking a close look at the differences in three schools selected for case study.

The librarians' perceptions of learning and how those perceptions changed were investigated over the course of the three years of involvement in Library Power. The librarians were found to describe learning on five levels:

Input, additions to the library collection;
Output, increased use;
Attitude, increased interest;
Skills, improvement in location of materials and information; and
Utilization, use of resources for content learning.

The librarians were aware that student learning involved more than providing resources and increased use at levels 1 and 2. They identified opportunities for learning as involving heightened interest, improved access skills, and ability to learn from a variety of resources. In each of the three years, approximately 85 percent of the responses were at levels 3, 4, and 5, with the highest number of the responses in the first year describing improved attitude at level 3, in the second year describing improved skills at level 4, and in the third year describing improved use for learning at level 5. This change indicates that across the Library Power initiative the librarians' grasp of the role the library plays evolved toward more collaborative and central participation in student learning.

An additional analysis examined the kinds of evidence the librarians cited to indicate that learning was taking place. Ten indicators of learning were found in the librarians' responses that ranged from independence in applying skills to test results. The most frequently mentioned indicators related to the librarians' observations of students in the library. They had observed students' independence in using the library, their reluctance to leave and tendency to return, and their comments and the expressions on their faces. These observations were given as indicating that students were learning in 60 percent of the librarians' responses. Indicators showing learning that was likely to be specifically integrated with curriculum content, such as "helps and teaches other students, shares ideas with others," and by the questions asked and connections made were found in 25 percent of the responses. And more documentable accountability such as final products, "recalls content at a later time," and test results were given in only 15 percent of the librarians' responses. The task of identifying and assessing learning related to the use of libraries is essential where school librarians assume a central collaborative role in the learning of students. More work is needed in this area to develop assessment strategies within the entire range of indicators of learning identified in this study.

The second phase of this study examined case studies to determine why some schools were having more success than others at developing and sustaining integrated, collaborative library programs that provided opportunities for student learning. Comparison of three schools revealed that Library Power was more effective where there was a commitment to an inquiry approach to learning shared by the librarian, teachers, and administrators. Where an inquiry approach was in place, the library was an integral part of the learning process. Without a commitment to constructivist learning that requires a variety of resources, the library was considered an extra activity in an already overloaded program. In schools where the library was considered essential rather than just good, a clear commitment to inquiry learning was in place on which to build a collaborative library program integrated with the curriculum. In these schools, Library Power was making a significant impact on student learning opportunities.

An important contribution of this study is to the development of methods to study the impact of libraries on student learning. The framework for evaluating libraries and scales for describing levels of learning and for identifying indicators of learning may be applied to investigate learning in other schools. Used to frame interviews or structure observations, these instruments can reveal what is being emphasized in a library program and what is the underlying approach to learning that forms the basis for collaboration between teachers and librarians. The framework and scales provide a way to identify why some school libraries are more successful than others at providing opportunities for student learning. In addition, these instruments may be adapted for use in workshops for librarians, teachers, and administrators to evaluate existing library programs in preparation for developing collaborative programs based on inquiry where students learn from a variety of resources in the content areas of the curriculum.

REFERENCES

Callison, D. (1986). "School library media programs and free inquiry learning." *School Library Journal* 32 (6): 20–24.

Harste, J. (1994). "Literacy as inquiry: An interview with Jerome C. Harste." *Reading Teacher* 47: 518–521.

Harste, J., Callison, D., and Jurewicz, E. (1994). *Visions of literacy.* Videotape produced by ITV and Special Projects, Indiana University. Portsmouth, NH: Heineman Educational Books.

Kuhlthau, C. (1993). *Seeking meaning: A process approach to library and information services.* Greenwich, Conn.: Ablex.

Kuhlthau, C. (1994). *Teaching the library research process* (2nd ed.). Lanham, Md.: Scarecrow Press.

THREE

Learning and the Digital Library

Delia Neuman

There are few doubts about the potential of the digital library for providing unprecedented access to information and ideas. There are numerous doubts, however, about the potential of this rich and still-mysterious venue for providing an optimal environment for learning. In fact, the very strengths of the digital library—its limitless information, variety of formats, affordance of unconstrained navigation, and support for combining material in myriad ways—are the sources of these uncertainties in formal learning environments. We know little enough about how to foster higher-level learning with "traditional" collections of print and nonprint materials. How, then, can we foster such learning in the vast and untracked terrain of the digital library?

Research in information studies traditionally focuses on accessing information rather than on learning from it, but the emergence of electronic information resources (EIRs) has been a catalyst for a range of work on the relationship of these resources specifically to learning. In addition, insights on learning and media accumulated by the field of instructional technology provide another important perspective on learning in electronic environments. Research and theory from both these fields suggest both caveats and opportunities related to children's prospects for learning in the digital library. Placing these insights within the larger context of "information literacy" provides a framework for understanding and addressing a variety of issues related to learning in this exciting new venue. The purpose of this chapter is to draw upon selected research and theory across this spectrum in order to present an array of insights about enhancing the potential of the digital library as an environment for higher-level learning in the school. Reflecting on our current limited knowledge about this complex topic, the chapter is introductory rather than exhaustive and is intended to offer a starting point for further discussion and research.

THE DIGITAL LIBRARY AS A VENUE FOR HIGHER-LEVEL LEARNING

Wozny's (1982) investigation of ninth-graders' use of online bibliographic databases in connection with an independent research project is one of the earliest studies in this field to draw attention to the potential of electronic information resources, not just to help young learners access information but "to introduce students to a broader world of information" (p. 40) and to provide "a new opportunity for assisting students developing search strategies" (p. 42). Ensuing years have seen a variety of other works designed to explore the broad relationship of EIRs to learning and particularly to the mastery of the concepts and skills required for conducting research (e.g., Aversa and Mancall, 1986; Callison and Daniels, 1988; Crane and Markowitz, 1994; Lathrop, 1989; Mancall, 1984; Neuman, 1993, 1995a, 1995b). Each of these works—along with a variety others—has had a role to play in shedding light on the complexities of learning with and through EIRs. Today, that light might profitably be focused on learning and the digital library.

Mancall (1984), for example, noted the importance of teaching logic and critical thinking skills in order to help students use online databases profitably. Aversa and Mancall (1986) suggested that students should be taught online searching specifically so that they can become knowledgeable about information and how to develop and refine their strategies for finding and using it. Callison and Daniels (1988), after working with forty-one juniors who searched for information on a variety of topics in a commercial EIR, noted that "the value of the online search experience for the high schooler" might well go beyond the acquisition of basic experience with using the technology to "the challenge to make information-use decisions based on facts, relevancy, recency, and authority" (p. 10). Lathrop's (1989) survey of seventy-three secondary school librarians in nineteen states focused specifically on online information retrieval as a research tool and addressed (among other concerns) instructional objectives, student training, and curriculum uses. More recently, Crane and Markowitz (1994) detailed a three-level model for teaching critical thinking through online searching, while Neuman (1993, 1995a, 1995b) identified a number of curricular and instructional issues to be addressed, helping high school students become competent and credible researchers with EIRs. All this work reveals a growing awareness that EIRs provide a critical venue for helping students learn concepts and skills that are essential in the information age—abilities to access, evaluate, and use information to build knowledge, to think critically, and to solve problems. The digital library, which provides an even richer and more complex environment than the individual components investigated in these studies, offers an even more extensive venue for helping students develop these essential abilities.

Neuman's (1995b) national Delphi study, related to learning and online and CD-ROM databases, for example, reported a number of findings that can readily be extrapolated to the wider world of the digital library. The Delphi panelists (twenty-five library media specialists who are experts in using these electronic information resources with high school students) rated over two hundred statements, including several that specifically addressed the importance of using EIRs to enhance students' research skills. Ratings of two statements in particular highlight the importance the panelists assigned to this function: "A goal of a database curriculum should be to help students master the higher-order thinking skills involved in designing, conducting, and interpreting research" (p. 284); "Database searching should be part of a formal research offering that covers the nature and processes of research, various tools, etc." (p. 284). These two statements were among only six from the entire study that garnered a final means of 4.0—"perfect scores" on the instrument's scale of 0 to 4. The panel's unanimous agreement with these statements, as well as Neuman's summary for the full study, underscores the importance of using EIRs as venues to foster higher-level learning: "The results confirm that the major issues related to schools' use of online and CD-ROM databases involve their role in students' development of the higher order thinking skills necessary to plan, design, and conduct competent and credible research in the electronic information age" (p. 284).

RESEARCH FROM INFORMATION STUDIES

Students' Interactions with Components of the Digital Library

Information studies research has also addressed the complexities of students' interactions with various kinds of electronic information resources in an attempt to identify successful and unsuccessful strategies and, further, to suggest design elements that might enhance students' use of these tools (Large et al., 1994a, 1994b; Liebscher and Marchionini, 1988; Marchionini, 1989; Marchionini and Teague, 1987; Neuman, 1993, 1995b; Perzylo and Oliver, 1992; Small and Ferreira, 1994; Solomon, 1994). Marchionini's continuing focus on students' mental models as they use EIRs has led to important insights related to both elementary (Marchionini, 1989; Marchionini and Teague, 1987) and high school (Liebscher and Marchionini, 1988) students' effective manipulation within these environments—and, by extension, within the digital library. Large et al.'s, Perzylo and Oliver's, Small and Ferreira's, and Solomon's work on elementary students' use of particular EIRs provides further insights that can be extended to learning and the digital library for this group, while Neuman's studies of high school students' use of these resources suggests such insights for older students.

Elementary and Middle School Students and the Digital Library

Marchionini and Teague (1987) were among the first to explore elementary students' use of electronic information resources, and Marchionini's (1989) finding that children as young as third and fourth graders could "unsuccessfully use [Grolier's] full-text, electronic encyclopedia with minimal introductory training" (p. 64) is heartening to teachers and library media specialists charged with helping their students master the textual components of the digital library. Large et al. (1994a) reported similar findings with sixth graders, investigating these children's use of Compton's multimedia encyclopedia and noting that they were able not only to navigate the database effectively but also to determine which alternative path (menu, keyword searching, or title browsing) was most efficient for retrieving verbal information for a particular search task (judged as simple or complex according to the number of possible search terms). Marchionini's (1989) notation that the students' strategies in a textual environment tended to be heuristic and interactive suggests that children have a natural affinity for the kind of exploratory and self-directed learning that is particularly well suited to the digital library. Large et al.(1994a) that students needed little training to navigate within a multimedia venue—one that included not only text but still images, sound, and video sequences—is also encouraging regarding students' independent learning in the digital library.

Large et al.'s work as well as the work of Perzylo and Oliver (1992), however, raises questions about students' ability to make productive use of the information that renders multimedia environments unique—at least for traditional classroom assignments. Large et al. (1994b) found that multimedia seemed to be more effective for leading to students' recall of simple topics than complex ones and noted that "in general the multimedia group failed to benefit fully from the dual coding of visual and verbal information" (p. 526). Perzylo and Oliver (1992) found that sixth graders were able to navigate the components of *National Geographic's Mammals* effectively but were hampered in their use of much of its material for their "summary papers" largely because they lacked the means and strategies of recording and incorporating the nontextual components that carried much of the information they sought. Students preferred to access the sound, video, photographic, and graphics information in the database—in that order—and read and digested only that textual information that was "brief in its extent and . . . selected intentionally [such as] the photo captions and the hypertext descriptions" (p. 237). For their assignment, however—a traditional written report—students used virtually no information but the textual material they were able to print out (primarily an essay) and incorporated other forms of information only through references in their narratives. Clearly, both the text-based nature of the assignment and the product's lack of printout capability for anything but textual materials all but ensured that students would not be able to use the multimedia information effectively for this task. Nevertheless, the researchers' conclusion that the students' performance reflected not only these factors but the fact that "students appeared to have no skills or knowledge in seeking and recording information from other than textual sources" (Perzylo and Oliver, 1992, p. 238) raises important cautions about the use of multimedia components of the digital library for learning.

Small and Ferreira's (1994) findings reinforce these cautions: these researchers found that middle schoolers (sixth through eighth graders) used a print resource and tended to take written notes as they read, and they engaged in more "extracting" behaviors than did comparable students who used a multimedia resource. The latter group, who reported that they liked the visual and sound components of the interactive videodisc used for the experiment, generally took only "mental notes" and performed more "browsing" activities. While the study did not address the relative information-gathering success of the two groups, it did note that students rated the multimedia source significantly higher than the print source on such factors as "accessibility, accuracy, comprehensiveness, consistency, controllability, currency, ease of use, organization, reliability and understandability" (pp. 100–101). This disconnection between students' preferences for multimedia formats and their inabilities to mine them for in-depth information suggests that students and teachers alike must develop new conceptions of the best ways to access, evaluate, and use multimedia information for learning. The strategies that teachers and students must use to optimize learning through the World Wide Web, for example—whose power stems largely from its ability to provide information in formats other than text—are still to be discovered.

Solomon (1993), too, investigated children's use of a particular kind of electronic information resource—in this case, the OPAC. Like Marchionini, he discovered that elementary students were generally successful in their use of this text-based EIR, and, further, that they became increasingly proficient as the school year progressed and they learned to maneuver more and more effectively within this environment. Unlike Marchionini, however, Solomon set out to identify the details of students' interactions with the OPAC so that he could suggest guidelines for designing these

EIRs to enhance students' opportunities for success. His results include a delineation of the reasons for students' breakdowns (i.e., in retrieval) that provide important insights into the relationship of OPAC use to learning. Solomon identified breakdowns in three capabilities—knowledge of specific skills, knowledge of rules, and contextual knowledge. The implication, of course, is that students must master these capabilities to operate effectively in this kind of environment. First, they must understand basic concepts related to reading, spelling/keying, and the nature and uses of an OPAC. Second, they must understand the OPAC's rules of syntax (e.g., with regard to spacing and punctuation); query formation (e.g., the use of nouns and plural forms); and focus (e.g., differentiating among author, subject, and title search). Finally, they must understand how to monitor an OPAC response and to take appropriate action, based on their content knowledge and their understanding of how the OPAC works, to proceed successfully.

In a later paper based on this initial study, Solomon (1994) further illuminated the relationship of OPAC use and learning by describing the connection between students' proficiency with the OPAC and the kind of instruction and assignments that different groups of students received. Solomon noted that one group had received clear-cut assignments ("Turn in a written report with the following pieces of information on your state") that allowed them to complete the task simply by entering the name of a state (e.g., Alabama) and retrieving pertinent information. Although this group had a high success rate with the OPAC, "the lack of challenge in their searching limited what they discovered about information retrieval. [They], as a result, were less able to recognize and respond to breakdowns than other students who had more variety in their OPAC experiences." These other students, who "were given assignments that required more in-depth [content] knowledge and more creative control actions at the OPAC . . . began to develop strategies that employed broader, narrower, and coordinate terms that would help them identify additional sources" (p. 47). Solomon concluded: the challenge of assignments that encouraged children to build on their interests or investigate subjects in some depth carried over to their information retrieval behavior at the OPAC. They needed to move beyond the simple subject search to discover, learn, and try many strategies to get information on their interests and to overcome OPAC breakdowns (p. 47).

Clearly, Solomon's insights about the relationship of curriculum and instruction to students' levels of learning with an OPAC can be extrapolated to the world of the digital library. If a sophisticated curriculum and creative assignments can enhance higher-level learning with such a basic tool as an OPAC, how much more important must these factors be in facilitating such learning in this richer and more complex environment?

High School Students and Text-Based Materials in the Digital Library

One of the earliest studies of high school students' use of electronic information resources was Liebscher and Marchionini's (1988) comparison of ninth graders' "analytical" (Boolean) and "browsing" searches in Grolier's full-text CD-ROM encyclopedia, which established that both groups performed successfully and relatively equally in terms of the mean numbers of search terms used and relevant articles retrieved. Their study raised interesting questions about the application of information retrieved to a learning task, however, because of their finding that the "analytical" group received higher grades on their final essays than did the "browse" group. Speculating about the relationship between the amount of planning required by each group at the query formulation stage and the subsequent "payoff" in terms of information use, the researchers analyzed the prepositional phrases in the students' final essays. They found little correlation between a student's grade and the overall number of such phrases—but they did find an "inverse correspondence between grade received and number of nonrelevant prepositional phrases" (p. 230). The authors theorized that students who used the simple browse strategy might have been unwilling to discard irrelevant information they had gleaned during their searches and that the "less[er amount of] internal organization of information . . . required at the query formulation stage" might have interfered with these students' abilities "to discriminate as well as [the analytical group] between relevant and nonrelevant information" (p. 230). Liebscher and Marchionini's questions about students' abilities to organize information in a way appropriate to the assignment—even within the restricted environment of a CD-ROM encyclopedia and for the limited task of using that information in a brief essay—raise more substantial concerns about the abilities and strategies students will need in the more diverse and less structured world of the digital library and with the kinds of products to which its information might be applied.

Neuman's studies of high school students' interactions with online and CD-ROM databases (1993, 1995a, 1995b) also attempted to identify the relationship of a particular class of electronic information resources to student learning. The original study, an extensive naturalistic inquiry of ninety-two freshmen's and sophomores' interactions with eighteen online and seven CD-ROM databases, yielded insights into the details of students' successes and failures in using these resources that are particularly salient to learning in text-based components of the digital library. Further analysis of these data revealed the details of basic differences between the structures inherent in databases and the conceptual structures that students bring to searching—differences so compelling that they seriously hampered students' independent use of these resources (Neuman,1995b).

High school students, of course, are novices in their understanding of research and its methods, in their familiarity with the topics they study, and in their development of the persistence and flexibility that characterize the mature adults for whom most online and CD-ROM products (and most components of the digital library) are designed. Fairly minor symptoms of these students' conceptual naiveté involved their frequent choices of inappropriate databases and their regular pattern of searching for authors in subject indexes and for titles in author indexes. Much of this, of course, reflects the nature of adolescent behavior—choosing whatever workstation happened to be available and beginning a search without paying attention to the information on the screen—and such difficulties can be overcome with patience and instruction. Others, however, suggest deeper problems. One student, for example, looked for articles on "moonshine runners" in a resource that dated from 1982 and explained that the topic was missing from the database because moonshine running was illegal, not because he was looking for historical material in a database of contemporary information. More seriously, a number of chemistry students included items related to organic chemistry in bibliographies for papers on topics in inorganic chemistry—not because they were padding their bibliographies but because, as their teacher concluded, these gifted freshmen were unaware that chemistry and chemical information are organized into two branches. If students are stymied at such basic levels and in such simple resources, how will they navigate effectively—let alone efficiently—in the more complex world of the digital library?

The data also revealed an incompatibility between students' needs and the complexity of the resources available to them. Noting that CD-ROM databases are often too simple and online ones too advanced seem almost too obvious for a scholarly observation. But the disparity between the needs of these students and the nature of the information in their electronic information resources was in fact a serious conceptual obstacle the students' effective use of these resources for learning. Most students—even advanced ones—need basic information related to curricular needs rather than either popular renditions or reports of cutting-edge research results. Thus, if the digital library is to be used to help the majority of students (1) master aspects of curricular content, and (2) develop the research skills necessary not only to complete school assignments but to serve as the basis for lifelong learning, then it must include information that is at an appropriate level of complexity both for students' levels of knowledge and for students' tasks. That is, to foster learning, the digital library—like any library—must include a range of resources to meet the needs of a range of users. Although Internet access to "world renowned" experts and their work has excited both educators and students, it is also important to make room in the digital library for information that is conceptually accessible to, and useful for, a student audience whose interests, needs, abilities, and goals make them a truly unique user group. Both the students and the adults in this study called for such basic EIRs as lists of textbooks and young adult trade books on curricular areas and for the creation of subject-specific EIRs that include academic information written for high school students.

A more interesting—and difficult—conceptual issue is the incompatibility between students' knowledge bases and conceptual structures and those inherent in databases. As novices, most students lack the vocabulary, the conceptual schemata, and the cognitive flexibility enjoyed by the experts for whom the majority of digital resources are designed. In this study, students' inability to generate synonyms, combined with their naivete about how electronic information resources are structured, often frustrated their ability to use even self-contained CD-ROM resources effectively. Extrapolating this situation to the larger world of the digital library raises concerns about how productively students might use this world for learning. Superimposed on the difficulties inherent in any keyword-searching system, how will students' linguistic and conceptual naiveté affect their chances of productive searching?

Students' limited command of synonyms reflected their inexperience with many of the ideas that adolescents go to school to master. One student's exasperation illustrates the problem: "You have to find a synonym. But if you don't know about [a topic], then how are you going to get a synonym?" How, indeed, are students going to find the words and generate the ideas they will need to access information across the digital library? Words are keys to concepts, and students' limited vocabularies suggests a conceptual immaturity as well as a linguistic one. In a self-contained electronic information resource like a CD-ROM, a built-in thesaurus similar to those routinely found in word processors could have helped by giving students access to information through vocabulary—and, therefore, concepts—that did not exist in their own conceptual structures. But no such tool existed in the CD-ROMs let alone in the online databases that these students used. Extrapolating the issue beyond this limited environment makes it even more complex because it raises questions about how students can access the most relevant and appropriate information across multiple resources without some mechanism that will expand their vocabularies and conceptual schemata. Lack of knowledge can thwart even simple explorations in subject areas students might want (or need) to study, and these novices might not even be aware that they had missed major and critical information.

Even beyond the difficulties engendered by their limited vocabularies, students' naïve—and often inflexible—conceptual structures about their research areas also hindered their ability to use the text-based electronic information resources in this study. First, it is important to note that the students' structures seemed to reflect almost exactly the structures imposed by curriculum categories in general and by teachers' assignments in particular; as school and public librarians well know, if the story assignment is a research paper on the Civil War, then the phrase "Civil War" may represent the students' entire understanding of the research task, at least at the beginning of a project. Not surprisingly, the students in this study were not always able to exceed the boundaries imposed by a teacher's explanation of a task. Also not surprisingly, without intervention, the students flailed about in both online and CD-ROM resources just as unproductively as students often do when they use "traditional" reference sources.

Discussing the individual resources themselves, students complained that "there are different categories than what you really want" and that they could not search either for such broad concepts as a particular decade (e.g., the 1960s) or such narrow ones as a particular year (e.g., 1865). Predictably, CD-ROM searches for such topics as "World War II," "Catholics in the 1950s," and "one-room schoolhouses" all proved fruitless. Unable to create conceptual categories that matched those inherent in the EIRs, students frequently gave up their searches. To succeed in the broader environment of the digital library, students will clearly need to develop a sophisticated understanding of the nature of information and of the ways it can be organized and explored.

One boy's search for "Vietnam-era draft evaders" illustrates students' conceptual naiveté as well as an even more complex problem: the conceptual rigidity with which some students approached their task. Using a CD-ROM index, the boy tried "Vietnam" repeatedly even when the word failed to generate any hits. After considerable prodding from the researcher, he finally tried another approach; he entered "draft" and found a subhead "draft resisters" and a sub-subhead for Vietnam. Interestingly, even though this tack enabled him to find his subject, he continued to insist—as he had throughout this session—that "draft" should have been a subhead under the main heading "Vietnam." It seemed clear, first, that he did not understand that information can be organized in more than one way, and, second, that this naivete made him incapable of adjusting his own conceptual hierarchy to find an article independently. Without the outside intervention that he needed to succeed, he probably would have walked away from his task—as many students did—convinced that the EIR held nothing for him.

This student was not alone in his inability to transcend the initial understanding he had brought to his task. Students complained about prompts that asked for more specific search requests—"There was no way I could make mine more specific"—and recommended more general categories. Students also complained, however, about categories they felt were too general: "I thought the [headings were] way too general for some of the topics that we needed to use" (note the phrase "topics that we needed to use"). Clearly, even in this constrained environment, there was a need to bridge the gap between students' conceptual structures and those inherent in databases. Within the larger world of the digital library, how can educators help meet students' need for flexible traversal of the barriers separating general and specific topics within those categories? Faced with possibilities not only within but across electronic information resources, how will these novices acquire the conceptual depth and flexibility necessary to find accurate and relevant information efficiently and effectively?

In summary, it seems clear that research from information studies has confirmed that the digital library is an essential venue for learning the concepts and skills necessary for conducting research and handling information in the information age. Moreover, this research has also indicated that elementary, middle school, and high school students can indeed profit from their use of such discrete components of the digital library as electronic encyclopedias, OPACs, and online and CD-ROM databases. Studies have also indicated, however, that looking closely at the details of students' interactions with these components raises significant questions about how to maximize electronic information resources for learning.

Some of this research intentionally incorporates insights from another field—that is, instructional technology—in order to address these questions. Research situated directly within that field offers additional avenues for further research into the use of the digital library as an environment for learning. In particular, insights from the segment of the field that is concerned with designing instructional materials suggest ways in which components of the digital library might be organized and developed to enhance their potential for learning.

RESEARCH FROM INSTRUCTIONAL TECHNOLOGY: LEARNING AND MEDIA

Interest in learning and media dates at least from the early part of the century when "educational museums" were created to house such audiovisual aids as stereoscopic pictures and lantern slides. In the ensuing years, each new technology in turn has taken its place in the march toward more sophisticated and more integrated learning media: instructional film, instructional radio, instructional television, programmed instruction, computer-based instruction, and now a medley of multimedia environments. Formal research programs emerged in the 1940s and 1950s with investigations of how military training films could be adapted to civilian instruction. Over the years, the learning potential of each new format—how to identify that potential and how to enhance it—became the central focus of researchers' agendas.

Until the last decade, most of the research in instructional technology—as in education in general—was grounded in behaviorist learning theory. Decades of studies conducted under this paradigm, however, produced results related to learning and various media formats that were, at best, equivocal (see R. C. Clark's 1983 article for the classic and compelling criticism of traditional instructional technology research that jolted the research community). Currently, instructional technology research and development are grounded in cognitive learning theory, which, of course, now undergirds research and practice throughout the teaching and learning community. This new theoretical focus, combined with more sophisticated research methodologies, offers strong new possibilities for understanding the nature and processes of learning in the digital library.

Theoretical Foundations for Research on Learning and the Digital Library

Explorations of the relationship of cognitive theory to instructional technology have in fact coexisted with behaviorist ideas in the instructional technology community for years, and the field has a long history of drawing on both traditions to explore the relationship of media and learning. For example, Robert Gagne's (1977) *Conditions of Learning*, originally published in 1970, became a classic when its third edition interwove principles from cognitive theory with those from instructional systems design. Other classic works in the field have also been reconceptualized and updated to reflect the most current understandings of how people learn.

Of particular theoretical significance to questions about learning and the digital library is the work of Robert Kozma (1991), whose article entitled "Learning with Media" crystallized and expanded many of the ideas that had been circulating in the instructional design community and established the foundation for conducting instructional technology research within the cognitive perspective. In this seminal work, Kozma described learning as an active, constructive process and defined "learning with media as a complementary process within which representations are constructed and procedures performed, sometimes by the learner and sometimes by the medium" (p. 179). As it has for all of instructional technology research, Kozma's review of research on learning with books, with television, with computers, and (briefly) with multimedia environments offers an important conceptual framework for research on learning and the digital library.

Kozma postulated that each of these media formats is distinguished by a cluster of characteristics that, taken together, make the particular format more and less suitable for particular kinds of learning tasks. The stability of print, for example, supports serial and sequential processing and the development of static (although not necessarily simple) mental models; the motion of video media and their concurrent presentation of information through several sensory channels support simultaneous processing and the construction of mental models that include dynamic and procedural components. The transformational ability of the computer—its ability not just to present information but to transform it from one symbol system (like numbers) into another (like a bar graph)—supports the learning of underlying abstract rules and principles that define the structure of knowledge. Multimedia environments, which combine the characteristics of all these individual media formats into an integrated and expanded whole, may help learners build and analyze mental models of complex problem situations. Kozma (1994) was quick to admit that "the cognitive effects of the more recently developed environments are speculative" (p. 206), but in a later article he offered his conclusions and insights as an argument for reframing instructional technology's long-standing debate on the contributions of media to learning:

> Perhaps we should ask, what are the actual and potential relationships between media and learning? Can we describe and understand those relationships? And can we create a strong and compelling influence of media on learning through improved theories, research, and instructional designs? (Kozma, 1994, p. 233)

Kozma's three questions as well as his recommendation that researchers explore "specific ways in which media capabilities may be used to influence learning for individual learners performing particular tasks in specific content areas" (1994, p. 237) offer particular guidance for research related to learning in the digital library—the largest and most complex multimedia environment learners have ever encountered. His inference that we are just beginning to ask the most important questions and to explore the most significant relationships suggest that the digital library is an exciting "learning environment" for theoreticians, researchers, and developers as well as for students.

Work from information studies described earlier provides some insights into the nature of student learning in that environment and the questions that remain to be answered: Liebscher and Marchionini (1988) Neuman (1993, 1995a, 1995b), and Solomon (1993, 1994) all suggest important capabilities that students must acquire to use text-based electronic information resources successfully. Large et al. (1994a, 1994b), Perzylo and Oliver (1992), and Small and Ferreira (1994) perform the same function for multimedia materials. Instructional technology—and particularly instructional systems design—provides insights into how components of that environment might be designed to foster that learning.

Designing Components of the Digital Library

One of the enduring works in instructional technology is Malcolm Fleming and Howard Levie's (1978) *Instructional Message Design: Principles from the Behavioral Sciences*—reissued in 1993 as *Instructional Message Design: Principles from the Behavioral and Cognitive Sciences*. The 1993 edition combines findings from both traditions of learning theory to specify over three hundred research-based guidelines for designing instructional presentations in various print and nonprint formats—and over two hundred of these address issues that can be applied to creating components of the digital library. This collection of principles for designing materials to enhance motivation, perception, general learning, concept learning, and problem solving is clearly relevant to enhancing the potential of those components as venues for learning.

Even such simple principles as "Purely decorative pictures should be used sparingly" (Fleming and Levie, 1993, p. 89) and "Logically organized text is better remembered than poorly organized text" (p. 208) provide useful insights about how components of the digital library might be organized and presented to increase students' likelihood of learning in this environment. More complex principles—such as "The acquisition of unfamiliar content can be improved via familiar examples, analogies, and metaphors, while such strategies are less essential for familiar content" (p. 215) and "The presentation of visually richer and more realistic best examples leads to a richer and better consolidated prototype resulting in increased transfer" (p. 244)—can also be mined for their applicability to creating elements of the digital library. Because these principles focus on designing instructional rather than informational presentations, they offer a critical perspective on preparing segments of the digital library that will be used by students. Applying such "design for learning" axioms as well as guidelines for ensuring optimal access and retrieval seems a fundamental prerequisite for enhancing the learning potential of the digital library.

A number of today's instructional technology researchers are exploring what are known as "open-ended learning environments"—settings that seek to integrate instructional and informational components and in which students perform tasks and processes that are similar to those they must perform to learn within the digital library. Michael Hannafin (1992), who has emerged as a leader in this effort, describes a range of individual settings that researchers are developing and testing in order to enhance our understanding of how students learn in electronic environments that do not just present concepts to be learned but that incorporate extensive information resources. "Macro-level environments" include both rich collections of resources and tools students use to explore them "to pursue interests or needs beyond the parameters typically provided in isolated lessons" (p. 58); "micro-level environments" offer similar arrays of materials but focus within more discrete domains. "Generative environments," such as the Jasper Woodbury series created by the Cognition and Technology Group at Vanderbilt University, consist of scenarios with embedded information that students must identify, evaluate, and manipulate to solve problems. "Mathemagenic environments" support access to various representations of content in a particular area (often through hypermedia links) and allow students to "move rapidly among networks of concepts [and] to construct their own sets of relationships within the network" (p. 59). According to Hannafin, these various settings can support either goal-directed learning—as do traditional instructional media—or exploratory learning. The question for instructional technology—clearly an echo of Kozma's (1994) questions noted above—seems to be how to adapt traditional design theories and methods to the creation of environments that can support both kinds of learning, perhaps within the same "package." The question for those who are concerned with learning and the digital library is how to extrapolate the insights gained through research in these individual settings into a wider world that includes many discrete resources and also requires traversal across and among them.

A great deal of discussion in instructional technology has focused on these settings, which have proliferated in recent years. Goodrum, Dorsey, and Schwen (1993), for example, described the conceptual and practical difficulties in designing an "enriched learning and information environment" that accommodates the difficulties that Perkins (1991) had identified for students operating within such a setting: high cognitive load, increased responsibility for managing their own learning, and need to adopt an unfamiliar learning process. Scardamalia and her colleagues (1989, 1992) have worked for years on the development and refinement of CSILE—"Computer-Supported Intentional Learning Environment"—a shell that allows students to create their own knowledge base related to classroom instruction by working collaboratively in an electronic environment to generate hypotheses, ask questions, and revise their understandings of that information. Reiber (1990, 1996) has explored how both animation and elements of simulations and games can enhance students' abilities to focus on and learn from multimedia "microworlds." In their exploration of the assumptions, methods, and implications for learning inherent in the various kinds of open-ended learning environments, Hannafin, Hall, Land, and Hill (1994) noted the lack of compelling empirical evidence of how open-ended learning environments influence learning and, further, discussed the difficulty of obtaining such evidence—these environments are "designed to promote fundamentally different kinds of learning" than the field is used to studying; its tools for understanding "different kinds of learning goals" and for "assessing the successes or failures of such systems" are underdeveloped; and its "design science for such systems" is "very weak" (p. 52). Clearly, the authors might be describing the state of our knowledge about designing materials to enhance learning within the digital library.

Thus, while instructional technology research is following Kozma's dictum to ask new questions, the field is less able to provide new answers. In the tradition of Fleming and Levie (1978, 1993), however, Hannafin and his group (1994) have compiled a set of empirically based guidelines for designing interactive multimedia that might provide some insights into how components of the digital library might be designed to enhance learning. In fact, their explanation of what they mean by "interactive multimedia" might stand as a definition for the digital library itself.

> Interactive multimedia dynamically link and manage organized nodes of information containing multiple symbol systems and images within a given medium or across different media. [They] provide user-directed, nonlinear methods for organizing and accessing information . . . ; support access to knowledge according to individual demands . . . ; permit direct access to individual elements contained in large databases . . . ; and provide user-centered interactive environments. (1994, p. 63)

Many of their twenty principles, along with corresponding implications for design, stress the importance of the organization of information and could be readily applied to designing components of the digital library to enhance their learning potential. Note, for example, Principle 4: "Knowledge to be learned needs to be organized in ways that reflect differences in learner familiarity with lesson content, the nature of the learning task, and assumptions about the structure of knowledge" (Park and Hannafin 1993, p. 70). Or the implication derived from Principle 16, which describes the importance of using visual representations to help structure students' knowledge and experience: "Provide concept maps to indicate the interrelationships among concepts and hypermaps to indicate the location of the learner relative to other lessen segments" (p. 78). Such aids to structure and orientation within the digital library could clearly enhance students' success in this environment. These and other heuristics suggested by Park and Hannafin directly address such "information retrieval" issues as the importance of students' conceptual structures to successful searching as noted above (Neuman, 1993, 1995a, 1995b).

For researchers, teachers, and school library media specialists concerned with learning in the digital library, this description of the state of the art related to understanding and creating learning environments raises hopes and cautions: although it is heartening to see the insights and advances that can be gleaned from instructional technology, we are still left with the fundamental question of how we can help students exploit individually and in the aggregate to achieve higher-level learning. Instructional technology might provide insights about learning within specific environments, but the field has not extrapolated its findings beyond those limited settings. A comprehensive approach that integrates these findings with findings from information studies is necessary to provide a conceptual framework for designing and presenting components of the digital library to enhance learning.

INFORMATION LITERACY: A CONCEPTUAL FRAMEWORK FOR "LEARNING AND THE DIGITAL LIBRARY"

In her thorough and useful overview of the development and current status of "information literacy," Behrens (1994) cites a number of definitions that have been proposed for this umbrella term. The definition included in the American Library Association's 1989 Presidential Committee on Information Literacy: Final Report—which she quotes as "the most frequently used today" (p. 315)—is striking in its interweaving of many of the concepts related to information studies and learning with media that have been discussed earlier.

> To be information literate, a person must be able to recognize when information is needed and have the ability to locate, evaluate, and use effectively the needed information. . . . Ultimately, information literate people are those who have learned how to learn. They know how to learn because they know how knowledge is organized, how to find information, and how to use information in such a way that others can learn from them. They are people prepared for lifelong learning because they can always find the information needed for any task or decision at hand. (ALA Presidential Committee Report, p. 1, quoted in Behrens, 1994, p. 315)

This definition makes explicit the link between information use and learning: it specifies the higher-order thinking skills associated with effective information use, states the importance to information literacy of knowing "how knowledge is organized," and stipulates that preparation "for lifelong learning" is the primary goal of information literacy. Its integration of concepts inherent to learning with those essential to information use suggests a theoretical structure that not only encompasses ideas from other information studies and instructional technology but anchors the two fields within a larger framework—a framework that provides useful guidance for considering the digital library as a learning environment.

Tools and procedures related to this information literacy framework have existed within the school library media community for years, and many can be mined for suggestions to support children's learning within the digital library. For example, Eisenberg and Berkowitz's (1990) "Big Six Skills" approach to library and information-skills instruction, Kuhlthau's (1993) work on how users seek meaning, and Stripling and Pitts's (1988) insights on teaching library research as a thinking process can be readily adapted to the electronic environment. A variety of work on resource-based teaching and learning can also provide direction for helping students become efficient and effective manipulators of EIRs. Neuman's (1995b) Delphi study suggests a number of specific information literacy concepts that students must master in order to use these sources in the service of higher-level learning: for example, "Understanding the general nature of searching" and "Understanding criteria for judging the value of particular citations" garnered perfect means of 4.0 from the study's panel of experts, while such other abilities as "Understanding the general nature of research," "Designing effective search strategies," "Identifying researchable topics," and "Generating search terms" all received mean ratings of over 3.9.

The series of standards for information literacy proposed by various states (for example, California Media and Library Educators Association, 1994; Colorado Department of Education, State Library and Adult Education Office, 1994) also provide broad conceptual guidance for addressing learning as well as information use within the digital library. Building on these ideas, the new national guidelines and standards for school library media programs published in 1998 by the American Association of School Librarians and the Association for Educational Communications and Technology provide an even clearer statement of the relationship between information use and student learning. They not only stipulate "information literacy standards for student learning," but also identify the links between these standards and the content and process standards of the full range of K–12 subject matter areas (Marcoux and Neuman, 1996). By specifying learning outcomes for information literacy and delineating the relationships of these outcomes to outcomes in such core subjects as English, history, mathematics, and so on, this document provides a powerful tool to assist library media specialists in fostering higher-level student learning through the use of information resources related to topics across the curriculum. The document also provides a framework for further research into the ways in which the various components of the digital library, individually and in the aggregate, might be marshaled to promote that learning.

CONCLUSION

"Learning and the digital library" has two distinct components: learning related to accessing, evaluating, and using the information resources available in this environment and learning related to mastering and building upon the ideas embodied within those individual resources. Research, theory, and practice from information studies provide guidelines for fostering the first kind of learning, while research, theory, and practice from instructional technology provide insights about the second. Concepts and guidelines from information literacy provide a framework for helping students, library media specialists, and researchers understand and address a variety of issues related to learning in this rich and exciting new environment.

These areas suggest three promising avenues for fostering higher-level learning within the digital library. Research from a variety of other fields—for example, reading comprehension, interface design, and problem solving—should also be investigated for the insights they can bring to enhancing the learning potential of the digital library. To help students achieve the maximum learning benefits afforded by the unmatched number and connectivity of the resources of this exciting environment, educators and system designers alike must draw from all these traditions. Optimizing the learning potential of the digital library for the children our schools will require the best thinking from all the disciplines that contribute to our understanding of how children learn. The challenges as well as the opportunities, like the digital library itself, are virtually unlimited and only beginning to be explored.

REFERENCES

Aversa, E., and Mancall, J. C. (1986). "Managing online information services in school library media programs." In S. L. Aaron and P. R. Scales, eds., *School library media annual 1986* (pp. 219–236). Littleton, Colo.: Libraries Unlimited.

Behrens, S. J. (1994). "A conceptual analysis and historical overview of information literacy." *College and Research Libraries* 55 (4): 309–322.

California Media and Library Educators Association. (1994). *From library skills to information literacy: A handbook for the 21st century*. Castle Rock, Colo.: Hi Willow Research and Publishing.

Callison, D., and Daniels, A. (1988). "Introducing end-user software for enhancing student online searching." *School Library Media Quarterly* 16 (3): 173–181.

Clark, R. C. (1983). "Reconsidering research on learning from media." *Review of Educational Research*, 53: 445–460.

Colorado Department of Education, State Library and Adult Education Office, and Colorado Educational Media Association. (1994). *Model information literacy guidelines*. Denver: Colorado Educational Media Association.

Crane, B., and Markowitz, N. L. (1994). "A model for teaching critical thinking through online searching." *Reference Librarian* 44: 41–52.

Eisenberg, M. B., and Berkowitz, R. E. (1990). *Information problem-solving: The Big Six Skills approach to library and information skills instruction*. Norwood, N.J.: Ablex.

Fleming, M. M., and Levie, W. H. (1978). *Instructional message design: Principles from the behavioral sciences*. Englewood Cliffs, N.J.: Educational Technology Publications.

Fleming, M. M., and Levie, W. H., eds. (1993). *Instructional message design: Principles from the behavioral and cognitive sciences* (2nd ed.). Englewood Cliffs, N.J.: Educational Technology Publications.

Gagne, R. M. (1977). *The conditions of learning* (3rd ed.). New York: Holt, Rinehart and Winston.

Goodrum, D. A., Dorsey, T., and Schwen, T. M. (1993). "Defining and building an enriched information environment." *Educational Technology* 33 (11): 10–20.

Hannafin, M. J. (1992). "Emerging technologies, ISD, and learning environments: Critical perspectives." *Educational Technology Research and Development* 40 (1): 49–63.

Hannafin, M. J., Hall, C., Land, S., and Hill, J. (1994). "Learning in open-ended environments: Assumptions, methods, and implications." *Educational Technology* 34 (10): 48–55.

Kozma, R. B. (1994) "The influence of media on learning: The debate continues." *School Library Media Quarterly* 22 (4): 233–240.

Kozma, R. B. (1991). Learning with media. *Review of Educational Research* 61: 179–211.

Kuhlthau, C. C. (1991). "Learning with media." *Review of Educational Research* 61: 179–211.

Kuhlthau, C. C. (1993). *Seeking meaning: A process approach to library and information services*. Norwood, N.J.: Ablex.

Large, J. A., Beheshti, J., Breuleux, A., and Renaud, A. (1994a). "A comparison of information retrieval from print and CD-ROM versions of an encyclopedia by elementary school students." *Information Processing and Management* 30 (4): 499–513.

Large, J. A., Beheshti, J., Breuleux, A., and Renaud, A. (1994b). "Multimedia and comprehension: A cognitive study." *Journal of the American Society for Information Science* 45 (7): 515.

Lathrop, A. (1989) "Online information retrieval as a research tool in secondary school libraries." In A. Lathrop, ed., *Online and CD-ROM databases in schools: Readings* (pp. 287–339). Englewood, Colo.: Libraries Unlimited.

Mancall, J. C. (1984). "Training students to search online: Rationale, process, and implications. *Drexel Library Quarterly*, 20, 64–84.

Marchionini, G. (1984). "Training students to search online: Rationale, process, and implications." *Drexel Library Quarterly* 20: 64–84.

Marchionini, G. (1988). "Browse and analytical search strategies in a full CD-ROM encyclopedia." *School Library Media Quarterly* 16 (4): 223–233.

Marchionini, G. (1989). "Information-seeking strategies of novices using a full-text encyclopedia." *Journal of the American Society for Information Science* 40 (1): 54–66.

Marchionini, G., and Teague, J. (1987). "Elementary students' use of electronic information: An exploratory study." *Journal of Research on Computing in Education* 20: 139–155.

Marcoux, B., and Neuman, D. (1996). "Into the twenty-first century: New guidelines and standards for library media programs." *School Library Media Quarterly* 24 (4), 213–218.

Neuman, D. (1993). "Designing databases as tools for higher-level learning: Insights from instructional systems design." *Educational Technology Research and Development* 41 (4): 25–46.

Neuman, D. (1996). "Into the twenty-first century: New guidelines and standards for library media programs." *School Library Media Quarterly* 24 (4): 213–218.

Neuman, D. (1995a). *High school students' use of databases: Competing conceptual structures.* Paper presented at the annual meeting of the American Society for Information Science, October, Chicago.

Neuman, D. (1995b). "High school students' use of databases: Results of a National Delphi." *Journal of the American Society for Information Science* 46 (4): 284–298.

Neuman, D., and Hannafin, M. J. (1993). "Empirically based guidelines for the design of interactive media." *Educational Technology Research and Development* 41 (3): 63–85.

Park, I. and Hannafin, M. J. (1993). "Empirically based guidelines for the design of interactive multimedia." *Educational Technology Research and Development* 41 (3), 63–85.

Perkins, D. N. (1991). "What constructivism demands of the learner." *Educational Technology* 31: 9–21.

Perzylo, L., and Oliver, R. (1992). "An investigation of children's use of a multimedia CD-ROM product for information retrieval." *Microcomputers for Information Management* 9 (4): 225–239.

Reiber, L. P. (1990). "Using computer animated graphics in science instruction with children." *Journal of Educational Psychology* 82: 135–140.

Reiber, L. P. (1996). "Computer-based microworlds: A bridge between constructivism and direct instruction." *Educational Technology Research and Development* 40 (1): 93–106.

Scardamalia, M., Bereiter, C., McLean, R., Swallow, J., and Woodruff, E. (1989). "Computer-supported intentional learning environments." *Journal of Educational Computing Research* 5: 51–68.

Scardamalia, M., Bereiter, C., Brett, C., Burtis, P. J., Calhoun, C., and Smith, L. N. (1992). "Educational applications of a networked communal database." *Interactive Learning Environments* 2 (1): 45–71.

Small, R. V., and Ferreira, S. M. (1994). "Multimedia technology and the changing nature of research in the school library." *Reference Librarian* 44: 95–106.

Solomon, P. (1993). "Children's information retrieval behavior: A case analysis of an OPAC." *Journal of the American Society for Information Science* 44 (5): 245–263.

Solomon, P. (1994). "Children, technology, and instruction: A case study of elementary children using an online public access catalog (OPAC)." *School Library Media* 23 (1): 43–53.

Stripling, B., and Pitts, J. M. (1988). *Brainstorms and blueprints: Teaching library research as a thinking process*. Englewood, Colo.: Libraries Unlimited.

Wozny, L. A. (1982). "Online bibliographic searching and student use of information: An e teaching approach." *School Library Media Quarterly* 11 (1): 35–42.

FOUR

Do Scribes Learn? Copying and Information Use

Joy H. McGregor and Denise C. Streitenberger

Picture a class of eleventh graders gathering information in the library for a research paper assignment. Some students stand at the reference shelves, reading titles on spines. They pull a book off the shelf and open it, perhaps to the front or the back or to a specific page. They either restore the book to the shelf or take it to their table. A few students linger around the microfiche readers, waiting their turn. Some of them search through the drawers of microfiche. At the computer catalog, several students punch the keys and stare at the screen. Several students are lined up to use the photocopier. Other students are seated at the tables, writing. Most of these students have a book open in front of them, and they look back and forth from the book to their paper as they write. Students at one table talk to each other. Others stand waiting to talk to the

Reproduced by permission of the American Library Association from *School Library Media Quarterly Online*, vol. 1 (1998), http://www.ala.org/aasl/SLMQ/scribes.html. Originally published in *Instructional Interventions for Information Use: Papers of Treasure Mountain VI*, edited by Daniel Callison, Ruth Small, and Joy McGregor. Hi Willow Press. 1997, 307–327.

teacher. The room is busy and not very quiet. In this beginning stage of their assignment, the students are locating and starting to gather information from the books, the microfiche, and the computers.

Two days after the above scenario, the scene has changed somewhat. The noise level is down and movement is lessened. Most students are now sitting at the tables, writing. The teacher is sitting alone at another table, reading and writing. Talk occurs at some tables, while other tables are quiet. Fewer students wander around, stand at bookshelves, or line up at the microfiche reader and photocopier. Those who are moving around complete their task quickly and return to a table where they might make a comment to another student or else sit down quietly and begin writing. At this point, most students have moved from locating sources to gathering information from those sources.

Now we look at the next week. The students are back in the classroom. They are surrounded by cards filled with notes and lists, some scattered, some sorted into piles. A few students are writing, others are shuffling cards. Still others are talking to each other and some are waving their hands in the air, trying to get the teacher's attention. The teacher is moving around the classroom, talking to students whose hands are raised, occasionally being interrupted by other students who come to stand beside her, occasionally stopping to talk to the whole class. The noise level is high. Now the students are trying to use the information they have gathered to write their research papers.

We have described the external, observable elements of a class of eleventh-grade students writing research papers—a common assignment in high schools across North America. But is there more going on than meets the eye? What is happening in terms of learning, the goal one would expect of a project such as this?

Research projects provide the opportunity for learning both skills and content (Resnick, 1989). Information gathering can provide skill development of several kinds. Students can learn to generate appropriate questions for research. They can acquire locational skills by examining a variety of information sources and formats. As they become familiar with these sources and determine how to use them, they can develop analytical skills that apply to using other, less familiar sources. Encountering information expressed in different ways and occasionally in disagreement should help students learn to deal with ambiguity. They can learn to evaluate the credibility and usefulness of information. They can learn to organize their thinking as they sort and categorize information. As they think about multiple pieces of information and determine the relationships between them, they should be learning how to synthesize that information. We also hope that as they gather and use information, they are developing an understanding of their topic (Bloom, 1956).

The writing process involved in producing a research paper has the potential of providing further learning. Teachers expect students to learn to synthesize ideas into a coherent product, organize information into a logical sequence, and communicate the synthesis cogently. Throughout a project such as this, as students seek meaning in the text they encounter and make sense of the information, they should be constructing their own understanding of the subject matter. The ideas they read and their own prior knowledge should meet in a "construction zone—a magic place where minds meet, where things are not the same to all who see them, where meanings are fluid, and where one person's construal may preempt another's" (White, 1989, p. ix). Their perceptual and conceptual changes will vary from one person to another, but the project should provide opportunity for change and growth to take place. As those changes occur, student writers should gain experience in solving problems based on the personal goals they set and revise as they move through the process.

Researchers like Flower and Hayes (1980) have shown us that better writers "develop flexible goals to guide their writing proc-

> esses, . . . rich enough to work from and argue about, but cheap enough to throw away" (p. 43). Poorer writers tend to spend little time planning, rushing to commit words to the page, and to hold tight to their initial formulations of a problem (Hull, 1989, p. 107).

Through practice in writing research papers, students should move along the continuum from novice to expert writers. But do students really gain these understandings as they work on research projects? How do interventions by adults facilitate this learning? Are there interventions that inhibit learning or that teach something other than what they are designed to teach?

DESIGN AND IMPLEMENTATION

Two naturalistic research studies observed forty-five eleventh-grade students carrying out research paper assignments. One project, described at the start of this chapter, took place in an English class in Texas in 1996. That project grew out of an earlier study in 1993 in which students in Alberta, Canada, wrote English and social studies research papers (McGregor, 1994). The original study generated a model of student thinking during research paper writing. One element of the model showed an orientation toward process or product. An apparent connection between strong product orientation and plagiarism was observed, but further research was needed to investigate this link. The Texas study was designed to explore student information use in general and also to probe the possibilities of the link between product orientation and plagiarism.

Students

The samples were purposefully selected to observe eleventh-grade students writing research papers as part of their normal educational experience. No effort was made to control either situation in any way, but the research sites were chosen to provide as much similarity as possible. Both schools have a good reputation academically and are located in small, middle-class communities, just outside major urban areas. The student participants, though, demonstrated a range of ability levels. The Canadian students were international baccalaureate (IB) students and the American students comprised a more heterogeneous group. The Alberta sample was selected to provide the richest data possible regarding student thinking, with the assumption that IB students describe their thinking most easily. The heterogeneous Texas sample was selected to observe a wider range of behavior.

Three teachers and two classes were involved in the Alberta study. One class was observed in both English and social studies and the other class observed in English only. The Texas study involved one English class of twenty-one students and one teacher.

In the Alberta study, students were observed and interviewed during the information collection phase of their papers. Audio taped think-aloud protocols of their paper-writing phase were also analyzed. In the Texas study, students were observed and interviewed throughout the information collection and writing phases. In both cases, research logs, notes, and final drafts of the research papers were collected and analyzed and sources of information were examined. The first study was conducted by one researcher and the second by two.

Adult Intervention

Although adult intervention was not the focus or the purpose of either study, it would have been impossible to conduct the studies without observing these interventions throughout. It is important to provide some description of this area because in both studies these interventions emerged as important to the resulting student research papers and to the learning of the students. The form of adult intervention differed with each class, as would be expected, since four different teachers and two librarians were involved.

In the Alberta study, two English teachers, one social studies teacher, and one librarian provided various forms of assistance to students. The English teachers introduced the assignment in class, provided a brief handout describing the format and grading rubric for the project, and further discussed the format and grading. One teacher spent considerably longer discussing format than the other. Elements of form emphasized in both cases were:

- number of sources of information required
- formal report style
- length
- extra elements required, such as a table of contents

Both English classes were instructed not to copy from the reference sources but rather to use their own words instead. Topic selection in both cases took place in the classroom by drawing teacher-designed topics from a hat. The same set of topics was used in each class. Once the classes arrived in the library, both teachers answered questions when asked, but usually stayed separate from the students otherwise. One teacher wandered around occasionally, monitoring students' efforts. The other rarely did.

The social studies teacher assigned an introductory exercise that required use of the books needed for the research papers in order to familiarize the students with the collection in the general topic area. He introduced the assignment in class and provided a brief handout with the grading scheme and formatting instructions for:

- number of sources
- citation style
- length

He provided the question students were to answer, which required critical analysis of the information located and a decision based on that information. Class discussion covered the process for coming to a conclusion about the topic. This teacher discussed ideas with students when asked, monitoring their progress throughout.

The librarian in the original study spent a few minutes at the beginning of the first period in the library with each class, introducing the materials to the students as a group and explaining the value and use of some of the most important resources. She was available to answer the occasional questions students directed her way. Most of the necessary books were preselected and assembled on a book truck, although students still went to the shelves to use reference sets and several other sources. Since the writing occurred at home, no teacher or librarian interaction took place once the classes left the library.

A great deal more instruction took place on writing research papers in the Texas study. It is likely that the difference in the composition of the classes (IB compared with heterogeneous) meant the students had had different prior experiences with research papers. The teacher introduced the topic in the Texas classroom in great detail, teaching the steps involved in writing research papers and demonstrating the major resources students would likely use. She provided extensive handouts that explained the specific requirements and grading of the paper, as well as note-taking, draft writing, formatting, quoting, citing sources, and editing. Prior to going to the library, she discussed the specific assignment requirements and note-taking in detail, but focused primarily on correct format, such as:

- what to include on note cards
- number of note cards
- how to write bibliography cards
- number of bibliography cards
- deadlines for turning cards in
- content of thesis statement
- content of outline

- number of paragraphs
- number of sources to be cited
- number of parenthetical references in each section of paper
- number and length of quotes
- number of sources to be included in bibliography

Students selected topics from a list of ninety-six possibilities or were permitted to select a topic not listed. No more than two students could select the same topic.

By the time the students arrived in the library to begin their information collection they had already been introduced to the most important reference sources. Therefore, the librarian simply discussed expectations for behavior in the library. The librarian was not involved with this assignment at any other time, except for one instance where she reprimanded a student for inappropriate behavior. Teacher intervention in the library during information gathering dealt with how to create note and bibliography cards. The teacher seldom intervened to advise what information was important, how to evaluate the information, or how to choose the best sources from multiple options.

Following information gathering, the Texas students spent class time writing their papers. Teacher intervention at this point was extensive. She demonstrated how to write a thesis statement and an outline, providing examples and instructing students to use her examples as format models by plugging the appropriate details into the sentence or phrase. She continually reminded them to cite sources appropriately. She provided editing instructions and exercises. Emphasis was primarily on the format of each of these elements. She helped individuals with these tasks (sometimes actually completing the task for the student), approved their thesis statements and outlines, and answered questions constantly.

In both studies, teachers and librarians assumed that students knew how to use information without assistance. They provided intervention on locational and formatting problems, but seldom on how to use the information once it was located. None discussed how to select appropriate information from sources, how to evaluate information for usefulness, how to reconcile conflicting information from various sources, or why quoting other writers might be useful or appropriate. No data were gathered to indicate whether or not this discussion had taken place on previous occasions. It is possible that the IB students of the first study were expected to be capable of carrying out that task independently. In the second study, the emphasis on format of note cards, bibliography cards, citations, and quotes dominated instruction, and though it was not specifically stated in the written objectives of the project, correct format and the elimination of plagiarism were clearly the focus of the assignment.

DISCUSSION OF OBSERVATIONS

Since it was possible for observation to extend through the entire library research project including the writing phase, and since teacher intervention was more extensive throughout the Texas study, this chapter will deal with observations primarily from that study, with some comparison between cases. Although each study incorporated both quantitative and qualitative data analysis, this discussion is based chiefly on quantitative analysis.

A finding from the original study—an apparent connection between a process/product orientation of a particular student and the way in which that student used information—was investigated further in the second study. All students in the Alberta study demonstrated an orientation toward the format of the end product rather than the process of gathering and synthesizing information for the content. Students were concerned about making their product fit the mold they envisioned based on prior experience and the instructions for the assignment. Those students who demonstrated little or no awareness of processes such as seeking meaning, making sense, or learning tended to exhibit a strong desire to make the final product "look good" or "sound right." These same students tended to copy a great deal from the original sources of information rather than paraphrase the information or synthesize the ideas. On the other hand, the students who demonstrated involvement in processes of seeking meaning, making sense, or learning did not copy from their sources. They synthesized, summarized, and paraphrased the information. The apparent relationship between the product/process orientation and the tendency to copy provoked questions regarding whether this was a chance connection or the nature of the relationship.

Students in the Alberta study received very little direction related to copying or plagiarism other than an early admonition not to do it. In the Texas study, however, the teacher constantly reminded students not to plagiarize and instructed them on how to quote and cite properly. She required them to copy all information word-for-word from the original sources to their note cards, which they handed in with their final papers and which she said she would check for plagiarism. It was impossible to know whether this strong emphasis on proper citation was due to the teacher's awareness of the researchers' interest or because it was an integral part of this teacher's instruction. The reason was irrelevant, since in either case students received instruction and coaching in avoiding copying and citing according to an accepted style. This element provided an unexpected opportunity to analyze the effects of such instruction.

The amount of copying was determined in both studies by comparing the students' final papers with the original sources listed in their bibliographies. Categories of copying were devised and described in the first study (see appendix A) and applied again to the second study. Portions of papers copied word-for-word were labeled E, portions copied very closely but with minor word or tense changes were labeled D, and portions copied with more extensive word changes but without altering the original sentence and paragraph patterns were labeled C. The amount of copying in each category was then determined and calculated as a percentage of the total paper. When students copied by changing some of the words but leaving the sentence and/or paragraph patterns intact (category C), it was assumed that they were attempting to paraphrase, albeit ineffectively. Blatant copying with little or no change (D or E) was interpreted as more indicative of an inability or an unwillingness to avoid plagiarism. Each paper was assigned a level, determined by the percentage of D and E copying. Papers ranged from type 1, which contained no copying to type 5, which contained 50 percent copying or more. Table 4.1 compares the amount of copying at the D and E levels in each of the English classes in the two studies. Only the English classes are compared, since the topics in both cases required reporting historical information. The decision-making requirement in the social studies assignment may have resulted in different thought processes and information-use strategies, rendering it less comparable to the English papers.

Table 4.1 Comparison of Copying Scores at D and E Level, English 1993 and 1996

	English 1993 (Alberta study) % D and E	*English 1996 (Texas study) % D and E*
Type 1 (no copying)	31.3	50
Type 2 (less than 15%)	21.9	40
Type 3 (15–29%)	15.6	0
Type 4 (30–49%)	12.5	5
Type 5 (50% or more)	18.8	5

Table 4.1 shows that blatant copying (D and E) was somewhat less in the Texas study, probably due to the many reminders to avoid plagiarism and the emphasis placed on proper citation. Only 10 percent of the papers in the Texas study were types 4 and 5 (30 percent or more of the papers contained information copied almost word-for-word). In the Alberta study, 31 percent of the papers were types 4 and 5. It would appear that the teacher emphasis on avoiding plagiarism was effective with many students, since the amount of blatant copying was considerably less.

ANALYSIS OF ERRORS

Traditionally, cognitive developmentalists have delved into thought processes by observing errors in written and spoken language. Through observing these behavioral errors, a means of identifying patterns in the development of cognition emerges (Ferreiro and Teberosky, 1982; Piaget, 1965). Based on this tradition, errors in the students' attempts to cite and paraphrase were analyzed in order to identify possible patterns in their thinking.

Citation Errors

An interesting phenomenon emerged in the 1996 research papers that did not exist in the 1993 papers. A large number of papers contained D and E categories of copying followed by parenthetical references, seemingly making them legitimate citations. Analysis showed that these portions of the paper were incorrectly cited in a number of different ways. Many included exact copies of the original text, cited, but without quotation marks. Others were very similar to the original, again cited and without quotation marks. To be correctly cited, these portions should either have been exactly the same as the source and enclosed in quotation marks, or paraphrased so that they were significantly different, including sentence patterning, with the source of the idea cited. Instead, they were a hybrid of the two—a token attempt or no attempt at paraphrasing followed by a parenthetical reference that indicated the students were very aware of the need to cite. Students may have omitted quotation marks from the exact quotes in these portions because they had already reached the limit of two long exact quotes allowed in the paper.

Other citational errors were found in the same sections. Citing the wrong source entirely was a common error. In some instances the correct source was included in the bibliography, and in others it was not listed at all. In other instances students combined two sources and cited a third. Incorrect citations also appeared amid consecutive citations of the correct source. Students making this error may have been concerned that they had cited the same source too often and changed a citation to give the appearance of using additional sources.

Students also cited the correct source incorrectly. Errors of this type included citations to the wrong page, combining two sources and citing one or the other but not both, or citing only a portion of a quote but including more than that portion.

Errors were found within the quotations themselves. Errors included misspelling from the original source to the note card, then reproducing the same misspelling in the paper. In some cases, words were completely changed from the source to the paper. Some examples of this error were these: "dissection" became "direction," "absurd" became "observed," "guilt" became "quilt," "hilly" became "chilly," "best" became "worst," and "envy" became "entry."

Paraphrasing Errors

Both the 1993 and the 1996 students had difficulty with the concept of paraphrasing. Paraphrasing was not defined for the Alberta students in 1993, while the teacher in Texas in 1996 defined paraphrasing as expressing "the thoughts of someone else in your own words"(teacher handout). The Texas students were informed that their own writing is distinctive and individual. This implies that sentence patterns, too, would be distinctive and not a replica of the patterns in the original source. Poorly paraphrased segments, labeled as category C on the copying scale, were considered to be copied, since they followed the original sentence patterns closely, with some word and phrase changes. These portions seemed to represent an effort to comply with expectations at some level, although not at the level of effectively expressing an idea in their own words.

Students in the Texas study received direct instruction in paraphrasing in the form of a handout. Guidelines included statements such as:

- a paraphrase often includes your interpretation of complicated phrases and ideas
- never use a word of which you do not know the exact meaning when paraphrasing
- make sure you understand the ideas in the passage
- look up any unfamiliar words or phrases
- turn the card over and try to write from memory the main idea that is expressed on the card

(Handout given to students in 1996 class)

Reproducing the original author's sentence patterns, but replacing some words with synonyms and shifting the position of some phrases, probably indicates that the student was still looking at the original sentence. This reproduction does not show understanding of complicated phrases and ideas, let alone interpreting them. Sometimes the word replacement involved simplification of the original word, which might indicate that the student understood that word. Often, however, the replacement word was just as complicated as the original, and the synonyms were thesaurus-like, not necessarily appropriate for the particular context.

Skillful paraphrasing (category B) requires making sense of what is read. An attempt to paraphrase, but poorly done (C), indicates that students tried to carry out a requirement of not plagiarizing, but might not have attempted to make sense of the whole idea or understood it well enough to express it their own way. Citing (D and E), but barely attempting to paraphrase, takes even less thought and indicates simply carrying out a requirement or possibly an expectation that paraphrasing wouldn't be assessed. Logically incorporating that original text into the paper may require some making sense of the idea, just as effective incorporation of a properly cited quotation requires sense-making, but very often the incorporation of such text was not effectively done. Connections and transitions from one sentence to the next were missing. A change from one source to another was very obvious because different voices were used.

WHAT DO THE ERRORS MEAN?

What can we learn about student thinking from these errors or error patterns? Can we make assumptions about what these errors might indicate? We cannot make absolute judgments and arrive at specific findings, but several interesting issues emerge, following a logical progression. What do the errors suggest about (1) whether students look for meaning in information, (2) whether they use that meaning to make sense, and (3) whether they construct their own understanding of that information?

Although some of these errors were likely typographical (hilly to chilly, guilt to quilt), others seem to indicate that meaning was not important. At the moment the word was changed, whether in transcribing from source to note card or from note card to paper, the student likely was not trying to incorporate the idea into his or her existing mental model of the topic. When the replacement word was a different part of speech or unrelated in meaning, there could be little making sense going on, either during note-taking or writing.

Almost half the Texas students put little effort into really making sense of their topic. They showed a lot of product-orientation, but in a more defined and directed sense than students in the first study. Their attention to citation of ideas, whether accurate or inaccurate, indicated that they were more aware of the format of that product element than the first group, probably because the interventions from the teacher emphasized this point so heavily. This was part of the teacher's goal—to make them aware of the need to cite words and ideas of others. She was successful in making them aware of that. Less than 5 percent of the aggregate total of their papers was copied without citation, compared with 22 percent in the Alberta study. She was less successful in getting them to cite accurately.

Seeking meaning leads to making sense, which in turn leads to constructing one's own understanding. Resnick states that "to learn about something, to come to understand it, is, in current cognitive science parlance, to construct a mental model" (1989, p. 4). Vosniadou and Brewer (1987) describe levels of change in developing mental models:

> Accretion refers to change that occurs through the gradual accumulation of factual information within existing schemata. Tuning describes the evolutionary changes in the categories used for interpreting information. . . . Restructuring refers to changes in knowledge that involve the creation of new structures. (p. 52)

An immature, inaccurate mental model can become more accurate and more sophisticated as understanding is constructed.

A prime concern coming out of the Texas study was how much students actually changed their mental models of either the topic they were studying or the procedure for using information from outside sources—how much they constructed their own understanding of their topic or the procedure. They spent a great deal of time and effort simply scribing—copying or nearly copying words and sentences from an original source to a note card and then from a note card to a paper. Some of this scribing led to legitimate copying, in the form of quoting appropriately from the source. Most of it led to inappropriate copying or plagiarism. The activity of scribing seems unlikely to lead to accretion, tuning, or restructuring. Perhaps minimal accretion occurs through copying words from one place to another, but the permanence of any factual information accumulated that way is suspect. Did new understanding really develop? Did the mental model really change? Since the students were not available for interviewing after some time had lapsed, it is impossible to know to what degree they actually constructed a personal understanding of their topic. If the intent of the assignment was strictly procedural—to teach students how to cite—even the mental model of that procedure was not well constructed, as indicated by the number and kinds of citation errors.

Students copied extensively, sometimes legitimately as in quoting from the original source and attempting to cite appropriately (according to an accepted style, as defined by the teacher), and sometimes unacceptably, by plagiarizing with no attempt to cite. Table 4.2 indicates the number of students in the Texas study that copied in those two ways combined. The kind of copying in this table is different from the kind of copying referred to in table 4.1, since table 4.2 combines the appropriate quoting and citing with the inappropriate plagiarism. Any attempt to cite, whether it followed the prescribed style or not, was considered an attempt to cite, while lack of any indication of a source for the copied information was considered plagiarized. Since both required copying word for word, or very close to it, from the original source, both were seen as involving a scribing type of task.

Table 4.2 Level of Copying (Both Appropriate and Unacceptable) (Texas Study)

% of total paper copied	*% of students*
15–29%	10
30–49%	5
50–74%	70
75–100%	15

One of the goals of the assignment was to teach students to quote and cite appropriately. This fact must be considered in all discussion of the scribing activity. The teacher probably did not intend, however, for students to simply string together a series of quotes and call it a research paper. Table 4.2 shows that 70 percent of the Texas students copied, either legitimately by quoting or illegitimately by plagiarizing, between 50 and 75 percent of their papers and another 15 percent copied, in the same manner, more than 75 percent of their papers. These numbers seem to indicate minimal constructing of students' own understandings. Based on the way in which scribed portions of the papers were incorporated into the context of the surrounding text, it is likely that the mental models of both the subject matter and the procedural knowledge of appropriate citation were inadequately developed.

SPECULATIONS AND FURTHER RESEARCH

In the Alberta study, teacher intervention relating generally to use of information, and specifically to avoiding plagiarism, was minimal. Based on the high degree of copying demonstrated by those students, the questions arose of why students copy and whether or not that tendency is related in any way to the level of process awareness. Are students who demonstrate processes of seeking meaning and making sense less likely to plagiarize? By extension, if there is a relationship between a lack of process orientation and the tendency to copy, it would seem that teacher intervention could make a difference to the situation. But what kind of intervention would make a difference? Because of the 1996 teacher's emphasis on avoiding plagiarism, the opportunity to explore a particular kind of intervention emerged. It appears, based on the primarily quantitative analysis of data from that study, that emphasizing avoiding plagiarism and appropriate citation does not eliminate the behavior, but modifies it to some extent. Whether the modification is beneficial to student learning is debatable. If this was the first time that a teacher had intervened in this way, perhaps students made a beginning in a long, slow process of developing an awareness of appropriate ways to use other writers' ideas. Further qualitative analysis of these data and of other data gathered through interviews and research logs in the Texas study may yield other observations.

In neither the Alberta nor the Texas study were librarians greatly involved in the library research projects. For the benefit of all information users, perhaps librarians could initiate improved communication and collaboration designed to enhance learning. Modification of long-standing educational practices could lead to students' constructing a better model of both subject matter and information use. As suggested by Pitts in a 1994 study of high school learners/information users, "careful, but not intrusive, monitoring of individual student progress throughout the unit will be necessary if the teachers involved are to provide appropriate expert support for the new learning and to identify problems and provide mediation" (p. 384).

New questions launch further exploration. How do teachers intervene effectively to increase learning of both topic and procedure beyond simple compliance with a requirement? How can librarians make a difference? If librarians and teachers work more closely together to mediate in the library research experience, can student learning improve? Could increased or different collaboration between teachers and librarians have an impact on information use? Do different assignment demands lead to different behaviors? What motivates students to copy? Further research related to these questions can expand our understanding of the construction of meaning and the development of mental models of information use.

APPENDIX A
CATEGORIES OF COPYING

No copying.
Paraphrasing, doesn't closely resemble original.
Paraphrasing, can easily recognize original pattern of sentences and paragraphs, but many words have been changed.
Copying, with phrases rearranged, omitted, some words added. Occasional synonyms used.
Copied word for word for the most part. May involve some omissions, slight rearranging, minimal changing of tenses, minimal use of synonyms.

EXAMPLES OF COPYING

Category C: *As it appeared in the original source*

The urban workers of France were a tiny minority compared with the nation's great masses of peasants. Yet their influence during the Revolution would be tremendous—out of all proportion to their numbers. (Banfield, Susan. 1989. *The rights of man, the reign of terror: The story of the French revolution.* New York: Lippincott, 16.)

As it appeared in a student's paper

The urban workers of France also formed part of the third Estate. They were a tiny minority alongside the nation's great mass of peasants, yet they had tremendous influence during the Revolution.

Category D: *As it appeared in the original source*

The Scottish witches associated, so it was believed, with evil spirits which appeared in the form of animals. Macbeth's witches also associate with evil spirits which appear in the form of cats and toads. (Winstanley, Lilian. 1922. *Macbeth, King Lear and contemporary history*. London: Cambridge University Press, 114.)

As it appeared in a student's paper

Witches were believed to associated [*sic*] with evil spirits which appeared in the form of animals. *Macbeth*'s witches associate with evil spirits in the form of cats and toads.

Category E: *As it appeared in the original source*

In the church a number of staging conventions evolved that were to remain in use throughout the Middle Ages. The acting space was divided into two parts: the *mansions* and the *platea*. The mansions (also called stations, seats, or *sedes*) were simple scenic devices for indicating the location of incidents. For example, a throne might be used to suggest the residence of Pilate. Each place was represented by a different mansion, and all remained in view throughout the play.

Since the action could not be performed in the limited space provided by the typical mansion, the actors used as much of the adjacent floor area as they needed. Often the same space was used in many different scenes. This generalized acting area was called the *platea* (or sometimes the place or playne). Thus, a series of mansions was arranged around a neutral playing space, and the performers moved from one mansion to another as the action demanded. (Brockett, Oscar.1974. *The theatre: An introduction.* 3rd ed. New York: Holt, Rinehart, and Winston, 119.)

As it appeared in a student's paper

A number of staging conventions evolved in the church that were to remain in use throughout the Middle Ages. The acting space was divided into two parts: the mansions and the platea. The mansions (also called stations, seats, or sedes) were simple scenic devices for indicating the location of incidents. For example, to suggest the residence of Pilate a throne might be used. Each place was represented by a different mansion and all remained in view throughout the play. However, since the action could not be performed in the limited space provided by the typical mansions, the actors used as much of the adjacent floor as they needed. Often the same space was used in many different scenes and this generalized area was called the platea (or sometimes the place or playne). This series of mansions arranged around a neutral playing space provided the 'stage' and the performers moved from one mansion to another as the action demanded.

REFERENCES

Bloom, B. (1956). *Taxonomy of educational objectives: The classification of educational goals. Handbook I: Cognitive domain.* New York: Longmans, Green.

Ferreiro, E., and Teberosky, A. (1982). *Literacy before schooling.* Portsmouth, N.H.: Heinemann.

Flower, L., and Hayes, J. R. (1980). "The dynamics of composing: Making plans and juggling constraints." In L.W. Gregg and E. R. Steinberg, eds., *Cognitive processes in writing* (pp. 31–50). Hilsdale, N.J.: Lawrence Erlbaum. Quoted in Hull, Glynda Ann. "Research on writing: Building a cognitive and social understanding of composing." In *Toward a thinking curriculum: Current cognitive research.* 1989 year book of the Association for Supervision and Curriculum Development, ed. Lauren B. Resnick and Leopold E. Klopfer, 104–28. Alexandria, Va.: ASCD, 1989.

Hull, G. A. (1989). "Research on writing: Building a cognitive and social understanding of composing." In L. B. Resnick and L. E. Klopfer, eds., *Toward a thinking curriculum: Current cognitive research. 1989 year book of the Association for Supervision and Curriculum Development.* Alexandria, Va.: ASCD.

McGregor, J. H. (1994). "Cognitive processes and the use of information: A qualitative study of higher order thinking skills used in the research process by students in a gifted program." In C. Kuhlthau, ed., *1994 School library media annual* (pp. 124–133). Englewood, Colo.: Libraries Unlimited.

Piaget, J. (1965). *The child's conception of number.* New York: W. W. Norton.

Pitts, J. M. (1994). "Personal understandings and mental models of information: A qualitative study of factors associated with the information seeking and use of adolescents." Ph.D. diss., Florida State University.

Resnick, L. B. (1989). In L. Resnick, ed., *Knowing, learning, and instruction: Essays in honor of Robert Glasser.* Hillsdale, N.J.: Lawrence Erlbaum Associates.

Vosniadou, S., and Brewer, W. F. (1987). "Theories of knowledge restructuring in development." *Review of Educational Research* 57 (Spring): 51–67.

White, S. H. 1989. Foreword in *The construction zone: Working for cognitive change in school,* by D. Newman, P. Griffin, and M. Cole. Cambridge: Cambridge University Press.

WEB LINKS

The ERIC Clearinghouse on Reading, English, and Communication at http://www.indiana.edu/~eric_rec/ has a variety of research and practice-based resources on writing in the classroom.

Widener University's Library has made available a thorough set of criteria to help students evaluate various sorts of Web pages, including advocacy pages and news pages. The librarians have expanded on traditional notions of accuracy, authority, and currency to apply them more directly to Web pages. These resources are available from: www2.widener.edu/Wolfgram-Memorial-Library/webevaluation/webeval.htm.

For an extensive bibliography of literature on mental models and conceptual change, see http://www.cbl.leeds.ac.uk/~paul/mentalmodsrefs.html.

FIVE

Composing Boolean Search Statements: Self-Confidence, Concept Analysis, Search Logic, and Errors

Diane Nahl and Violet H. Harada

Today's students live in an electronic world in which information doubles every two years and personal computers in the home and workplace are necessary survival tools. As a result, it is apparent that among the life skills these students need to succeed in the twenty-first century is the ability to manage the ever-expanding amount of information they are encountering.[1] The key to effective use of these new information sources lies in the students' ability to analyze problem statements and adopt problem-solving strategies in constructing search statements. This analysis involves higher-level thinking skills to retrieve, select, and evaluate information required "in breaking down a topic into its key concepts or facets, recalling synonyms from long-term memory, and combining the results with logical connectives in an orderly and iterative manner."[2] It may also require using tools that help locate and generate synonyms and related terms such as dictionaries, thesauri, and controlled vocabulary lists.

Library educators view this emphasis on problem definition and analysis as part of a shifting paradigm in effective learning principles that involves a process approach rather than a source approach in instruction.[3] Kuhlthau identified a model for information searching involving a complex mix of cognitive and affective stages that she validated through a series of investigations at the high school and college levels.[4] Eisenberg and Berkowitz detailed a problem-solving approach as the framework for their "big six information skills."[5] Along similar lines, Stripling and Pitts established thought levels of research and reactions that provide the foundation for a ten-step model in conducting research as a thinking process.[6] Among the fundamental steps these models share is the presearch phase, which requires students to create effective search statements before going online. Borgman, Moghdam, and Corbett refer to this phase as learning necessary "system-independent skills . . . including concepts of problem analysis, planning, and strategy development."[7] The focus of this research was on how secondary students could acquire these presearch skills through brief written instructions before going online. Studies in three areas related to information searching were reviewed: problems encountered by novice users engaged the search process; the influences of language ability, affect, and gender differences in end-user searching; and written point-of-use instructions as an intervention strategy.

PROBLEMS ENCOUNTERED BY NOVICE SEARCHERS

Much of the earlier research in teaching electronic information searching has been reported in special library, corporate, of cognitive and affective stages that she validated through and academic settings.[8] A critical conclusion in many of these studies is that the mechanics of computer searching are not the major stumbling block; however, concept and term identification and confusion in understanding the logic of Boolean operators are definite hurdles.[9]

These findings have been corroborated by a growing body of research in lower education where investigations of both elementary and high school students using information-retrieval skills also underscore students' lack of general information-seeking strategies.[10] In a Delphi study involving twenty-five library media specialists across the United States, Neuman concluded that the major problems students encountered in using electronic information sources were in "generating search terms, designing effective search strategies, and overcoming mismatches between personal ideas of how information is organized and how information is actually organized in databases."[11]

Solomon, in a detailed analysis of more than nine hundred OPAC (online public access catalog) transactions of elementary students, discovered some of the following breakdowns in their search strategies: mismatches between the children's natural selection of search terms and the actual subject headings used in the online catalog's database, limited uses of synonyms, word forms (students tended to use singular rather than plural forms of nouns), and confusion with homonyms (e.g., "Wales" and "whales").[12] He also found that at more advanced levels of searching, students simply did not have sufficient knowledge in the subject area to suggest alternative terms. Moore and St. George also reported that selecting keywords was a major obstacle in the information-retrieval process for sixth graders in New Zealand.[13] In their study, the efficacy of the search depended on the individual's ability to match keywords and to see relationships among differing aspects of a topic. They observed that few children at this age level were able to plan, monitor, and regulate cognitive strategies.

In a study of high school students using an online catalog, Chen noted that students used natural-language expressions that were incompatible with the online catalog's controlled vocabulary.[14] By viewing videotaped records of student performance at the OPAC stations, she observed that students often used strings of words or major phrases extracted directly from the search problems to use as search terms.

INFLUENCES OF LANGUAGE ABILITY, AFFECT, AND GENDER DIFFERENCES

The critical nature of a student's linguistic-processing capabilities was reported by Chen in her analysis of the searching behaviors of high school students of average and below-average achievement.[15] She found that using appropriate search vocabulary was "clearly related to language ability, including grasping main concepts in a statement, identifying potential keywords, and generating related search terms."[16]

The complex interrelationship of cognitive and affective skills in search sessions has been addressed in several other investigations. Kuhlthau discovered that secondary students worked through a seesawing pattern of confusion and optimism that paralleled their struggle to explore and focus on topics and engage in collecting, evaluating, and using information.[17] Recognizing the need to understand better the cognitive processes and affective states that constitute Boolean search attempts by users, Nahl created written point-of-use instructions to which affective elaborations had been added.[18] Data from her experiment revealed that novice end users derived significant benefits from reading the enhanced point-of-use instructions. The positive effects included the facilitation of both cognitive skills (e.g., comprehension and assessment of Boolean search statements) and affective skills (e.g., self-confidence in search decisions or their acceptance of instructions).

Although gender-related differences may apply to learning new technologies, few studies have directly examined gender differences in relation to communication media. One such study by Eastman and Krendl examined sex-related differences among middle school students in the context of learning to search an electronic text.[19] The psychological literature has traditionally reported that girls excel at verbal tasks while boys are better at spatial and abstract tasks.[20] Eastman and Krendl reported that girls showed significantly higher scores on the final products, including organization, presentation, and referencing ability in their written themes.[21] Results from comparison of the computer achievement measures, however, showed little difference between the two groups. For example, boys and girls were found to be equivalent in number of successful searches, quantity of errors, and total number of pages accessed.

WRITTEN POINT-OF-USE INSTRUCTIONS

Although there is no general agreement on a best method, several studies on learning methods in end-user searching identified certain advantages of written worksheets: they can be used as part of classroom instruction or at the reference desk; they encourage end users to plan their strategies with some thought to search modifications; and they make the logical combinations of terms more explicit. In a survey of twenty-five studies describing different modes of instructional delivery, Mader found that academic librarians reported use of point-of-use guides (52 percent) almost as frequently as hands-on (56 percent) and one-on-one (56 percent) assistance.[22] Based on responses to a questionnaire on knowledge about keyword and Boolean searching, Ensor noted that college students and faculty who were aware of such library handouts as a keyword instruction method gave more correct responses on nine of ten statements of keyword searching knowledge.[23]

The practical realities of limited staffing and the labor-intensiveness of individualized instruction (most secondary-school library media centers have only one or two professionals) accentuate the need to consider alternative and supplementary instructional methods presented in written formats. Although research indicates that instructions provided by information retrieval systems themselves do not always assist students in constructing search statements, locally designed instruction sheets and search hint sheets may help end users to define their topics and plot search strategies.[24]

Several resources currently being used in school library media centers were particularly useful in preparing the student instructions, worksheet, and quiz for this study. Wehmeyer's foundational work in identifying patterns in a search strategy clarified the importance of focusing on alternate term selection, especially synonyms and related terms.[25] Kuhlthau also included the identification of descriptors and alternate subject headings as essential components of information searching.[26] Stripling and Pitts provided concrete examples of teaching research as thinking process.[27] Winn's work in identifying relationships between search words offered clear instructions, especially for the language and wording of explanations using OR and AND Boolean operators.[28] Problem-analyzer worksheets devised by Hunter and Lodish were also examined for their content and ease of use as graphic organizers for students to take a problem statement and break it down into several main terms and their related terms or synonyms.[29] Of the publications examined, the Pennsylvania Department of Education's guide on problem definition provided the most detailed lesson plans on formulating focused research questions.[30]

The Problem

The preponderance of the evidence from these studies reveals that concept analysis is a complex amalgam of linguistic processing subskills, including the student's ability to identify key ideas in a search query, to generate subject words and related terms, and to combine them with logical connectives. Studies also indicate a need to better understand both the interplay of affective states with these cognitive processes and gender differences in relation to students' perceptions of self-efficacy. The novice searcher's need for some form of mediated assistance in analyzing research questions and in constructing effective search statements is evident. As information specialists and curriculum consultants in a school setting, library media specialists must be able to analyze the problems that students encounter in their information searches and devise methods to increase students' proficiency in information retrieval.

The aim of the present study was to investigate the effectiveness of brief written point-of-use instructions in helping secondary students to acquire an understanding of term selection and search logic in order to create Boolean search statements in a presearch activity. Several cognitive subskills contribute to the ability to create a viable search statement.

In traditional communication theory, decoding is the process of looking at a coded statement and translating it into ordinary language; encoding is the process of creating a coded statement by following certain rules. A search statement is coded with Boolean logic operators and brackets and with search terms that often must include word variations and synonyms.

Students learning to write search statements acquire encoding skills. Students acquire decoding skills when they are given search statements to analyze. For example, students can be shown a set of reasons for selecting an answer in a decoding task. By analyzing the rationales students chose, the researchers were able to identify categories of reasons that provide clues about the depth of the students' understanding. Affective subskills include students' perceived level of confidence in their answer to a decoding or an encoding question or in their ability to complete a series of tasks. In recent studies, continuous self-confidence has emerged as a significant factor in search success.

In the current study, the researcher hypothesized that the way in which point-of-use instructions are written can influence decoding, encoding, and affective subskills in presearch tasks. For example, the instructions can be minimal or can also include a worksheet to permit practice with Boolean logic and term selection. This study investigated the effects of these differences in instructions on acquiring decoding, encoding, and affective skills. In addition, the data permitted detailed analysis of the types of errors novices make in creating search statements. The subjects in the study were 191 secondary students, primarily juniors and seniors, from six schools on the island of Oahu. The schools are distributed throughout the island: five are public and one is private. Students participated in class groupings, either in their classrooms or in the school library media center.

Independent Variables

Three scenarios were set up in order to assess the potential effectiveness of brief written instructions for electronic searching. The least intervention on the instructional continuum consisted of a booklet that contained an essay about searching but that carefully avoided specific instructions on Boolean logic or term selection. In the next level of intervention, the booklet contained specific brief instructions on Boolean logic, term selection, and search statement composition, in addition to a worksheet already completed with an example. The third level of intervention added a blank worksheet, to be completed by students who were then shown the correct answer for comparison. In addition, all students completed a form requesting information about their gender, grade level, and prior experience with computers, word processing, and electronic searching. After reading the instructions and before taking a quiz, students were directed to look over the ten quiz questions and to predict the number of questions they could answer correctly. Then they were asked to rate how confident they were in that number.

Confidence levels were also assessed for each question with a three-point rating scale: How confident are you that your answer is correct (very, somewhat, not at all)? The confidence scores were totaled separately for decoding questions, for encoding questions, and over all questions.

Test Conditions

Students were randomly assigned to the scenarios within existing classroom groupings. The test was administered in classroom settings or library media centers by the investigators and graduate research assistants who acted as proctors. The test booklets consisted of three parts: a three-page search instruction section, some with a blank worksheet of a new example to solve and some with a completed example of an ideal solution; next, the one-page information form; and finally, the ten-item quiz. Instead of the search instructions, a third group read a three-page essay about searching that provided a context for the activity, but lacked instruction. Students were instructed verbally to read the booklet, follow all the written instructions and directions, and complete every answer.

Those who received the worksheet version were instructed to raise their hand when they had completed it. A proctor then handed them the correct example and instructed them to compare it to their own answer. When students were finished, proctors checked their booklets for omissions and allowed students to complete them if needed. One hour was set aside to administer the test, but students were always finished well within forty minutes, and the quickest finished in fewer than twenty minutes.

Dependent Measures

The presearch quiz included six questions designed to measure decoding subskills. Students were asked to identify main concepts for a search by extracting search terms directly from a given query;

e.g., "Why do teenagers join gangs?" required them to extract the terms "teenagers" and "gangs." Other questions required them to compare two search statements and answer a question, e.g., students were asked which of the following two statements would retrieve the most articles: "Health AND Fitness" versus "Health OR Fitness."

Cognitive-reasoning scores were based on students' choices among three rationales, only one of which was correct. For example: "Why did you select that particular search statement? Circle the letter of the reason that best fits yours."

Because I want both health and fitness together.
Because health spas are for better fitness.
Because searching for either health or fitness gives me more leeway.

Encoding subskills were measured by four questions that required students to compose search statements based on written topical queries, e.g., "Why do dolphins migrate?" The search statements were analyzed and scored for correctness of term selection, correct application of Boolean logic, students in practicing subskills, and number and type of errors. Conceptual and logical errors were categorized using a typology of search errors developed in a previous study.[31]

Acceptable term lists were developed to guide scoring for questions with variable answers (i.e., questions that asked for words) that could be searched for a given query or questions that required search statement composition. Separate scores were assigned for decoding and for encoding portions of the test, and confidence scores were obtained for each of the ten quiz questions. Cognitive-reasoning scores (multiple-choice items) were obtained for each of the six decoding questions (percent correct in both skill areas).

RESULTS AND DISCUSSION

The analysis of variance (ANOVA) results in table 5.1 show that there were no significant differences between the groups for the type of instructions, either with a worksheet, with a worked-out search statement example, or without either of these. Though the group with the worksheets had slightly higher decoding, encoding, and cognitive scores, the treatments were too weak to detect significant differences, and the trend was not strong.

Two possible explanations offer themselves: one is that the tasks were too easy and did not require instructions. For instance, the group that received no instructions ($n = 19$) answered 60 percent of the quiz questions correctly for the combined decoding and encoding scores. If the test was more difficult, the expected effect might be more likely to occur. A second explanation is that the treatment effect was too weak because students did not read the instructions completely. Students were allowed to consult the instructions at any time during the quiz, but the proctors reported that students typically spent fewer than five minutes scanning the instructions before beginning the quiz. Clearly it is not sufficient

Table 5.1 Effect of Instruction Type on User Performance

		Instruction Type			
Scores	*[max]*	*Worksheet* N = *86*	*Example* N = *86*	*Essay* N = *19*	p
Decoding	[8]	6.26	6.06	6.32	0.637
Encoding	[80]	51.72	49.79	47.42	0.667
Term selection	[40]	23.15	22.66	27.16	0.278
Boolean logic	[40]	28.69	26.68	20.79	0.063
E + D	[88]	57.98	55.85	3.74	0.667
Reasoning	[6]	4.10	4.21	5.05	0.020
Cognitive	[94]	62.08	60.06	58.79	0.754
Confidence	[30]	23.92	24.30	22.63	0.206

to hand students point-of-use instructions; a way must be found to ensure that they process the instructions. In the future it is planned to integrate worksheets and feedback information throughout the instructions to involve students in practicing subskills.

Decoding and Encoding Skills

Decoding tasks are primarily recognition tasks involving students in selecting correct answers from among the incorrect ones. Encoding tasks are more demanding of students because they are required to apply both term selection and Boolean logic and in the vocabulary skills necessary for appropriate term selection; scoring approximately 60 percent correct in both skill areas. This corroborates Chen's finding that students' language capabilities are critical in generating appropriate search terminology.[32] Vocabulary skills necessary for information retrieval include identification of main concepts, potential search terms, possible synonyms, broader and narrower terms, and related terms. This problem needs to be addressed by teachers and media specialists throughout the curriculum through the teaching of these term selection skills explicitly as components of the search process.

Prior Experience

Subjects categorized themselves in terms of their experience by estimating how many times they had used computers for word processing and database searching. This self-selection appears in tables 5.2 and 5.3 as high, medium, and low levels of experience. The results show that students who reported that they were more experienced (high or medium) with either word processing or searching performed significantly better on all cognitive and affective measures (encoding, decoding, confidence). Table 5.4 shows what happens when students categorized their skill levels

Table 5.2 Word Processing: Experience and Performance

		Experience with Word Processing			
Scores	*[max]*	*High* N = *70*	*Med* N = *53*	*Low* N = *68*	p
Decoding	[8]	6.46	6.23	5.84	0.056
Encoding	[80]	52.94	53.34	45.56	0.054
E + *D*	[88]	59.40	59.57	51.40	0.041
Reasoning	[6]	4.37	4.47	3.94	0.060
Cognitive	[94]	63.77	64.04	55.34	0.031
Confidence	[30]	25.41	24.87	21.76	0.001

Table 5.3 Online Searching: Experience and Performance

		Experience with Searching			
Scores	*[max]*	*Worksheet* N = *86*	*Example* N = *86*	*Essay* N = *19*	p
Decoding	[8]	6.95	6.47	5.92	0.005
Encoding	[80]	57.30	56.20	46.83	0.007
E + *D*	[88]	64.25	62.67	52.74	0.004
Reasoning	[6]	4.85	4.55	4.02	0.006
Cognitive	[94]	69.10	67.22	56.76	0.003
Confidence	[3]	25.90	26.02	22.77	0.001

Table 5.4 Computers: Experience and Performance

		Experience with Computers		
Scores	*[max]*	*Skilled* N = *80*	*Novice* N = *110*	p
Decoding	[8]	6.55	5.93	0.005
Encoding	[80]	54.94	47.31	0.012
E + *D*	[88]	61.49	53.24	0.008
Reasoning	[6]	4.56	4.03	0.007
Cognitive	[94]	66.05	57.26	0.005
Confidence	[30]	26.23	22.39	0.001

globally (i.e., viewing themselves as either novice or skilled in using computers).

Similarly, self-proclaimed novices performed significantly worse on every measure, indicating that some degree of success in searching depends on previous practice with computers. The consistency of the effect of experience is impressive, since no keyboards or computers were used in this test. Future research needs to examine how experience with word processing contributes to such presearch tasks as appropriate term selection and correct application of logical operators.

THE IMPORTANCE OF SELF-CONFIDENCE AS A SEARCHER

It is interesting to note that the effect of experience extends to the affective domain of behavior. Students reporting less experience with computers had significantly lower confidence in the correctness of their answers to each question, and rightly so, because their encoding, decoding, and cognitive-reasoning scores were significantly lower than those reporting high confidence. It is evident that self-confidence is a determining factor in success. Therefore, it is worthwhile to continue to explore how self-confidence can be strengthened and developed as a skill.

Table 5.5 shows the effect of self-confidence on success very clearly. The subjects were divided into two groups (high/low) at the midpoint of the scale on the basis of their total confidence ratings (maximum = 30) over all ten questions. The students who were more confident in their answers scored significantly higher than the less confident students on every cognitive measure. This result confirms that found by Nahl in studies with college students.[33] If confidence is a skill that can be acquired, as argued by some psychologists, then researchers and practitioners have an opportunity to develop new forms of instruction with a focus on con-

Table 5.5 Effect of Confidence on Performance

		Confidence		
Scores	*[max]*	*High* N = *126*	*Low* N = *63*	p
Decoding	[8]	6.53	5.48	0.001
Encoding	[80]	52.63	46.14	0.039
E + D	[88]	59.17	51.62	0.020
Reasoning	[6]	4.59	3.58	0.001
Cognitive	[94]	63.75	55.20	0.009

fidence building.[34] These results appear to show that students who develop positive self-perceptions acquire an affective advantage, which allows them to avoid various cognitive errors. On the other hand, negative self-image or pessimism is an affective disadvantage that leads students to avoid opportunities to learn.

GENDER AND SELF-CONFIDENCE

Table 5.6 explores the effect of gender and shows that males and females do not differ on the cognitive measures. Despite their equal knowledge and cognitive abilities, however, the confidence

Table 5.6 Effect of Instruction Type on User Performance

		Gender		
Scores	*[max]*	*Male* N = *97*	*Female* N = *94*	p
Decoding	[8]	6.21	6.14	0.760
Encoding	[80]	50.20	50.66	0.878
E + D	[88]	56.40	56.80	0.898
Reasoning	[6]	4.33	4.16	0.380
Cognitive	[94]	60.73	60.96	0.943
Confidence	[30]	24.90	23.00	0.004

of female students was significantly lower.[35] Another demonstration of this effect is that 74 percent of the males rated themselves as highly confident, while only 57 percent of the females did so, despite the fact that their cognitive scores were identical. These results are quite complex, and further research is needed to isolate the contributing factors. On one hand, higher self-confidence is related to greater success; on the other hand, females who scored equal to males are less confident. It is evident that both personal experience as well as cultural factors of gender enter into the search process.

ERRORS IN SEARCH STATEMENTS

Seven types of errors in writing search statements were identified in a previous study of undergraduates.[36] The secondary students in this study committed all of these errors and contributed two new categories that were added to the typology and results. Error analysis data will assist practitioners who instruct students and prepare written instructions for searching databases because they can focus on strategies and intervention, which will decrease the number of errors students make.

Lexical Errors

The most serious error (50 percent of all errors in the sample) was of type 7, "Neglecting word-form variations" (mean = 4 errors per search statement). As table 5.7 shows, all students committed this error (100 percent). Each of the other eight error categories averaged less than one error per student (range = .08 to .83). Solomon also found that without explicit instruction, students have insufficient awareness of the degree of diversity of natural language and of the need to control the variations of individual concepts or terms in search statements.[37] For example, in the

Table 5.7 Mean Number of Errors Per Student for Each of the Nine Search Statement Error Types

Error Type	*Example**	*% Students Committing Error*	*N = 36 Mean*	*Standard Deviation*
1. Making a Boolean inversion	dolphins *OR* migrate	44	0.44	0.45
2. Not using Boolean operators	dreams *AND* daydreams	28	0.61	1.23
3. Using common natural language	airplanes and *pollution of air;* *dolphins migrate to different places to find food*	36	0.72	1.19
4. Omitting concepts	dolphins *("migrate" is missing)* dreams *("sleep" is missing)*	31	0.58	0.97
5. Adding unnecessary concepts	white tigers AND *world* air OR *habitat*	22	0.28	0.57
6. Using inappropriate alternate terms	dolphins OR *whales* daydreams OR *wondering*	42	0.83	1.25
7. Neglecting word-form variations	dolphins OR *migrate* white tigers AND *extinction*	100	3.94	0.23
8. Misspelling or inappropriate syntax	dolphins OR *porpoises* AND migration dreams AND *daydreams*	22	0.28	0.57
9. Using "funny Boolean logic"	(dreams OR daydreams) AND (daydreams OR dreams)	8	0.08	0.28

*Italicized terms in search statements illustrate the error type.

query, "Why do dolphins migrate?" students often wrote "dolphins AND migrate," ignoring the forms "migration" and "migrating" and the singular form "dolphin." Clearly, this is a skill that needs to be addressed in online search instructions. Because word-form variation was not addressed in the instructions used in this study, the results provide a baseline level for comparison in future studies with instructions that focus explicitly on this problem.

Over one-quarter of the students (22 percent) committed error type 8, "Misspelling or inappropriate syntax." Despite the examples shown in the instructions, some students invented new punctuation forms for search statements, such as colons and ampersands. Misspelled words peppered some search statements, but most students did not have such problems (78 percent). It would be useful to test how specific instructions that alert students to these problems might help in strengthening their motivation to prevent and correct these errors.

Semantic Errors

Semantic errors reflect a lack of understanding of the meaning and scope of the concepts that lie within a given query. In the presearch activity, students must analyze query statements to determine what the essential concepts are, then which search terms to use to represent the concepts, and finally, how to combine these terms logically using Boolean operators. Students need to understand that sometimes terms can be taken directly from the wording of the query, but sometimes alternate wording must be added to define a concept, and sometimes two concepts must be combined with the AND operator to create the desired topical intersection, or perhaps two alternate terms must be combined with OR. Some basic criteria for making such decisions were addressed in the instructions with brief explanations and illustrative examples in a stepwise manner.

Almost half the subjects (42 percent) committed a type 6 error,

"Using inappropriate alternate terms" (e.g., "dolphins OR whales"). This is a conceptual problem in understanding the scope of a concept (including whale migration expands the scope of the query to sea mammal migration). There is a conceptual boundary between the dolphins concept and the whales concept that makes a finer distinction between terms. Success in information retrieval often depends on making such conceptual distinctions. The majority of the students (58 percent) did not commit this error, showing that instructions can be an effective means for reducing errors of this kind. Almost half of the students (42 percent) were not able to delimit concept categories correctly, indicating the need to include practice in presearch concept analysis in instructions and exercises, a recommendation made by both Neuman and Chen.[38]

More student-friendly systems include interactive help that guides students through the term selection process with online thesauri and offers choices among search statements, among other innovations. An overarching concern linked with term selection is helping students develop adequate content knowledge in the subject areas. Solomon and Moore and St. George identified this lack of sufficiently developed mental models as a crucial factor in successful information searching.[39]

Additional conceptual problems were evident in error type 4, "Omitting concepts." Nearly one-third of the students (31 percent) simply did not include one of the main concepts required by the query. For example, for the query "How do the types of dreams and daydreams we have affect how well we sleep?" the search statement was simply "dreams." Similarly, nearly a quarter of the students (22 percent) committed error type 5, "adding unnecessary concepts." For example, for the query "How many white tigers exist in the world today?" they included untransformed terms directly from the query, which could cause search failure, such as "white tigers AND world." If the query had been "How many white tigers exist in India today?" an acceptable search statement would have been "white tigers AND India." In this case, however, "world" is an unnecessarily restrictive concept that would eliminate material on white tiger populations simply because the word "world" did not appear in the online record.

For the query "What is being done to improve the air quality on commercial airplanes?" students added concepts that were beyond the scope of the query such as "air OR habitat." These error types were explicitly addressed in the instructions used in this study, and over two-thirds of the students were successful in avoiding them. This indicates that general instructions may help the majority, but for others more emphasis on concept analysis is needed.

More than one-third of the students (36 percent) committed error type 3, "Using common natural language" with or without Boolean operators (e.g., "airplanes AND pollution of air"). Another example violates the rules of concept analysis and search term selection: "dolphins migrate to different places to find food." Chen observed new searchers entering long phrases and even sentences instead of breaking their queries into concepts and terms to be combined in various ways.[40] A few cutting-edge systems now allow users to do this, while the computer parses the unnecessary terms and creates a Boolean statement itself.[41] For the present and near future, however, searchers need the skill of topic analysis to transform their terms into the system's terms.

Logical Errors

Logical errors involve the misuse of Boolean operators in search statements. For example, the search statement, "dolphins OR migrate" should use AND instead, whereas "dreams AND daydreams" should use OR. This is clearly a Boolean inversion error (type 1, table 5.7). Almost half of the students (44 percent) committed this error, showing that Boolean thinking needs additional training because it is so different from the everyday use of the terms "and" and "or."

More than a quarter of the students (28 percent) committed

error type 2, "Not using Boolean operators" when one is needed to combine concepts. Natural-language grammar represented in the phrase "dolphins migrate" somehow opposes in the student's mind the Boolean requirement of inserting the AND operator into the expression. Instructions, therefore, need to deal explicitly with this kind of grammatical rigidity. There are systems that do not require searchers to insert AND because it is the default operator; however, many systems still require it. Many World Wide Web search engines use OR as the default operator. Students need to understand which of the operators is being employed by default in order to control the results better. Only 8 percent of the students created idiosyncratic or "funny" Boolean logic, showing that the instructions helped to formalize their thinking with search logic.

CONCLUSIONS

Though producers make claims about the user-friendliness of their databases, novice searchers experience a variety of difficulties using these systems. The students in this study achieved overall scores averaging 60 percent correct in applying online searching concepts and committed nine types of errors in composing search statements for simple queries. On the average, every search statement had two errors in it, and every student committed eight errors in writing four search statements. Students who reported high confidence throughout the task had significantly higher scores on every measure. The findings suggest that students who have developed habits of positive self-perception gain an affective advantage that allows them to avoid cognitive errors.

Clearly, online searching involves a complex skill set, including vocabulary knowledge and concept analysis for adequate term selection, an understanding of search logic for correct application of Boolean operators, and a high degree of self-confidence. Systems that do not require the insertion of Boolean operators by searchers nevertheless employ such operators in their search engines. Thus, students must understand the functioning of the search engine in order to control the output.

IMPLICATIONS FOR ONLINE INSTRUCTION

The complexity of the task requires a reexamination of the organization and delivery of instruction, which includes the following possibilities: breaking down cognitive skills in the presearch operations into such subtasks as identifying main ideas and keywords; brainstorming and evaluating appropriate use of alternate terms; and understanding differences among synonyms and related terms and between broader and narrower terms. Breaking the instruction into smaller segments allows for practice and reinforcement of successful performance. Library media specialists must analyze the specific types of lexical, semantic, and logical errors students are making in search statement composition and incorporate explicit instruction that alerts students to these problems. This type of diagnostic learning requires information-searching experiences that are introduced, reinforced, and expanded upon across grade levels and content areas rather than presented as "one-shot" instruction. Building adequate content knowledge in the subject areas among students is a critical first step in successful information searching. To develop their own mental models, students need to examine information in a range of resources. They also need to pool and discuss their findings with peers in order to generate research questions that are personally meaningful. A crucial underlying assumption is that teachers and library media specialists are working in collaborative teams as they plan, implement, and evaluate instruction. Given the importance of affective habits in influencing cognitive errors, and given that they are based on pessimistic rather than optimistic interior dialogue, instruction should focus on confidence building. Possible instructional strategies include:

- Feedback and discussion at critical points in the search operations;
- Cooperative-learning opportunities such as peer mentoring and buddy tutoring;
- Reflective logs to describe and analyze self-progress;
- Adding features in the system design that enable novices to think in retrieval terms about their searches;
- Including vocabulary assistance (e.g., spell checking, word-form variations, and a thesaurus that suggests narrower, broader, and related search terms);
- Including search statement syntax assistance (e.g., let searchers know that punctuation is incorrect, predict the results of statements, and suggest Boolean combinations); and
- Including orientation, advice, and reassurance throughout the search (e.g., make help systems truly interactive and relevant to what is happening at the moment, warn searchers of common errors, let searchers know when they are correct in formatting search statements and selecting terms).

ACKNOWLEDGMENT

The authors wish to acknowledge Rebecca Bichel, Irene McEnerney, Karen Reitz, Diane Scot, and Kelly Yamashiro, graduate students in the School of Library and Information Studies, University of Hawaii, who assisted in data gathering and analysis for this study.

NOTES

1. Judy Ala and Kathy Cerabona, "Boolean Searches: A Life Skill," *School Library Journal* 38 (Nov. 1992): 42; Mary E. Johnson and Barbara S. Rosen, "CD-ROM End-User Instruction: A Planning Model," *Laserdisk Professional* 3 (Mar. 1990): 35–40.

2. Trudi Bellardo, "An Investigation of Online Searcher Traits and Their Relationship to Search Outcome," *Journal of the American Society for Information Science* 36 (July 1985): 241–250.

3. Carol C. Kuhlthau, *Seeking Meaning: A Process Approach to Library and Information Services* (Norwood, N.J.: Ablex, 1994); Daniel Callison and Ann Daniels, "Introducing End-User Software for Enhancing Student Online Searching," *SLMQ* 16 (Spring 1988): 173–181.

4. Ibid.

5. Michael B. Eisenberg and Robert E. Berkowitz, *Information Problem-solving: The Big Six Skills Approach to Library and Information Skills Instruction* (Norwood, N.J.: Ablex, 1990).

6. Barbara K. Stripling and Judy M. Pitts, *Brainstorms and Blueprints: Teaching Library Research as a Thinking Process* (Englewood, Colo.: Libraries Unlimited, 1988).

7. Christine Borgman, Dinch Moghdam, and Patti Corbett, *Effective Online Searching* (New York: Dekker, 1984).

8. Elizabeth Aversa, "Teaching Online Searching: A Review of Recent Research and Some Recommendations for School Media Specialists," *SLMQ* 13 (Summer, 1985): 215–220.

9. Pat Ensor, "Knowledge Level of Users and Nonusers of Keyword/Boolean Searching on an Online Public Access Catalog," *RQ* 31 (Fall 1992): 60–74; Sharon Mader, "Teaching End Users to Search Online Information Retrieval Systems: Lessons from the Field," in *Online Searching: The Basics, Settings, and Management*, ed. Joann H. Lee, 2d ed. (Englewood, Colo.: Libraries Unlimited, 1989), 63–66; Gary Marchionini, "Information-Seeking Strategies of Novices Using a Full-Text Electronic Encyclopedia: An Exploratory Study," *Journal of the American Society for Information Science* 40 (Jan. 1989): 54–66; Diane Nahl, "Affective Elaborations of Boolean Search Instructions for Novices: Effects on Comprehension, Self-Confidence, and Error Type" in *Proceedings of the American Society for Information Science* 32 (October 9–12, 1995): 69–76.

10. Diane Barlow, Brenda Karnes, and Gary Marchionini, "CD-ROM in a High School Library Media Center," *School Library Journal* 34 (Nov. 1987): 66–68; Penelope A. Moore and Alison St. George, "Children as Information Seekers: The Cognitive Demands of Books and Library Systems," *SLMQ* 19 (Spring 1991): 161–168.

11. Delia Neuman, "High School Students' Use of Databases: Results of a National Delphi Study," *Journal of the American Society for Information Science* 46 (Aug. 1995): 284–298.

12. Paul Solomon, "Children's Information Retrieval Behavior: A Case Analysis of an OPAC," *Journal of the American Society for Information Science* 44 (June 1993): 245–264.

13. Moore and St. George, "Children as Information Seekers," 161.

14. Shu-Hsien Chen, "A Study of High School Students' Online Catalog Searching Behavior," *SLMQ* 22 (Fall 1993): 33–39.

15. Ibid., 33.

16. Ibid., 37.

17. Carol C. Kuhlthau, "An Emerging Theory of Library Instruction," *SLMQ* 16 (Fall 1987): 23–28.

18. Nahl, "Affective Elaborations," 69.

19. Susan T. Eastman and Kathy Krendl, "Computers and Gender: Differential Effects of Electronic Search on Students' Achievement and Attitudes," *Journal of Research and Development in Education* 20 (Spring 1987): 41–48.

20. Geneva D. Haertel, "Literature Review of Early Adolescence and Implication for Programming," in *Early Adolescence: Perspectives and Recommendations* (Washington, D.C.: GPO, 1978): 93–203; Norman R. F. Maier and Gertrude G. Casselman, "The SAT as a Measure of Problem-Solving Ability in Males and Females," *Psychological Reports* 26 (June 1970): 927–939.

21. Eastman and Krendl, "Computers and Gender," 41–48.

22. Mader, "Teaching End Users," 63–66.

23. Ensor, "Knowledge Level of Users," 60–74.

24. Mader, "Teaching End Users," 63–66: Nahl, "Affective Elaborations," 69–76; Diane Nahl, "CD-ROM Point-of-Use Instructions for Novice Searchers: A Comparison of User-Centered Affectively Elaborated and System-Centered Unelaborated Text (Ph.D. diss., University of Hawaii, 1993); Rachel Naismith and Joan Stein, "Library Jargon: Student Comprehension of Technical Language Used by Librarians," *College and Research Libraries* 50 (Sept. 1989): 543–552.

25. Lillian B. Wehmeyer, *The School Librarian as Educator*, 2d ed. (Littleton, Colo.: Libraries Unlimited, 1984).

26. Carol C. Kuhlthau, *Teaching the Library Research Process*, 2d ed. (Metuchen, N.J.: Scarecrow, 1994).

27. Stripling and Pitts, *Brainstorms and Blueprints.*

28. Patricia G. Winn, *Integration of the Secondary School Library Media Center into the Curriculum: Techniques and Strategies* (Englewood, Colo.: Libraries Unlimited, 1991).

29. Beverly Hunter and Erica K. Lodish, *Online Searching in the Curriculum: A Teaching Guide for Library/Media Specialists and Teachers* (Santa Barbara, Calif.: ABC-CLIO, 1989).

30. Pennsylvania Department of Education, *Problem Definition Process: A Guide to Research Strategies* (Harrisburg: Pennsylvania Department of Education, 1989). ED 314 062.

31. Nahl, "Affective Elaborations," 69–76.

32. Chen, "Study of High School," 33–39.

33. Nahl, "Affective Elaborations," 69–76; Nahl, "CD-ROM Point-of-Use Instructions," 197.

34. Albert Bandura and N. E. Adams, "Analysis of Self-Efficacy Theory of Behavioral Change," *Cognitive Therapy and Research* 1 (1977): 287–310; Albert Bandura, "Human Agency in Social Cognitive Theory," *American Psychologist* 44 (1989): 1175–1193.

35. Eastman and Krendl, "Computers and Gender," 41–48.

36. Nahl, "Affective Elaborations," 69–76.

37. Solomon, "Children's Information Retrieval Behavior," 245–264.

38. Neuman, "High School Students' Use," 284–298; Chen, "Study of High School," 33–39.

39. Solomon, "Children's Information Retrieval Behavior," 245–264; Moore and St. George, "Children as Information Seekers," 161–168.

40. Chen, "Study of High School," 33–39.

41. Peter Jacso, "General Encyclopedias on CD-ROM: A Close Analysis of These Major Reference Products," *Link-Up* 11 (Sept./Oct. 1994): 27–28; Peter Jacso, "General Encyclopedias on CD-ROM: A Look at the 1995 Editions," *Link-Up* 12 (May/June 1995): 20, 22; Peter Jacso, "Not Just a Pretty [Inter] Face—New Windows-Based CD-ROM Programs," *Information Today* 11 (June 1994): 30–32.

Six

"If You Don't Have It, You Can't Find It": A Close Look at Students' Perceptions of Using Technology

Jinx Stapleton Watson

Rarely do adults ask students to reflect on their learning. This study looks closely at a sample of eighth-grade students' perceptions about their experiences with technology, especially the use of the World Wide Web. Employing a phenomenological methodology of both examining a single student story and analyzing a collection of student voices, several themes and questions emerge. Students' personal attributes of self-confidence, resilience, and openness to learning about the new technologies and their skills in reading the Web and managing information may offer new questions for teachers and information professionals.

Accustomed to gathering and reporting data quantitatively and statistically to measure how much students learn, schools rarely listen to students' talk and reflections on what they know or how they learned it. Kuhlthau, Turrock, George, and Belvin (1990) remind

This is a reprint of an article published in September, 1998 in the Journal of the American Association of Information Science, 49 (11), pp. 1024–36, which can also be accessed at *http://www.interscience.Wiley.com/*

us that "in the field of library and information studies, very little is known about what goes on inside the user." This qualitative study examines students' perceptions of their experiences in using the World Wide Web. As students continue to use electronic resources for their school work and their leisure interests, teachers, librarians, and information professionals need to know how young people make sense of their access to and retrieval of information. "When information seeking is viewed as a process of construction, the user's experience becomes a critical component for analysis" (Kuhlthau, 1993a). In order to get to know about some real-life experiences, I invited a number of eighth-grade students to reflect about their personal experiences with technology. My major purpose was to gather information from students about their own perceptions in using the new technologies. Specifically, I wanted to know what they mean when they say that they use the World Wide Web as a new resource for their studies and leisure. I wondered if they would disclose information about how they felt, that is, their levels of confidence, pleasure, or frustration, and whether they would reveal unexpected or surprising insights about the skills needed to access information.

In order to express what they knew tacitly, students sometimes shaped a narrative to recount particular episodes in their experiences. Schank (1990) writes that "stories digest experiences." The students recalled ordinary moments in thinking about their use of the Web, and their stories and anecdotes supplied the data in which I then sought meaning. By analyzing their musings on encounters with this technology, we may gain some insight into how these students feel and what they think about their experiences. This kind of insight and understanding may inform us about student users' construction of the relations between using the Web, the outcome of its use, and their own information problems (D. Raber, personal communication, October 17, 1997). If we believe that "people make it [the Net] work," we must see how students make the Internet work for school and personal interests (Janes and Rosenfeld, 1996). A supply of narratives may reveal some of the idiosyncratic and universal attitudes and skills that students acquire as they use new technologies. As I reflected on and engaged with the students' words, my resulting text interprets the students' thinking. The study, therefore, provides qualitative data for others to read first-person voices from the schools and one professional's response. Such a study may offer practitioners insight for listening to the users of the new technologies, for the "major purpose of library research must be focused on the question of how libraries can intervene usefully in individual sense-making processes" (Dervin, 1977). Educators and policymakers may need to add student voices as an important element in thinking about users of this and other technologies. As recipients, users and leaders in using electronic resources for learning, students' ways of being with technology may inspire us to think in fresh ways.

BACKGROUND

Five years ago, the Tennessee State Department of Education's initiative in technology funded public schools for the purpose of purchasing hardware and software for individual classrooms. In 1992, Tennessee school districts received the first of their state funding from the Basic Education Plan (BEP) to develop "twenty-first-century classrooms" (Tennessee Code Annotated 493-351). The legislation supported the purchase of both hardware and software, with flexibility for local administrators and teachers to make selections. During their first year, the district of Maplewood (names of town, teachers, and students have been changed for purposes of this study), designated all fifth grades as "twenty-first-century" classrooms. Each fifth-grade classroom in the district received five computers, including one for the teacher's use. Each year since then, the district designated the subsequent grade as recipient of the state "seed" money. As a result, in the school year

1996–97, students in the original "twenty-first-century" fifth-grade classroom, found themselves in the eighth grade, their fourth "twenty-first-century" classroom.

In Maplewood, these technology classrooms included four student computers with CD-ROM drives, which were networked to a teacher computer; one networked printer, a laser disk player, a videocassette recorder; Internet connectivity, and, in some instances, scanners and a digital camera. Authoring and multimedia presentation software were included.

In the fall of 1996, many Maplewood district eighth graders entered their fourth year with technology in the classroom. For the most part, they encountered eighth-grade teachers receiving their first year of training in this technology. (The phenomenon of novice teachers and more expert students is not the focus of this study. Nevertheless, it raises interesting questions as students become more and more computer literate and as adults continue to acquire their first skills in using technology. Certainly, questions of expertise connote issues of roles, power, and status. And indeed, some of these themes emerged in this study.) The purpose of this study was to reveal the students' own experience and their reflections on using the technology as a tool and resource.

METHODOLOGY

Regarding research methodologies, Mellon (1990) suggests that "methods of naturalistic inquiry should be selected where in-depth understanding of human actions is the primary focus." I wondered about students' experiences with technology, in general. I held no preconceived ideas, no hypothesis, but rather, came to students with an invitation to hear them talk about their experiences using electronic resources, especially the World Wide Web. This study is embedded in a constructivist perspective whereby the researcher asks participants to construct meaning of their own experience. Making meaning of one's experiences often conveys both cognitive and affective qualities. That is, as one wrestles with meaning, one cannot help but reveal how one feels about the issues, for, "meanings are constructs that people hold of themselves and their worlds" (Belkin, 1990). Affective information is not often offered explicitly. Bruner (1964) reminds us that a basic cognitive task is to "go beyond the information given" As a result, I engaged in the interpretive task of examining the students' words in order to construct my own knowledge of the cognitive and affective qualities of these particular student users of the Internet. Therefore, as listener, as practitioner, as researcher, I, too, engaged in constructing meaning of the students' meanings. Page (1997) suggests that "when we have comprehended an author's account, we are obligated to offer our response to it . . . [and] we acknowledge our role in making its meaning."

The cognitive system for making meaning is basically narrative (Bruner, 1990). Therefore, phenomenological inquiry elicits story as content and offers narrative analysis as methodology to make sense of a key question. It offers the researcher a process by which to reveal or uncover elements in students' thinking as they engage in the process of reflection through their stories. Because students sought to make meaning of their experiences and I sought to make meaning of their narrative, I employ two uses of story in this research: First, the collection of students' experiences in the form of anecdote or story, and, second, the rhetorical device for my writing as I come to some understanding of the students' stories. The study represents my reading of the students' transcribed interviews.

THE INTERVIEW

With no predetermined hypothesis, I structured very few questions, listened carefully to the thread of the students' talk, and allowed myself to be open to the themes they, themselves, raised. As in a reference interview, the questioning process can be "virtually content-free . . . and the respondent provides the content—the unique perceptions" (Dervin, Jocobson, and Nilan, 1982). I offered one umbrella question, "What do you mean when you say you use technology?" I followed up with a second and third question when necessary, "Teachers tell me that your classroom has many computers. What does it mean to you to tell people that you use the computer?" And, "Tell me about using the Internet and the World Wide Web." I interjected additional questions only to probe, such as, "How did you know how to do that?" "How did you feel when that happened?" "Tell me more about what happened then." Students gave me permission to tape record their statements. I took very few notes in long-hand and used none of my own notes as data.

The interviews took place in a small conference room in the school media center. Students recognized their surroundings and seemed motivated to talk. They were not shy or reticent, and although the interview represented our first meeting, we were able to establish rapport within a few minutes.

RESPONDING TO THE INTERVIEW DATA

Stories and anecdotes were embedded in much of the interview and conversation I had with each student. As I reviewed the transcripts, I sought a sense of narrative. That is, I selected excerpts that described moments really showing what a student did or thought about, rather than words that philosophized about their activities with the Internet generally. Therefore, from each transcribed interview, I located and shaped a key narrative. Often, a stunning excerpt represented the gist of the student's exchange with me. For example, many students echoed Alice's statement, "If you don't know what you're looking for, you're out of luck."

And Polly captured it most succinctly by reminding us, "If you don't have it [the subject], you can't find it." The stories I selected to read and comment on caught my attention for their potential contribution to what we may want to know about students' sense and feeling about technology. In an attempt to interpret, to probe for the meaning of what was being said in stories, I read and analyzed each student's narrative content closely. Schank (1990) reminds us that "there is no one way to understand this story . . . when someone hears a story, he looks for beliefs that are being commented upon . . . and finds them by looking through the beliefs that he already has." Immersed in the students' brief text, I sought possible interpretations of their ideas and feelings about engaging with the new tools and resources of technology. The immersion in text and narrative analysis offered one technique for examining phenomena embedded within each student's words.

As an extended exercise, I analyzed the content across stories in order to encounter larger directions. From this content analysis, I derived two broad directions or categories I labeled: students' personal attributes and students' particular skills in using technology. These two categories serve as a way to organize my response to the students' responses. Others (Kuhlthau, 1993a) have acknowledged that searching for information involves actions, thoughts, and feelings, and indeed, students revealed both cognitive and affective attributes as they spoke of their experiences.

Each of the students' points, which I have considered significant enough for comment, I label as "questions." The notion of framing questions to be considered comes out of the phenomenological tradition, inviting continued inquiry from future readers. As Bruner (1994) remarked, "Great stories open us to new questions." That is, in phenomenological work, no definitive answers may be presumed, but rather, the researcher raises questions she considers fruitful for further and continued consideration. In illuminating the voices of student experience, I frame their attributes and skills as questions to invite readers' further thought. These questions may act as points for continued exploration. The students' stories and my subsequent close reading of their narratives represent a form of inquiry about which further inquiry can take place (Clandinin and Connelly, 1995). I note that several questions emerge from each of the larger directions or categories of attributes and skills. The first category I address—students' personal attributes in relation to their use of technology—raises two questions: The question of self-confidence or voice of authority, and the question of understanding time. The second category—the students' particular skills in using technology—include the question of reading information and a question of managing information.

The outcome of this study produces no theory or hypothesis, because what students say about their experiences with technology and especially the World Wide Web varies with the purpose, context, or setting of technology use. However, transferability or identification may occur. As Clandinin and Connelly (1990) remind us, the language of qualitative research presents a language of the whole. Therefore, a reader of this study might need to question, "How does this story connect with my own experiences as a learner, teacher, and user of technology, especially the World Wide Web?"

THE STUDENT PARTICIPANTS

I sought participants who had been enrolled in the Maplewood District school for all four years of the "twenty-first-century" classroom legislation. The prompt for soliciting participants included an invitation to "talk about your experiences with technology with someone from the university." Out of nearly fifty students (two classes), twelve eighth-grade students volunteered to be interviewed individually for approximately one-half to three-quarters of an hour to discuss their experiences with technology. On the scheduled week for interviews, of those original twelve students, two were absent and one had to catch up on classroom work. Of the nine participants, five were male and four female. Three males had access to online computers at home, and two males used the local public library online computer "nearly every night" for as many thirty-minute sessions as they were permitted. Therefore, all five males had access to, or made time to use, the Internet above and beyond the school setting. Two of the females had access to word processing and computer game programs at home. None of the females' home computers had online connectivity. Although the school's early morning and late afternoon online computer lab, supervised by a teacher, was available to all students, only two of the male students with computers at home said that they stopped by the lab from time to time "when there's a report due" or if the "librarian needs help backing up disks." I did not request knowledge of the participant students' grade-point average, conduct record, or social economic status. Nor did I inquire as to why they chose to participate in this study. And finally, I did not ask for nor diagnose the level of expertise in using the Internet. That is, I received no information from teachers about the students' actual experience or success with using the Internet as a tool and as a resource.

The students each selected an "alias" name and they and their teachers were given a first draft of my findings, which they read for veracity. None offered criticism of the findings and all seemed to concur with my written statements. The following students' stories appear in the directions which I label personal attributes: Vel, Elisha, J. R., Bryce, Lauralee, and Will. The direction labeled particular skills included stories and anecdotes from Bryce, Elisha, Alice, Vel, Polly, and J. R. I did not use the interview of one student. He spoke in generalities and wanted to philosophize. He found it difficult to remember moments or instances of his own use. He told me more about his brother's experiences working at the Apple Corporation in California.

LIMITATIONS OF THE STUDY

The nine students represent a convenience sample due to their affiliation with a single school, which might not represent the thinking or attitudes of other Tennessee students with "twenty-first-century" classroom experience. Whether this represents an extreme sample from the state would be worthy of examination. Maplewood District is generally noted for its commitment to excellence in education. Average teacher salaries are higher in this district than any other in the state (Annual State Salary Review, 1997), and much of the annual budget comes from local property tax, unlike its neighboring school districts. Therefore, the average social economic status of the community school might indicate that public school students in this town have benefited from family and community interest in strong educational programs. The variables of social economic status or academic achievement are not addressed in this study.

A second limitation includes reliability of the students' perceptions. In soliciting students' comments, I had no way to check their experiences. My only source was the interview data. A follow-up of this study might include two additional data sources: (1) observation of students using the Internet to evaluate search strategies and (2) an analysis of work produced from using the Web as a resource. These two data sources would serve to check the affective area of confidence level and the cognitive area of skill in using the Internet as a tool and as a resource.

DISCUSSION

Students' Personal Attributes: Questions of Confidence or Voice of Authority

Three stories illustrate the sense that students gain self-confidence and express authority with their understanding and use of technology for school work. In the following stories, Vel seems to allude to a comfort, a feeling of familiarity with electronic sources for both school work and recreation. Elisha's comments indicate a spirit of resilience in using the technology, and J. R. acknowledges learners' openness and vulnerability, which suggests a sense of confidence from these student users.

> Vel: A question of familiarity. "I use them at school and I go to the public library and use them. . . . Ever since I was in the fifth grade, so that would be about three or four years now. . . . I feel like I got it down pat. Or if I don't, I feel like I'm a very independent person so I don't like to ask for a lot of help. Like if I just don't understand it, I'll ask for help, but I'll try to figure it out. I just don't give up easy."

Vel offers us three reasons for his self-confidence, which he asserts as "got it down pat." First, he feels used to working with "them" (computers) because he says that he has used computers since the fifth grade. Put another way, as an eighth grader (thirteen years old), Vel has worked with computers in some capacity for approximately one-third of his life. The familiarity that comes from his "three to four" years of experience suggests that using computers is not threatening or overwhelming. Second, Vel has access at school and at the public library. For him, accessibility may signify familiarity as well. Accessibility may suggests that one can stay current, that is, not endure long lapses of time between use, requiring brush-up sessions, or feeling out of date. Knowing that one has access and knowing how to access technology may suggest a kind of powerful knowing. In an emergent culture such as one that unfolds before us technologically, learners must feel assured that they can have access, belong to, and stay close to the changing culture, rather than fearing its new iterations.

Third, Vel's personal and self-named attribute of independence suggests that he has a conscious sense of himself and some awareness of how he goes about solving problems. This meta awareness of his own problem-solving style is important in new learning. As Vel progresses in gaining new computer skills, he does not appear to be daunted by more complicated projects, but rather, will figure them out or, when pressed, will ask for help. Vel is not unusual in his claim for independence. Kuhlthau, Belvin, and George (1989) examined library users' perception of the role of mediators. In their work, no mediator was identified for 70 percent of the participants. Vel suggests that he "doesn't ask for a lot of help," but acting as a "very independent person" can offer Vel both strengths and weaknesses in his searches. Further probing of this affective stance might reveal that other issues keep him from requesting help from professionals, family, or friends.

In sum, Vel's stated self-confidence stems from a sense that he is in charge of the computer. Having something "down pat," suggests that he is in charge and on top of his processes in using technology, in contrast to acting as a passive participant in his interaction. Experience, maintaining access, and personal attributes help shape this student's confidence in using electronic tools and resources. In this portion of the interview, he is not specific about what he seeks nor his level of success in searching electronically for information. He simply wants to communicate the ease with which he approaches "them." Perhaps if Vel lost a certain level of experience through his lack of access, he might lose a degree of self-confidence in using the electronic tools.

> Elisha: A question of resilience. "We're doing . . . a paperless project. We look on the Internet for all different kinds of information on future energy sources. . . . We do the whole report on a disk. We do all our charts and graphs on a disk. We transfer information on the Internet to our disk in the word processing. I think it's pretty cool. It's a lot better doing than having to write everything and it's lot easier to keep up with. You pretty much just have to learn how to look up information on the Internet. Then you have to open the

word processor and have the Internet open. Then you copy it and paste it onto your document in the word processor. . . . There were some Web sites that my science teacher gave me to look up data for future energy sources and also, for projected usage and past usage . . . and you can go to the Net Search and type in future energy sources and it'll give you a list of titles . . . sometimes you just have to look and see. I mean, some will have pretty much nothing that you really want. Others won't look like they have it but they do. It's pretty much trial and error, unless it has a really distinct title."

Elisha's sense of confidence and voice of authority shows in her clear and concise synthesis of her latest assignment. We can infer from this narrative that she has not been perplexed by either the content of the assignment or the skills required to report her work in a paperless fashion. She speaks directly, offering the steps in sequence and, most notably, uses the language of a seasoned word processor. By employing the vocabulary of adult users of technology, Elisha shares the technological culture. In order to say "open the word processor and have the Internet open" suggests that she understands how to access both operations. Using phrases such as "copy it and paste it onto your document" shows some word processing skills.

But the notable aspect of Elisha's self-confidence comes from her mention of "trial and error" searches. Certainly debatable as a pedagogy, K–12 teaching methodologies rarely encourage students to engage in trial and error learning of new knowledge. When teachers of any field introduce new skills and concepts, they typically demonstrate, that is, they model, specific steps and skills in order for students to practice before going on to more advanced steps (Tennessee Instructional Model, 1984). To suggest that she can tolerate the "trial and error" process, Elisha shows a resistance to the typically held school notion of producing one right answer. Trusting a trial and error search reveals a kind of forgiveness for coming up dry or on the wrong track. Elisha mentions the variability in sites; undaunted, she resorts to a kind of inclusive thinking, which suggests that she is willing to check out a number of sites and titles in order to come up with the information she seeks. She compares and contrasts. The flexible thinking, a tolerance for ambiguity, which resists rigid and linear thinking, reveal Elisha's voice of authority in her resilience. She enters the world of many Web sites and evaluates them by titles and content. She follows tracks and gets off tracks, but she understands that this kind of work does not represent failure. On the contrary, her experience illustrates to her that this kind of thinking is required to connect with needed sources.

Elisha's use of the vernacular, "it's cool," reveals that the assignment meets with little resistance from this adolescent. Yet another student uses the word "hip" in describing the project. The accolades suggest that, for now, either because it is new, fun, or because using technology suggests some authority or power they have recently embraced, some students welcome what might have once seemed a dreaded research assignment. Elisha and Vel offer statements illustrating degrees of self-confidence and resilience, never alluding to developing or refining their own search strategies. For them, a level of success represents knowing how to access by performing trial and error searches.

> J. R.: Questions of openness and vulnerability. "We don't ask for help in core subjects because we've been in these courses for all these years now and hey, they are things that we are expected to know. And you don't want to feel like all your classmates are ahead of you and you're asking a question and everyone's like, 'Man, I've known that since back in the sixth grade' . . . that doesn't really apply for much in computers because most of the time everyone around you, including the teachers, are as clueless as you are. So, if you ask a question everyone's like, 'Yeah, what's going on there?' because no one else really knows much. . . . You know, it's new to them. So it's just like when you're little, starting out in school, you know you

could ask anything . . . everybody is so new to it so you're not worried about what are people going to think if I ask this question . . . and the teachers here are very modest. They're not putting themselves on a pedestal. The teachers here, with the exception of a few, have no problem with asking me, a student, for help with computers."

More than revealing that he has some expertise with computers and serves as a support to some teachers, J. R. points out that, because the general use of technology is still in its infancy, most students assume that fellow users share similar expertise and frustrations. Indeed, he alludes that student users are basically novices. Given that assumption, asking questions about and requesting help for using technology are sanctioned as worthy ways to learn, as opposed to asking questions about basic or "core" subjects. From his point of view, making oneself vulnerable by showing ignorance and asking questions of teachers or classmates is sanctioned typically in one's early years of schooling when school is new to all. To carry out J. R.'s line of thinking, as long as technology remains in a continuing state of change and development, many users may long feel themselves "clueless" or "modest" about their expertise. If it is true that students in this generation feel more or less equal to each other in their technology skill levels, one might expect to see a new kind of classroom culture emerge, where peer support is more visible, where levels of expertise are more blurred than in "core subjects."

J. R. makes a reference to teachers suggesting that they may operate on a similar level of expertise as some of the students. As novices, he notices that teachers, too, may ask for help, even of students; yet they do not seem to mind the vulnerability of showing their lack of expertise. The exchange of roles between teacher and student occurs only infrequently in schools. For many reasons, school culture typically demands both formal and informal boundaries between student and teacher. And yet, with the emergent technologies, schools may find that teachers not only query the students but ask students to teach, inform, model, and answer problems they cannot necessarily answer themselves.

J. R. illuminates an interesting contradiction. That is, in not knowing "what's going on there," students show a certain self-confidence by purposefully making themselves vulnerable in asking questions and seeking help. Logic presumes that students who lack self-confidence might not ask for help or know how to frame questions for assistance. Thus, in listening to Vel, Elisha, and J. R., one might return to them to probe for clues of justified self-confidence or mere bravado, which hides frustration.

With these few interview segments, we hear students' construction of a user-friendly computer/Internet reality. Contrary to hearing "anxiety and uncertainty" (Kuhlthau, 1993a) expressed by these student users, the comments raise many questions. Is the confidence expressed by these students associated with using the technology as a tool, rather than as a resource? What constitutes each student's skill level in searching for information, generally, and on the World Wide Web specifically? Have teachers or students evaluated final products of research and writing to assess levels of competence in searching and synthesizing ideas? Does such assessment improve search strategies? Do their four years of twenty-first-century classrooms constitute a feeling of familiarity that moves these students away from what we might term novice users? If one does not perceive oneself as a novice, perhaps one does not experience the anxiety attributed to inexperienced users. Nevertheless, the overall tone of all the students' interviews was one of openness, confidence, and ease in speaking to me about their experiences with technology. They did not show anxiety in responding to the invitation to speak of their experiences. They did not share any uncertainty in revealing their stories of use.

Students may please themselves with their growing sense of self-confidence in using technology; adults may be surprised at young people's growing voice of authority. Nevertheless, the phenomenon of familiarity must be examined in light of continued and greater access for technology users. The phenomenon of resilience in learning, a willingness to engage in "trial and error" rather than systematic and prescribed approaches to accessing information, may offer educators and curriculum designers new ideas for pedagogy. Certainly, the notions of seeking information through "trial and error" methods may challenge the mode of producing "one right answer" for standardized tests. And finally, the blurring of traditional roles suggests that school culture may assume new dynamics, where teachers and students work together in more collegial ways, creating a true "learning organization" (Senge, 1990).

Students' Personal Attributes: Questions of Understanding Time

In talking with the eighth-grade students about their uses and experiences with technology, they revealed three mature notions of the concept of time. Bryce suggests that expediency is in order and that users of technology must be mindful of how they spend their time, for several reasons. Lauralee talks about the pleasure of having time for browsing, as she discovers the pursuit of ideas. And finally, Will discusses the need for patience as an attribute for accessing information.

> Bryce: A question of expediency. "Time is a very precious commodity. . . . [And] on the Internet this can be a financial issue . . . but if you don't have to worry about time constraints or where you have to be in fifteen minutes or how much you're going to have to pay, the Internet can be specific, up to date, and quick. So really, when we are looking for something on the Internet, to find something quickly is always to our advantage but sometimes, we don't find the most specific thing or the best information we can. . . . It depends on how easy it is to find that information. If you're doing something very, very specific, like my project on triboluminescence, it could take a long time, say maybe thirty minutes or more to find informa-

> tion. But something very widespread like the legalization of marijuana or trade embargoes around the world, some current event topic, it's pretty easy to find information on something such as that.

As a user of the Internet, Bryce reveals his understanding of both the financial and the existential issues of time. He honors the element of expediency because he is aware of the value of time in life, generally, and because he knows that some users pay for their Internet connection. Bryce is intrigued with the efficiency the Internet can provide. He states that even if users have no time constraints on their browsing, the Internet can provide current information quickly. In his statement, Bryce tries to compare the efficiency of searches between "widespread" and "very specific" topics. He claims that searching a "current event" topic will offer easier access than esoteric, little-known areas. Nevertheless, "subject knowledge may contribute to retrieval success" (Sugar, 1995) and what Bryce neglects to reference is the quality of the information accessed. His "thirty minutes" may represent a careful search around a familiar topic in which he knows his questions and parameters. Searches by others for "widespread" topics may represent more superficial looks at information where quantity and diversity may, indeed, surface more quickly.

Nevertheless, Bryce appreciates that time is precious and in this light, for him, a key value in using the Internet remains the expediency. He values subject currency and specificity as well.

> Lauralee: Questions of the pleasures of browsing. "I don't think you need time. I think people like a lot of time to browse. But you don't really need a lot of time to go where you need to go if you know your question. . . . Sometimes you'll go to somewhere completely different than where you wanted to go. Because if you look up something like the moon, there must be tons of matches. You could be looking for information on the colonization of the moon, and you would get a poem. So a lot of the matches don't give [a] good explanation of what they are. So you really have to click in to them to see

what they are sometimes . . . and sometimes when you are just bored, you just want to get on and just go somewhere. And you don't know what you want to find out. And sometimes an idea will just pop up into your head and you'll think, 'well, I want to learn more about that.' So you'll go to something. You really just go wherever you want and there's really no destination. You're just kind of floating around I guess . . . like walking in an unfamiliar place. You don't know where you are going, but you are not afraid of getting lost."

Lauralee shows delight about the browsing process using the World Wide Web. She appreciates the idea that one browses sites slowly when one doesn't know the question. But, according to her experience, when one knows what one seeks, there is no need for using a lot of time. She understands that the "matches" may not be one's own "match," which often happens when the browser doesn't know his question. She understands that even if she is pretty clear and specific about the topic she researches, she may have to "click in to them to see what they are" to make sure of the match. This does not seem to bother her. Finding a poem rather than the scientific information she seeks does not discourage her from continuing to seek information. She knows you have to check out the "match" to see what it really contains. Here, Lauralee alludes to the content of the search rather than to the search process itself. She does not mention specific strategies for seeking information, but rather, discusses and evaluates the content in light of whether it simply matches the original question of subject matter.

But Lauralee is most exuberant when she talks about the delight of finding information when she has randomly determined the starting point of the search. Not knowing "what you want to find out" describes browsing at its finest, with no time limits, for the sheer joy of connecting with an unplanned topic, and digging as deeply into a question as one pleases. She describes her pleasure as "floating around"—a metaphor suggesting weightlessness, sensuousness, or a lack of accountability. As a student, she has begun to encounter the joys of knowing, seeking information, and playing around with ideas for their own sake rather than for an end product or grade.

Lauralee distinguishes between needing time and liking to have the time to browse. Rather than feeling the press of time, she perceives the element of time as positive, as the necessary and pleasurable currency for the recreation of exploring ideas. She implies a distinction between browsing "if you know your question," which might not require a lot of time, and browsing when "an idea will just pop up into your head" and you have "no destination," interesting distinctions that serve to remind us of different functions of information searches.

> Will: Questions of patience. "The good news about computers is that they've got what you're looking for, it's got a lot of information; the bad news is that there's too much of it, and sometimes you can't find it. . . . You try and find a specific thing, right, and then it says there's like 900,000 or 9,000 files found on it. Like you have to find one out of nine thousand. . . . Virtually anything you want is on the Internet. . . . You have to be real patient."

Will shows awareness of the magnitude of this new world of information. Now more accessible to young students such as Will, he is impressed with the size of this information source yet seems to question his capacity to tap into it. He likes the grandness of the Internet, perhaps experiencing a feeling of having the world at his fingertips. Yet, at the same time, he has named his coping strategy for handling so much information—patience.

Will feels positively about seeking information and seems to be undaunted by the scope of his tasks. By mentioning that "you have to find one out of 9,000," Will suggests a mystery, a hunt, some suspense or competition that characterizes his relationship to the act of finding what he seeks. He plays this game carefully, with patience, believing that what he needs exists on the Internet.

These student voices raise questions of time for browsing and searching, for accessing and reading information on the World Wide Web. All three of these narratives around using technology and understanding time offer insight about how some students perceive their "precious" time, their sense of browsing, and their patience in searching. And by noting the two broad directions of personal attributes—having self-confidence and understanding time in using technology—we sense that students may require different conditions for seeking information than presently structured in the schools. Questions of making time to explore on the Internet offer many challenges to policy-shapers and curriculum developers for schools. Under what conditions would schools and libraries offer time for students to "float" around on the Internet with no predetermined topic for research? As students grow in their competence with technology and explore intellectual issues on their own on the Internet, management of what students learn and how students learn may look radically different from what we see currently in the schools. Indeed, questions of how students engage with the Internet and how that may influence their reading skills, for example, raise challenges for teachers.

Students' Particular Skills: A Question of Reading

Within the question of reading, three areas arise. Bryce discusses the role audio and graphics play in reading. His talk is labeled "questions of reading with many senses." Bryce made several references to "skimming" as a strategy for reading. The second excerpt is labeled "questions of skimming as a reading strategy." And Elisha sheds light about differences between reading for pleasure in books and for information on the Internet. Her narrative is named "questions of reading as 'treasure' and 'resource.'"

> Bryce: Questions of reading with many senses. "The Internet has more pictures and sound and other media than a book. Like books

> don't have animated things like Java. So you'll look at pictures and hypertext links rather than reading words just straight out of a book. So a lot of times you'll read less thoroughly on the Internet. . . . Java allows color picture animations even with sound. So when you're on the Internet you could hear a real time audio clip, watch a video as it loads, watch Java animation. It adds a lot to the experience of browsing that you don't get from a book . . . your imagination is used differently than reading a book. It can be stimulated by the intriguing animations. In fiction writing you create the story line in your head. That's all good but for nonfiction or factual information, pictures definitely add a lot."

Bryce raises many issues regarding the act of reading text and pictures. He suggests that the combination of graphics, audio, and hypertext links offers a rich medium for the reader. He proposes that instead of perceiving the imagination as inferior or passive, these sensory additions challenge the imagination in different ways from reading straight text. Without assigning the role of "imagination" strictly to fiction reading, Bryce sees that it can, indeed, be stimulated in accessing information and images from the Internet. He further makes a distinction between the role of visualization in reading fiction "where you create the storyline in your head" and nonfiction where "pictures definitely add a lot." He is clear that they cannot be compared, but rather, offer two different kinds of experiences, engaging different kinds of cognition.

Bryce offers yet another key insight when he suggests "you'll read less thoroughly on the Internet." The word "thoroughly" suggests a kind of attending to. Both in speaking and decoding text, listeners and readers attend to different kinds of information about words, including phonology or how to pronounce; the syntax of the text, which asks readers if it "sounds right" grammatically; semantics, which projects meaning; and the pragmatic, which checks context (i.e., Is this fantasy? Is this slang or offensive text?) (Dewdney and Mitchell, 1996). Bryce may be thinking that the audio clip, the graphics, or typography, in their "intriguing animations," offer more accessible cues for information about words than what readers find in close, deep, or "thorough" readings of stand-alone text. In decoding and comprehending print, readers must construct many levels of meaning and information on their own. For Bryce, "thorough" reading on the screen is not as necessary when multisensory cues such as he describes are provided. And finally, perhaps, the two kinds of reading—from print and from screen—are simply different, providing qualitatively different comprehension experiences.

Many of the students commented that graphics, as well as the text, serve as powerful points for their information gathering.

> Alice: "You can see the pictures on the screen. It's not like you are imagining them by yourself. . . . You have to read the book to find it, but on the computer you just click on an icon and you can see it . . . on the screen."

She knows the difference between engaging the imagination in reading text from books and seeing the picture, which expands and enhances the text's message. Yet another student, Vel, perceives the pictures and graphics as a motivator for his reading.

> Vel: "They might have a picture of the new car and then they might have a paragraph beside it and I might read it . . . and they've got the writing printed a certain way and I might like it and I might read it."

Here, Vel comments on both pictures and the typographies; each intrigues him to read the text for information.

Keeping in mind current research on learning styles (Gardner, 1983), educators might consider such multisensory and visually attractive cues for reading as ways to pull some readers into text. Nevertheless, seasoned readers of text will know the important difference noted above by Bryce and Alice; when one reads words, one has the power to imagine what the topic might look like, sound like, smell like. Words offer cues to the imagination. In employing multisensory cues to help decode text, the interpretation of the information will offer more of the authors' and programmers' nuances of understanding. In these instances, a reader's imagination and comprehension are challenged in ways different from what reading text alone may do. The lure of visually exciting screens does not offer a substitute for exercising one's imagination from reading stand-alone text, whereby one employs comprehension skills far superior to simple decoding or taking information from the screen. Bryce points out the important distinction between reading fiction and nonfiction; he notes an appropriate function of graphics for reading nonfiction and information and suggests they may inspire new reading strategies.

> Bryce: Questions of skimming as a reading strategy. "If you have something to do [on the Internet] you can't read it as thoroughly as if you had unlimited time. You don't pay by the hour with a book. And [with the Internet], sometimes you'll find yourself just skimming because the Internet has more pictures and sound and other media than a book."

Bryce is not apologetic about skimming for information. He is aware of the cost of Internet service for some. We know from a previous story that he values time, is expedient, and can assume that he uses the reading strategy of skimming in order to cover as much material as possible. His reference to reading less thoroughly on the Internet is not a negative one because he notes that both graphics (which can be decoded quickly) as well as words (which are decoded at a slower rate) can offer needed information. In a classic textbook on teaching reading, Huey (1977) suggests that

> We have never canvassed the possibilities of improving the total word-form, for particular words. . . . If by using capitals or by changing the shape, size, or even color of constituent letters we bring into prominence the total word-form and characterize it better, total form will thus come to play a still larger part than at present in mediating the recognition of what is read. Such recognition in larger units favors speed in reading and lessens the strain on eye and mind. (p. 423)

But skimming as a single reading strategy raises many questions. Well known are the courses that teach "speed" reading or strategies of skimming. They endeavor to liberate word-by-word and line-by-line readers in order to accelerate reading speed and to influence greater comprehension of large quantities of information. Such courses make "reading and studying into a conscious activity, in which students are aware of which passages they choose to read and at what level of detail" (Lambert, 1997). Given the nature of browsing or surfing on the Internet, will students learn also to employ thoughtful, critical reading strategies such as close reading to appreciate authors' intentions or to "search out implicit structure of a text" (Lambert, 1997)? Should we be concerned if students learn to read or only choose to read electronically by "surfing," or "gliding and tapping into what you want" as Will calls it? As a complex act, reading offers many levels of challenge and pleasure. Certainly, skimming empowers readers. And, ironically, skimming as a reading strategy is often difficult to teach to novice readers who lack the confidence to free themselves from word-by-word and line-by-line decoding. As educators, however, we must understand the differences among the various strategies and purposes of reading. Elisha notes differences between different kinds of reading.

> Elisha: Questions of reading as "treasure" and "resource." "Books are always going to be a treasure to me. . . . I can really get into a fantasy in a book rather than surfing on the net. I find wanting to have an adventure more in reading a book than going on the In-

> ternet. . . . The computer for me is more of an information resource. I find I am more interested when it's on the computer because it seems more in depth and up-to-date. I find it more appealing to go into the computer and have such a choice instead of one book, maybe . . . and it's easier to read. You kind of just sit there and you scroll down. It keeps my attention better, because of its brightness and being right there, I guess.

Elisha's insight offers a sense of balance. A reader, she helps look at key differences in being with a book compared to being on the computer. As metaphors, both "treasure" and "resource" share meaning of value and potential support. "Treasure" refers to an elusive, yet emotional dimension not necessarily seen in the notion of "resource," a more neutral support. "Getting into a fantasy" suggests getting lost, immersing oneself in a pleasurable experience. Saying it "keeps my attention better," Elisha paints an active picture of physically and cognitively interacting with the Internet. She chooses material from various sources, initiates when to "scroll down," and cannot escape its bright presence, a far different experience from curling up with a piece of fiction for pleasure or adventure reading, which may only happen in her head.

Paying attention to balance challenges educators to orchestrate the materials and resources for their curriculum development and delivery. Balancing reading assignments of fiction and nonfiction and requiring both curling up with books and logging onto the Internet require thoughtful pedagogy and pacing. As two very distinct and qualitatively different reading activities, students' intellectual lives should be charged with engaging in reading for pleasure and for information. They must not only read, but know the difference among various kinds of reading.

Of all the themes these student interviews raised, educators must raise the questions of reading as essential to their pedagogy. How critically or deeply do students read when they work with hypertext or read on the Internet as compared to reading print in books? What kinds of new reading strategies should teachers account for as students switch reading activities between paper and screen? Given the lure of electronic resources, will we create blocks of time in which students not only are allowed to browse on the World Wide Web but spend time getting lost in a book? What cognitive skills diminish as graphics and audio stimuli offer ready-made interpretations? Which reading skills expand? Essential questions of reading might shape new ways in which teachers conceive of using electronic sources in their teaching.

Students' Particular Skills: A Question of Managing Information

Throughout the interviews, students raised questions about quality in technological resources and wondered how to handle great quantities of information. Several students discussed how much information appeared before them at an instant and how much of it appeared irrelevant or useless. Alice and others suggest, first, that one needs to know one's question. I have labeled the first skill area, questions of knowing what you want to know. As a second step, students have to learn strategies to conduct searches on the Internet. J. R. shares his thinking in the section labeled questions of search strategies.

> Alice: Questions of knowing what you want to know. "Browsing is just flipping through things, seeing what all is there. It's kind of like flipping through the channels on TV, typing different things in to see what pops up on the screen. And you know, if you don't like it you can flip to another thing. If you don't know what you're looking for, you're out of luck. . . . For looking up 'solar energy' I didn't even know what I was supposed to do and so I just typed in 'solar energy' and I kept getting all these other things like 'solar energy, the book.' I'm like, 'no, solar energy.' Then there was a person named 'Solar Energy.' And it was like all kinds of things, so I just clicked 'solar energy: science.' Basically I had to find it out on my own. It took

like three days to figure it out. . . . There are so many things out there. On the computer you don't really know what all is in there. But you can find anything that you want. You just have to find a way to do it."

In this story, Alice offers a picture of familiarity with the initial browsing process, making the analogy with selecting television programs. But it would appear, for her, that her analogy stops there when she says that, "If you don't know what you're looking for, you're out of luck." Television browsers often act passively, checking to see whether or not they can be intrigued by a presentation to remain with a channel. But the Internet search feels different, more active, as the students refer to initiating a search and evaluating a match. Vel echoes this as he suggests, "When you first get on the Internet you have to have a subject to get on there." And Polly states it most directly, "If you don't have it, you can't find it." These students show that in order to make use of the Internet, one needs a focus, a question. And more productively, Belkin (1982) reminds us that "it is more suitable to attempt to describe that anomalous state of knowledge (ASK), than to ask the user to specify her/his need as a request" for information. Students must know what they want to know, beyond suggesting a discrete but ambiguous subject.

Shaping the research question seems to challenge the students. Alice spent three days trying to figure out specifically what she wanted to know. The broad topic of "solar energy" offered too many possibilities to search and by not figuring out what it was about solar energy she wanted to know, she found irrelevant connections. Polly adds to this frustrating picture when she tells us,

> Polly: "So sometimes it seems like you end up with things with no connection whatsoever, or so far out there in connection that it might as well not be. It's annoying when you end up with those things and you only have so much time to do it in, and you can't find anything."

Seekers of information must learn to frame or shape their initial question. Polly feels impatient with lost search time. Although it took Alice three days to learn that she had to undergo a process of refining her search, she became more clear that she had to figure out, "on her own," what she wanted to know. Even within the subset of "solar energy: science," Alice then went on to find additional subsets for past and projected uses of solar energy. Knowing what one wants to know represents one key to success in searches. Shaping questions for Internet searches differs little from searching print materials. Feeling confused about how to go about the process of finding information often maps back to the initial question that many students have not considered thoroughly enough. A second key to search success might include assistance. The students interviewed for this project do not mention seeking help from a mediator—a teacher or media specialist—but rather, mention figuring out search strategies "on their own."

Nahl and Tenopir (1996) suggest that users "need information about searching itself." Teachers and librarians can train students to search on their own by first teaching them to ask themselves such questions as, "What is it about 'solar energy' that you want to know?" And further, "And what about that is it that you care to learn?" thus helping to establish the topic even further by identifying the user's true information need. Teaching students overtly how to go about the business of seeking and writing up information offers students a model of digging mindfully into subject matter, rather than encouraging superficial searching and scanty thinking. The "trial and error" searches, the three-day searches represent fairly low cognitive efforts. If students care to research topics with serious effort, they must pay attention to their cognitive need to know and practice strategies that connect the seeker to the sought material.

Thus, once the research question is established, searchers must employ explicit strategies to seek information. J. R. offers insight into the delight of finding so much information and discusses his strategies for coping.

> J. R.: Questions of search strategies. "There's just much more selection on the Internet. . . . Sometimes it's good that it has so much, because it is very broad. It has a lot of information from a lot of different places and even from different times. I was looking for something and it had like 12,000 matching topics. You narrow it down by giving it specifics . . . what words to use. . . . But in narrowing and scrolling down, looking for what you need, you'll find something [else] interesting. You get sidetracked on it. But that also can be a pitfall because when you get to something like that, you have to know how to find that one thing out of the 12,000 that you are looking for."

J. R. appreciates the breadth and depth of the information so readily accessible from his Internet searches. But he is very aware that it can overwhelm. "Narrowing" represents his key search strategy and he understands how to use specific words to direct the search. Nevertheless, in simultaneously "narrowing" and "scrolling down," he notes the temptation of getting sidetracked into more possibilities. For him, this can be both good and bad news. At no point did J. R. mention employing "broadening" as a search strategy. Although he suggests that "you have to know how to find that one thing," he does not divulge how one might recognize it. More startlingly, his statement suggests that, just as with a needle in a haystack, you must know exactly what you seek and then must recognize it. His allusion to "specifics" or words to use does not employ the more sophisticated language of "terms." One senses that J. R. has learned by trial and error, that he has had some moderate success in his searches, but that the awe of so much response to his query continues to impress.

Students must employ basic search skills to access the Internet productively. These skills may include general research concepts such as defining the topic, negotiating parameters of both the topic and the search sources, and learning to use search terms and skimming for information. As for all research, both print and electronic, students must learn to evaluate their sources. And finally, student searchers must know how to synthesize their information and write their findings in their own words, citing the sources in appropriate ways.

Some students will teach themselves these skills from home and recreational browsing. Some students will learn these skills in school from peers or teachers. Research must address issues of initial learning of how to use the Internet for searches. How much can novices gain both from the playfulness in undirected browsing balanced with the structure of learning direct search strategies? Do trial and error searches enhance or impede the initial learning of tried-and-true search strategies for information retrieval? What methodologies best support the initial learning of retrieving information from Internet sites? These student voices help raise questions for additional research.

CONCLUSION

In reviewing the students' perceptions, we gain insight into how they, themselves, have begun to construct a working understanding of the relations among the information problem that they bring to the search, the Internet as tool and resource, and the outcome of their search. If the adults who work with student users understand students' constructs, perhaps they can gauge what users have in common and what is idiosyncratic in electronic searching. The study raises questions for professionals engaged in teaching students how to seek and retrieve information. The questions suggest areas for professional development for teachers and media center directors as they begin to embrace electronic and print resources for student research. The areas include assessing students' levels of self-confidence in using the Internet both as a tool and as a resource; knowing how to structure both overt and open-ended lessons in search strategies; and appreciating and employing different kinds of reading strategies.

First, the positive attitudes and self-confidence exhibited by these nine research participants provide interesting dimensions of youthful users, but may not indicate success in their information retrieval overall. Professionals who research stages of adolescent development may offer insight into notions of justified self-confidence or the veneer of bravado that students exhibit as they talk about their expertise with technology. Were these students novices or could their four years of familiarity with twenty-first-century classrooms label them as seasoned users? Understanding better students' sources of self-confidence with technology would offer information for meeting individual needs. This research suggests a level of student confidence only with using the Internet as a mechanism—a tool. None of the stories alluded to evaluating the Web sites for content excellence. Few mentioned accuracy and adequacy of the information retrieved from their searches. Information professionals must be clear about the differences between comfort level with the technology and depth of appreciation and critical assessment of the content students encounter.

Because of their "guinea pig" status as twenty-first-century classroom students, many of these students learned on their own, as peers of their teachers who were learning as well. We may continue to see this collegial setting for a number of years ahead as schools seek to change their pedagogies to accommodate the use of the Internet as a resource. These early years of developing curricula and teaching strategies that integrate print and electronic resources may offer an informal approach by learning in a collegial atmosphere. The informality of a developing technological school culture offers issues to notice. Different from the print-alone culture, students may know more about how to use the technology than the adults. How can we harness the real self-confidence and use this affective variable in assisting students' learning overall? Our continued understanding of students' cognitive and affective development (Kuhlthau, 1993b) may offer a beginning framework for learning how to introduce, how to pace, and how to measure students' capabilities with using the Internet.

Second, questions of continued technology training and professional development will begin to drive the quality of use in the schools. Research into how best to assist teachers and school media professionals in learning how to facilitate students' learning on the Internet is needed. Throughout the narratives, students made very few references to intermediaries such as teachers and media specialists. Only Vel, when pressed by my question, "How did you learn to find Web sites?" responded, "The [public] reference librarian!" Certainly schools need to engage in creative and developmentally appropriate ways to introduce students of all ages to the notions of vastness and currency of the Internet's content, as well as to elegant and efficient strategies for accessing the information. Schools may have to entertain questions of time and schedules to enable students to complete both leisurely browsing and efficient searches. And further, if research and search strategies are overtly taught, then how do schools schedule time to perform the searches, which are, by nature, unpredictable? Typically, students research outside of school time. If professionals want to assist students, coach them in their newly learned search skills, do computer labs and school media professionals assume new roles during traditional class time?

Third, threaded throughout their narratives, students made references to the process of reading. As we introduce technology into the schools and set expectations for using the Internet as a resource, we must be mindful of the different kinds of reading employed in gathering ideas. Educators and students must understand that we both skim and perform close readings on text, depending on the task of seeking knowledge. Therefore, questions of how to select a suitable process of reading, depending on the purpose, must be made more explicit for students. As they enter an Internet world with multisensory cues for decoding, which invite them to skim, students must not forget the processes of reading deeply for meaning and evaluating, as traditionally expected with print. The goal of learning how to access information and then comprehending it at many levels does not change because one can skim so much more easily on the Internet. Continued research might offer us ideas about how to recognize and practice the differences in how to read and comprehend print text and Internet text.

The students who shared their stories and insights about their use of technology illuminate key issues for educators. Eager to share, these students offer memorable stories of encountering the Internet. If we listen to their voices, we hear their confidence and their openness in using technology. If we listen carefully, we gain insight into rethinking how we teach such core subjects such as reading, research skills, and writing. As we consider students' perceptions, we gain insight into how to assess and utilize their own construction of what it means to use technology such as the World Wide Web.

ACKNOWLEDGMENTS

Thanks to Sue Diehl who helped make this study possible by sharing her expertise, her school media center, and her time to put me in touch with teachers and students. Thanks to Dania Meghabghab and Doug Raber for technical assistance in reviewing this article.

REFERENCES

Belkin, N. (1982). "ASK for information retrieval: Part I. Background and theory." *Journal of Documentation* 38: 61–71.

Belkin, N. (1990). "The cognitive viewpoint in information science." *Journal of Information Science* 16: 11–15.

Bruner, J. (1964). "Going beyond the information given: The Colorado Symposium." In *Contemporary approaches to cognition* (pp. 41–70). Cambridge, Mass.: Harvard University Press, 1964.

Bruner, J. (1990). *Acts of meaning*. Cambridge, Mass.: Harvard University Press.

Bruner, J. (1994). *Four ways to make a meaning*. Cassette recording, unnumbered, presented at American Educational Research Association, New Orleans.

Clandinin, D., and Connelly, F. (1990). "Stories of experience and narrative inquiry." *Educational Researcher* 19: 2–14.

Clandinin, D., and Connelly, F. (1995). "Teachers' professional knowledge landscapes." New York: Teachers' College Press.

Dervin, B. (1977). "Useful theory for librarianship: Communication, not information." *Drexel Library Quarterly* 13: 16–32.

Dervin, B., Jacobson, T., and Nilan, M. (1982). "Measuring aspects of information seeking: A test of a quantitative/qualitative methodology." In *Communication Yearbook* vol. 6. An annual review published for the International Communication Association (Beverly Hills, Calif.: Sage), 419–444.

Dewdney, P., and Mitchell, G. (1983). "Oranges and peaches: Understanding communication accidents in the reference interview." *Research Quarterly* 35: 520–536.

Gardner, H. (1983). *Frames of mind*. New York: Basic Books.

Huey, E. (1977). *The psychology and pedagogy of reading*. Cambridge, Mass.: MIT Press.

Janes, J. W., and Rosenfeld, L. B. (1996). "Networked information retrieval and organization: Issues and questions." *Journal of the American Society for Information Science* 47: 711–715.

Kuhlthau, C. (1993a). "A principle of uncertainty for information seeking." *Journal of Documentation* 49: 339–355.

Kuhlthau, C. (1993b). *Seeking meaning: A process approach to library and information services*. Norwood, N.J.: Ablex.

Kuhlthau, C., Belvin, R., and George, M. (1989). "Flowcharting the information search: A method for eliciting users' metal maps." *ASIS '89: Proceedings of the 52nd ASI Annual Meeting* 26: 162–165.

Kuhlthau, C., Turrock, B., George, M., and Belvin, R. (1990). "Validating a model of the search process: A comparison of academic, public and school library users." *Library and Information Science Research* 12: 5–32.

Lambert, M. (1977). "Read better, sleep more." *Harvard Magazine* 99: 66–68.

Mellon, C. (1990). *Naturalistic inquiry for library science*. New York: Greenwood Press.

Nahl, D., and Tenopir, C. (1996). "Affective and cognitive searching behavior of novice end-users of a full-text database." *Journal of American Society for Information Science* 47 (1996): 276–286.

Page, R. (1997). "Teaching about validity." *Qualitative Studies in Education* 10: 145–156.

Schank, R. (1990). *Tell me a story: A new look at real and artificial memory*. New York: Scribner's Sons.

Senge, P. (1990). *The fifth discipline: The art and practice of the learning organization*. New York: Doubleday.

Sugar, W. (1995). "User-centered perspective of information retrieval research and analysis methods," In M. Williams ed., *Annual Review of Information Science and Technology*, (vol. 30, pp. 78–101). Medford, N.J.: Information Today.

Tennessee Instructional Model. (1984). *Module on retention*. Nashville: Tennessee State Department of Education.

Seven

Children's Information Choices for Inclusion in a Hypothetical, Child-Constructed Library

Linda Z. Cooper

Literature tells us that children think differently than adults.[1] Professionals who work with children concur with this information. It should follow, then, that the information interests and needs of children are different than those of adults. This, too, has been addressed in research.[2] That children's thoughts and information needs are different from those of adults is hardly surprising. The scope of children's experience is different than that of adults. Their life world is different from that of an adult; therefore, different things—different *information*—will be important to them. The adult world recognizes this and has attempted to accommodate children's information interests and needs in various ways. For example, the children's library is almost always a separate entity from the adult's library. Material in the children's library is presented in formats and on reading levels that adults have deemed appropriate for children and, hopefully, in keeping with children's needs, interests, and levels of understanding.

Understanding is constructed by a process in which new information is scaffolded on to a schema or mental structure that is already in place. This mental structure has been built upon previous experience.[3] In order to have meaning, one must be able to relate new information to information already processed and stored.[4] If that connection cannot be made, then the new information will have no meaning since it will relate to nothing within the realm of the individual's experience.

PROBLEM

Children, probably more so than any other user group, have almost all of their information needs filtered and interpreted by other people. Very often it is an adult intermediary who must interpret a child's request and access the material that they *think* the child is looking for from the selection of information made available in the library by other adults. Although the intermediary will do his or her best to fill the child's request, the situation is still one in which the two parties involved—adult and child—have basic differences in their experiences and understandings. Even the most well-intentioned librarian can only hope that the material s/he produces or guides a child to is the information the child actually is looking for. A librarian may unintentionally steer a child towards information they feel is best for the child rather than what the child actually wants. This, of course, can happen to an adult user but is more likely to happen to a child user because of the considerations stated above. Children have little control over their circumstances in general and tend to use what is made available to them. A child may accept an adult's suggestion simply because adults make most of his or her decisions anyway.

The library serves many people, both individuals and broader population groups. Adult individuals and groups, however, share some common traits in both physical and intellectual development and in scope of experience. For example, most adults are proficient at scanning and tracking. Most adults who come to the library can read to some extent. Adults may also share commonalities of experience that are within the realm of growing up in a common culture. These are skills and experiences that children have not yet accomplished. Although individual adults will have their own personal perspectives regarding information, they do share some commonalities that make it easier for them as a group to interact with a culturally organized corpus and/or its intermediary. The child's difference in perspective is not only personal and sociocultural, but also developmental and experiential.

Since both intermediary support and decisions regarding what information will be contained within or made available through the library is controlled by adults, the entire corpus of information available to children in the library has been chosen by people with whom they have a fundamental difference in experience and perspective. A serious issue regarding intellectual access for the child thus exists. True freedom of intellectual pursuit supports the realization of an individual potential that may only be truly known by the person within whom that seed of interest or talent lies.

How can we move to make information in the library available to children and give them some control over their own intellectual development rather than force-feeding them in our attempt to nurture? First, we might ask children what their information interests are rather than assuming we know what they are. It is also important to examine how children think about the library in order to provide the most direct, unfettered access possible to support their intellectual pursuits.

RELATED LITERATURE

Sociology

Humans understand things by putting them into categories.[5] When confronted with information, we examine it in relation to everything we have previously experienced, our *stock of knowl-*

edge, and classify it according to type—we *typify* it.[6] It is widely accepted in the literature of education that new information will be more readily understood if it can be related to a previously held *schema* or mental structure. "The act of rendering some given event equivalent to a class of other things, placing it in an identity class, provides then one of the most primitive forms of going beyond information given."[7] Typifications, therefore, help a person create a schema so that meaning can be constructed from the new information.

Since each individual has a unique personal history, his or her accumulated experiences, or stock of knowledge, are different. Each person will, therefore, perceive information in relation to his or her personal stock of knowledge and understand it in a uniquely personal way that can be thought of as a personal typification. A child, his or her caretaker, and a commuter will each perceive a snowstorm and its consequences differently. The storm will mean something different to each, and each will typify the storm from his or her perspective. Therefore, our personal typifications or categories for information clearly color the meaning that information has for us.

Nevertheless, members of a community are able to converse about a wide variety of topics with a presumption that the general meaning of words is commonly understood. We can do this because we share broader cultural typifications about the meaning of information. The caretaker, the commuter, and the child can converse about a snowstorm with some confidence that they are speaking about the same thing. When members of the community share these common understandings about information and can communicate effectively, they have achieved *intersubjectivity*.[8]

In addition to both the personal typifications and the broader cultural typifications discussed above, there are also typifications shared by groups of people who have close common interests or *thought communities*.[9] We must be able to mentally categorize information in the manner of various thought communities in order to negotiate our day. For example, before I go skiing, I need to negotiate the method of typification/categorization used by the sporting goods store to find the most suitable equipment. After skiing, I may need to understand the method of categorization used by the drug store in order to find analgesics. On the way home, I may stop at the library and will need to understand the Dewey decimal system in order to find either nonfiction to guide my next sportive efforts or fiction to take my mind off them entirely. Every thought community I encounter will typify information from its own perspective.

What does all of this have to do with libraries and information seeking? The library is a thought community within the larger culture. It has specific ways in which it typifies the information it contains. If the user cannot make the cognitive leap from his or her personal typification of information to that of the thought community of the library, the information-seeking process will break down without the assistance of an intermediary. The user will have to depend on an intermediary's interpretation of his or her request in order to satisfy an information need. The "type" of information available in a library can be ascertained through examination of its collection, which does not, however, tell us what users think should be there. It only tells us which of the information available the users choose. The user's typification of what information a library ought to contain can only be known through communication with the user.

Developmental Psychology

If, as stated above, people's understanding of information is closely related to their stock of knowledge, then the developmental stage of an individual will impact this understanding. People in an earlier developmental stage will likely have a smaller stock of knowledge than people in a later developmental stage. As development progresses, the stock of knowledge will increase and, based on this new information, understandings will change.

Piaget's theory of development posits four stages through which all children move in the same order and at approximately the same time. The sensorimotor stage occurs first and lasts until about age two. It is largely concerned with the child's physical interaction with his or her environment. In the preoperational stage, symbols begin to replace objects in the child's conceptualizations. This period extends from approximately age two to age six. The concrete operational stage of development occurs from age six to eleven. Children during this stage are able to perform logical problem solving using concrete objects. The final stage, formal operations, begins at around eleven years and is a period when higher-level mental operations are formed. Children are able to reason without the use of concrete objects and are able to deal with the abstract.[10]

Research in the area of cognitive psychology also supports the idea that children's classificatory behavior moves from concrete to abstract as they get older.[11] "[Y]oung children's representations are instance bound, whereas older children are able to free themselves more from particular instances to form more 'logical,' abstract concepts."[12] It makes sense that a younger child with a smaller stock of knowledge will have less experience on which to conceptualize abstractly.

Vygotsky's social model of cognitive development rests on the connection between children's cognitive development and their social experiences.[13] He posits that children's cognitive development is shaped by interaction with their culture. They acquire knowledge through their culture, but they also learn to perceive in a manner in keeping with their culture. This is a move toward cultural intersubjectivity.

Vygotsky also addresses the movement from egocentric to socialized behavior that children experience as they develop.[14] This, too, is related to a move toward intersubjectivity with one's culture. Successful communication with one's culture is necessary for "survival" in both the social and physical senses. One needs to be able to think like others in his or her culture in order to get along in it. Personal typifications may satisfactorily categorize personal experiences, but the child must move toward mastery of cultural typifications in order to communicate successfully with others. Markman, for example, has observed that children quickly learn to organize categories in a manner that is most culturally acceptable or important.[15] Zerubavel states that "the difference between children's and adults' cognition has to do with the fact that they are at different stages of their cognitive development not only as human beings but as social beings."[16] According to Levi-Strauss, the use of more or less abstract terms to delineate concepts is not "a function of greater of lesser intellectual capacity, but of differences in the interests—in their intensity and attention to detail—of particular social groups within the national society."[17] As survival in the thought communities of the school and the library becomes of greater interest and importance to children, they will modify their understandings of concepts so that they will be in keeping with those communities. So it is to be expected that children's typifications of what should constitute a library will change from a personal perspective to a more social perspective.

Categories

Within the vast literature addressing category development, Eleanor Rosch's work with basic level objects in natural categories is particularly important to this study. "[B]asic objects are shown to be the most inclusive categories for which a concrete image of the category as a whole can be formed, to be the first categorizations made during perception of the environment, to be the earliest categories sorted and earliest named by children, and to be the categories most codable, most coded, and most necessary in language."[18] Basic level objects are those in the middle of a hierarchy. For example, in the hierarchy *canine*, *dog*, *poodle*, the member *dog* is the basic level object. "The basic level is the highest level at which members have similar shapes and at which a mental image can reflect the whole category, the level that is most quickly identified and has the most commonly used label, the first understood by children and to enter the lexicon of a language, and the level at which most of our knowledge is organized."[19] Given these qualities, it would seem that the members that young children would include in the category or typification of "information important to have in a library" would tend to be basic-level objects.

Children and Culturally Typified Libraries

Adults design information systems, including libraries. These systems are based on the cultural typifications of the wider community and the library. Literature indicates that children and adults think differently,[20] so the information systems in place may not be supportive of children's information-seeking behaviors and, in fact, may be considered intellectual barriers to information for children. Although childlike thinking will eventually develop into adult thinking, approximately ten years of potential intellectual development are not supported by most current information systems.

If information seeking for the average adult user is at times daunting, the problems confronting the child information seeker can be considered legion. They include barriers of language sophistication, reading ability, life experience, and developmental considerations (i.e., scanning, tracking, fine motor coordination).[21] According to Piaget, very young children tend to be individualistic and self-centered and expect others to have their perspective.[22] This leads to problems in the use of a culturally typified information system even if children can read well enough to use the system. Kuhlthau has advocated that school library media programs be based on the developmental states of children and young adults in order to meet their information needs.[23] This chapter reports on an inquiry that moves toward actualizing this idea through examination of children's own articulations regarding the contents of a library.

THEORETICAL ISSUES

The library is a cultural institution that hypothetically supports the intellectual needs of all members of its community. The material contained in and made accessible through the library is chosen and organized by adult members of the thought community of the library. Literature reviewed indicates that people understand information through a process of typification in which we categorize information based on a stock of knowledge acquired through previous experience. Although each adult member of the community will have his or her own personal typifications for information, as adult members of a common culture, there is also much shared understanding, or intersubjectivity, that has been attained through years of cultural experience. Children, however, do not have the same cultural stock of knowledge to which adults are privy, and so their understanding of information may differ from that of the adult community. It cannot be assumed that an adult's best guess regarding a child's information needs is in keeping with the manner in which a child thinks. Therefore, in order to best support children's information-seeking needs, it is important to examine the manner in which children think about information. If our understanding of information is reflected in the manner in which we classify or typify that information, the information that children classify as belonging in a library should reflect their understanding of the concept of the library and what it should contain. Insight into this area may enable the library community to better support the needs of its child users.

This study examines information that participants categorize as "important to have in a library" and how this typification of what information should constitute a library changes between kindergarten and grade 4. If children's information interests and needs differ from those of adults, it follows that as children get older (i.e., approach adulthood), their information interests and needs will change. It seems likely that these will change in keeping with their enlarging social and intellectual worlds. It is in the child's best interest to be able to communicate efficiently and effectively with his or her culture, and it follows that as a child gets older, his or her typifications for information will change in keeping with those of the surrounding culture. This acculturation is necessary if the child is to survive physically, intellectually, and emotionally in his or her culture and is bound to have a profound influence on the manner in which a child thinks about information.

PRAGMATIC ISSUES AND LIMITATIONS

Several important issues impact the interpretations that can be drawn from this inquiry. I personally believe that inquiries into children's information behaviors and preferences yield the most valuable insights when they are conducted in a situation that is normal or natural to the participants, as opposed to one that they might perceive as different or "not normal." In this study I was the participants' school library media specialist. I was interested in the information behaviors and preferences of the population I served. The most straightforward method of learning about these things seemed simply to ask the children in as normal a situation as possible, that is, in a regularly scheduled library class as part of their curriculum, which was supportive of critical thinking skills. Inviting another person (not the children's school library media specialist) to ask the children what they thought would have changed the situation from "normal" to "not normal." Although I made every effort to convey to the children that the project was to examine their choices for inclusion in an imaginary library of their own design, not what was in the library already or what another librarian might choose (see description of session below), it is impossible to calculate the exact extent that children's responses may have been affected by this situation. I felt that even with this limitation it was better to ask than not to ask with the hope that some insight into their information choices might be revealed. Observation of their information choices on a weekly basis, of course, would only have indicated their preferences regarding material already in the library and not what they would like to have in the library.

This project was conducted in the context of a real-life unit of study in a school library media center. As such, the situation and needs of the participating students came before issues of research reliability and validity. For example, the number of children participating at each grade level varied widely because that was consistent with the number of children on each grade level with whom I worked. Kindergarten through second-grade children numbered between 120 and 150 on each grade level. Third- and fourth-grade participants numbered about fifty children on each grade level. However, since the project was part of a real school library curriculum, it would have been inappropriate to exclude children in order to produce a more balanced number of responses from each grade level. Another option would have been to pull children into the project who were not normally in these classes. This too would have changed the data collection situation from "normal" to "not normal." Still another option would have been to include all children in the project but discount the responses of some in order to balance the amount of data from each grade level. Again, I was most interested in examining responses of all participants in order to glean as much insight as possible in an effort to improve library service to the children. The effort to balance data comparison on grade levels is described below.

In this project, children discussed their information interests in whole class situations rather than individually with me. The notion of individual interviews with children rather than group discussions was discarded for two reasons. First, pulling a child out of class to be interviewed changes the situation from one supportive of a curriculum-based project satisfying district, state, and national standards to one in which the child is removed from a learning situation and interviewed for purposes of "research" during what should be his or her classroom time. Second, removing a child from his or her class group to be interviewed individually by the school library media specialist is extremely unusual. The child would very likely view such a situation as a "test" situation and this would certainly impact the child's responses. Participating children were accustomed to group discussions, encouraged to engage in critical thinking, and expressed their opinions frankly during their regular visits to the school library. Individual interviews would have placed unusual stress on the children as well as removed them from their normal educational routine.

Children in the second grade had participated in a pilot exercise of the project the previous year (as described below), and this may have affected their responses for this project. Nevertheless, they participated in the project, and their input is included here. One year looms large in the totality of experience and stock of knowledge of an average seven-year-old child. In addition, it is noted that these children were now in different classes. Their new knowledge, experience, and group circumstance all affect their information choices.

Limitations are self-evident in that the findings reflect only the information choices of children who participated in this project. Since the project was conducted in an authentic school setting during regular library classes, rather than in a laboratory or contrived setting, all the variables that normally impact such a situation will impact the data and findings here. There were methodological problems of data collection and interpretation associated with the real-life circumstance, but an attempt to gain insight in this area warrants report, and an effort should be made to collect children's responses in as natural a circumstance as possible.

PROJECT GOALS

The goals of this project are to gain insight into participants' information preferences for inclusion in a child-constructed library, and whether and how these interests change with increasing grade level.

METHODOLOGY

This chapter reports on part of a larger study,[24] the purpose of which was to gain insight into participants' typifications of library information by having them design a hypothetical library. Their library would contain information chosen and arranged on shelves by the participants in a manner they felt would be conducive to easy access. Through examination of participants' choices of information for inclusion, as well as decisions regarding which information should be shelved together and what those shelf categories should be named, it was hoped that a deeper understanding of their perspectives regarding library information would be attained. The larger project, therefore, began by challenging participants to begin the construction of their hypothetical library through selection of the information they felt would be important to include. This chapter reports on their response to that first challenge. The larger project was conducted during the weekly library session of each class over a period of five weeks. The portion of the project described in this chapter was conducted during one of those sessions.

Population and Setting

Approximately 500 children from two public schools in kindergarten through grade 4 participated. Children in kindergarten through grade 2 attended a primary school, and the entire population of that school participated. Children in grades 3 and 4 attended an intermediate school in the same school district. Both schools are located in a largely middle-class suburban neighborhood. The ratio of girls to boys participating in the study was approximately equal, and the majority of participants were Caucasian. Ten children in grade 4 were members of a special education/inclusion class. They regularly attended library class with a full-size grade 4 class. Sessions for kindergarten through grade 2 lasted approximately twenty-five minutes. Sessions for grades 3 and 4 lasted approximately twenty minutes. Both time lengths represent the approximate lengths of the normal weekly lesson portion of library class. These sessions, as well as all sessions of the larger project, were conducted as part of the children's regular library lessons. All sessions were conducted in keeping with the best interests of the children, within accepted educational practices, and satisfied state and national standards.

Description of Project

For each class of participants, one regularly scheduled library session in the spring of the school year was devoted to the project described in this chapter. I began by suggesting that since the students had been coming to the school library media center for some time, they might have an idea of what was and was not available in the library. The notion of desired information not being available in their school library was introduced to encourage students to consider the broader scope of their information interests. I asked the students to visualize an empty library and to hypothesize that they could fill it with whatever they choose.

In the session conducted with the first class of children, I began by giving each student an opportunity to respond to this question. It quickly became evident that this was creating a stressful situation for the student when it was his or her turn to respond. I, therefore, changed the response situation to one that was voluntary and spontaneous. Students were invited to brainstorm what information they thought should be included in a library. This method elicited many more responses and was the method used for the balance of this first session and with all other classes at all levels. I was careful to give all children an opportunity to contribute if they wished. All responses were listed on large chart paper as they were suggested so that the children could see them. At the conclusion of the brainstorming session, children in kindergarten through grade 2 voted by a show of raised hands on how many thought each of the suggestions was indeed important for a library collection. In this way, even if a child had not verbally responded during the brainstorming, he or she was able to contribute an opinion by a simple raise of hand. Children in grades 3 and 4 brainstormed in a similar manner. However, time constraints in the block-scheduled school day did not permit a vote on the importance of suggested terms in grades 3 and 4.

ANALYSIS AND RESULTS

When each class had participated in this session, responses were sorted by class, grade level, and across grade levels. In this way, it was apparent which information children on each level thought most important to include in the library, how grade levels differed in their choices, and what similarities existed between grade levels.

The things that each class in kindergarten through grade 4 classes suggested as being important to have in a library were first examined in the order in which the children suggested them. Data were examined in this configuration because one suggestion could impact the next suggestion offered, so it would be possible for many ideas to be offered based on the first idea suggested. For example, it was noted that in one kindergarten class, immediately after one child had suggested "dead people" as something important to have information on, the next child suggested "bones." Similar patterns were noted elsewhere in the children's suggestions. In addition, there were instances of connected thought patterns separated by one or two suggestions. This separation may be explained by the fact that often several children wished to make suggestions at once and needed to take turns speaking. Notation of all of these would be very lengthy and these connected suggestions did not affect the overall results of this session significantly. In any real-life classroom situation, such as the ones in which this research was conducted, it would be impossible for children's ideas not to impact each other to some extent. It is noted that the incidence of longer strings of related suggestions increased with grade level, calling to mind Vygotsky's comments regarding a decrease in egocentrism as children get older.[25] That is, the younger children in this session were more focused on their own personal thoughts, while the older children were more tuned in and responsive to the comments of their peers. This suggests a move toward intersubjectivity within the older classes. For example, the following is a series of connected suggestions from a fourth grade class: animals, dogs, horses, monkeys, cats, rats, tigers, birds, ponies. Each of these suggestions contains an animal word. The following example is from grade 3: *Bailey School Kids*, *Cam Jansen*, *Animorphs*, Beverly Cleary, *Amber Brown*, *Sabrina the Teenage Witch*, R. L. Stine. Each of these is either part of a print or nonprint series or is series-like. Beverly Cleary authored the *Ramona* series and R. L. Stine authored the *Goosebumps* series.

Since class size was approximately 20 children, terms receiving twenty to twenty-five votes were back-checked to see if all votes came from a single class. Data were examined in this manner in the event of an entire class voting a term important because, possibly, they may have recent experience regarding that term. For example, if a class recently addressed a particular story in the classroom, all children in that class might vote that story important, thereby affecting the results of the grade as a whole.

The following terms were voted important by large numbers of children in a single class:

- *Are You Afraid of the Dark* (twenty children in one kindergarten class voted this important)
- Dragon Slayers Academy—(twenty-one votes in one grade 1 class)
- movies—(twenty-one votes in one grade 1 class)
- Chris Van Allsburg—(twenty votes in one grade 2 class)
- *Charlie and the Chocolate Factory*—(twenty-one votes in one grade 2 class)
- *Jumangi*—(twenty votes in one grade 2 class)
- computer games—(twenty votes in one grade 2 class)
- states—(twenty-one votes in one grade 2 class)

Overall, the final grade lists of important things to have in a library were not seriously affected by entire class votes.

Recall that the number of participants in each level of kindergarten through grade 2 far exceeded the number of participants in grade 3 or 4. Therefore, responses from grades 3 and 4 were combined so that they comprised a participant group more comparable in number to the other levels. Kindergarten classes suggested a total of 156 different important things to have in the library, grade 1 suggested 211, grade 2 suggested 168, and grades 3 and 4 combined suggested 224. It is beyond the scope of this report to consider all 759 of these suggestions. A method of addressing needed to be determined. Recall also that a class vote on the most important suggested terms was not taken in grades 3 and 4 due to lack of time. Terms that were suggested three to six times by this combined level totaled twenty-two and represent 10 percent of the total number of different terms suggested by grades 3 and 4. The twenty-two terms receiving the most votes on each of the other grade levels represent 14 percent of kindergarten terms, 10 percent of grade 1 terms, and 13 percent of grade 2 terms. Given the circumstances, these top twenty-two terms on each grade level, a total of eighty-eight terms, will be addressed here to compare the most often suggested terms on each level.

Information terms suggested most often on each grade level or combined levels are presented in three ways:

Table 7.1 presents the terms suggested as most important to have in the library by all levels. This shows us the overall information interests of each level.

Table 7.2 presents information terms within this pool mentioned by two or more successive grades levels. This shows us commonalities of interest as they change across grade levels.

Table 7.3 presents information terms within this pool that are unique to each level. This shows us the difference in information interests that are unique to each level.

DISCUSSION

Suggestions from kindergarten and grade 1 have quite a bit in common. Examination of table 7.1 indicates that just over half of the kindergarten and grade 1 most frequently mentioned information choices are animals or fictional characters that are animals. About a quarter of them are series (either books or television shows) or series types of material (Dr. Seuss books are not really a series but the illustrations and presentation of the books are series-like in their similarity). The most sophisticated of these terms is *fossils.* Inclusion of this term is most likely explained because it

Table 7.1 Important Things to Have in a Library

Kindergarten	*Grade 1*	*Grade 2*	*Grades 3 and 4*
dinosaurs	dogs	computers	outer space/solar system/ planets
animals	Rugrats	books	baseball
dogs	animals	dictionary	pet/pet care/raising puppy
rabbits/bunnies	*Animorph*	tables/chairs	*Animorphs*
books	dictionary	encyclopedia	biographies/famous people
monkeys	snakes	chapter books	gymnastics
Arthur	dolphins	paper/pencils	jokes
cats	*I Spy*	fiction	PlayStation/Nintendo
Clifford	sharks	animals	animals
sharks	dinosaurs	Arthur	Baby Sitters Club
Little House on the Prairie	cats	nonfiction	birds/birds of prey
Rugrats	books	*I Spy*	dogs
Goosebumps	shelves	Rugrats	fiction/fiction diaries
fossils	aliens	word searches	football/*Football Digest*
sports	computers	shelves	*Goosebumps*
snakes	word searches	Baby Sitters Club	history
Harry the Dirty Dog	Godzilla	magazines	how-to books
I Spy	sports	CDs and tapes	magic
chapter books	Dr. Seuss	bathroom	monkeys
birds	whales	librarian	movies
rainbows	wolves	Back Street Boys	mysteries
dragons	dragons	*Animorphs*	soccer

had been addressed in the classroom, since it is not normally a term found in the scope of these children's life world. Most of the terms suggested by kindergarten and grade 1 are basic-level terms.[26] Most of the terms suggested by the kindergarten were either animals or things within their life world. This includes book titles and characters with which they are familiar and concrete things such as dogs, rabbits, cats, and books. Although some of the animals suggested by these grades, such as sharks or dolphins, are somewhat exotic, it is likely that these children have seen them at

Table 7.2 Information Interests Shared across Top Interests of Grade Levels

Kindergarten	*Grade 1*	*Grade 2*	*Grades 3 and 4*
animals	animals	animals	animals
sports	sports	sports	sports
books	books	books	
Rugrats	Rugrats	Rugrats	
I Spy	*I Spy*	*I Spy*	
dinosaur	dinosaur		
dogs	dogs		
cats	cats		
snakes	snakes		
dragons	dragons		
	Animorphs	*Animorphs*	*Animorphs*
	dictionary	dictionary	
	computers	computers	
	word searches	word searches	
	shelves	shelves	
		fiction	fiction
		Baby-Sitters Club	*Baby-Sitters Club*

Table 7.3 Information Interests Unique to Grade Level Top Interests

Kindergarten	*Grade 1*	*Grade 2*	*Grades 3 and 4*
bunnies/rabbits, Clifford, sharks, *Little House on the Prairie*, fossils, *Harry the Dirty Dog*, rainbows, Curious George	dolphins, aliens, Godzilla, Dr. Seuss, whales, wolves, cheetahs	table/chairs, encyclopedia, paper/pencils, nonfiction, magazines, CDs and tapes, bathroom, librarian, Back Street Boys, windows	outer space/solar system/planets, baseball, pets/pet care/raising puppies, biographies/famous people, gymnastics, jokes, PlayStation/ Nintendo, football/ *Football Digest*, history, how-to books, magic, movies, mysteries, soccer, Amber Brown

an aquarium/zoo or at least have had stories or other information regarding the animals related to them. Certainly, the majority of suggestions are within what one would assume to be a kindergarten/grade 1 child's stock of knowledge.

Table 7.1 indicates that the most often suggested terms in grade 2 include many concrete items found in or that comprise a library that are not necessarily information packages (i.e., books) but rather architectural features such a shelves or "accessories" such as word searches. Recall that the previous year these children did a pilot exercise for part of which they constructed a floor plan of a library and, therefore, may be sensitive to doors, windows, shelves, and furniture in the library. Grade 1 responses included several of these types of terms in their suggestions, but grade 2 included many more. Grade 2's stock of knowledge regarding what things are traditionally in a library is broader than that of the previous two grades, and they frequently included terms such as *encyclopedia*, *fiction*, *nonfiction*, *magazines*, *CDs and tapes*, and *librarian*. It is almost as though they are suggesting what they believe *should* be in a library, rather than what they would personally like in a library. According to Erickson, children of this age are experiencing conflicts of initiative versus guilt.[27] They want to please and they need routine and consistency. These things were reflected in grade 2's responses. Their knowledge here and desire to construct what appears to be a very traditional library is reflective of social influence on the way they are thinking about the library and can be considered a move toward intersubjectivity with the thought community of the library.[28]

The most often mentioned terms in grades 3 and 4 reflected students' higher reading level and broadening interests. There is an overall growth in sophistication of information interests and a decrease in the use of basic-level terms to articulate information choices.[29] More sophisticated genres are mentioned such as biography, fiction diaries, and mysteries. The popularity of electronic games is evidenced by the inclusion of terms such as Play Station and Nintendo. Only six animal or animal-related terms are mentioned as compared to thirteen at the kindergarten level.

Table 7.2 shows shared information interests in two or more levels reflected in the top responses examined. Two terms that are suggested by all levels are animals and sports. Series material is also mentioned on all grade levels. The importance children have given to animals, sports, and series books is not surprising. These information interests are reflective of both developmental considerations regarding children's ability to relate to concrete information[30] as well as their need for a vehicle to provide both needed security and continuity[31] while allowing children to broaden their intellectual horizons. Series books provide a scaffold of familiarity that supports children so that they can work on constructing a larger stock of knowledge.[32] Kindergarten and grade 1 share the most common information interests, and these are reflected largely in material about animals. Grades 1 and 2 share a developing interest in the components that make up a library—dictionaries, computers, shelves. Books continue in kindergarten through grade 2 to be the information package that these children agree is of great importance to have in a library. Grades 3 and 4 appear to have fewer information interests in common with the other grade levels. In this study grades 3 and 4 are located in a different building than the lower grades. Perhaps the physical separation of the primary school building and the upper-level building supports an intellectual separation as well. Entire schools often engage in schoolwide activities (i.e., a schoolwide read-a-thon with a particular focus), which may contribute to building a thought community.

Table 7.3 shows the differences in the most frequently articulated information interests across all levels. Examination of these differences shows that information choices unique to kindergarten and grade 1 are reflective of a more physical, perhaps visceral, nature—they are mostly animals, they are alive. Children's lexicon of experience at this age is not vast, but they do know about being alive and have a keen interest in things that sleep and eat and grow and move. This is something concrete to which they can physically relate and is not socially grounded.

The uniqueness of grade 2's responses is that they are at the same time both concrete and social, that is, most of the terms unique to grade 2 are concrete objects. However, they are concrete objects with a social purpose. They are the traditional trappings of a library, and their interest in this area demonstrates a move toward socialization. It is interesting that a year after these children had participated in an exercise to construct a library floor plan that they still focused on this particular aspect of the library. At this age children are still very concrete in their thinking. They understand the library through its concrete components rather than its abstract concepts. But the fact that they have chosen these things as important components of a library suggests a growth in social awareness. Rather than focus on things they can relate to in a personal/visceral fashion, they have selected concrete items that comprise a socioculturally designated place in which sociotypified activities are preformed: a library.

Examination of terms in table 7.3 that are unique to grades 3 and 4 indicate a growth in the interest of socially typified group activities with socially constructed rules (gymnastics, baseball), an awareness of the importance of cultural instruction (how-to books), a widening "world interest" (outer space), and a move toward an interest in more abstract concepts (history). An interest in "jokes" points to increased socialization and the ability to understand humor that is not merely egocentric. The terms unique to this level are more socially oriented. They are things people do together or learn from one another. They are reflective of a growth in socialization and in a socioculturally typified view of the information that ought to be contained in a library. These children are moving toward intersubjectivity with their community.

Table 7.4 compares the most frequently mentioned information interests of children in this study with the twenty terms children

Table 7.4 Frequently Requested Terms by Children, According to Solomon and Cooper

Solomon's list (high to low)	*Cooper's data (grade levels frequently mentioning terms)*
cats	K 1 2
dogs	K 1 2
mystery	4
animals	K 1 2 3 4
magic	4
poetry	[mentioned less frequently by grades 2 and 4]
dinosaur	K 1
drawing	[mentioned less frequently by grades 3 and 4]
horses	[mentioned less frequently by grades K, 1, 3, 4]
weapons	[not mentioned]
karate	[mentioned less frequently by grade 1]
baseball	4
rabbits (bunnies)	K
sports	K 1 2 3 4
ghosts	[mentioned less frequently by grade 4]
insects	[mentioned less frequently by kindergarten]
monsters	[not mentioned]
birds	K 4
fiction	4
science	2 3

requested most frequently in an earlier study by Paul Solomon.[33] Results from data in this study are largely in keeping with Solomon's results. Solomon's terms *weapons* and *monsters* were not mentioned at all by children in the present study. The terms *karate*, *ghosts*, and *monsters* were mentioned in the present study, but not frequently (and, therefore, not included in tables 7.1–7.3). However, the interest indicated by children in the present study for *Animorphs*, *Goosebumps*, "dragons," "aliens," and "Godzilla" would seem to somewhat match *weapons*, *karate*, *ghosts*, and *monsters* in nature. The difference is that in this study, several of the terms that participants used to articulate these interests reflect media influence. Even terms that were originally books (*Animor-*

phs and *Goosebumps*) eventually morphed into television shows, and participants' knowledge of them may be through media exposure. Solomon's terms *poetry*, *drawing*, *insects*, and *horses*, while not among the most frequently selected information terms by children in the present study (and, therefore, not included in tables 7.1–7.3), were mentioned several times by his participants.

IMPLICATIONS AND FURTHER STUDY

Based on participants' information choices, a move from personal typification toward intersubjectivity with the thought community of the library is indicated by an overall move in choices of information important to include in a library from those things found in a narrow life world to those found in a broader, more sophisticated life world. As noted earlier, such a move toward cultural intersubjectivity was expected. In addition, participants' interests reflect a move from a kindergarten and grade 1 interest largely in animals and information they can relate to on a visceral/somatic level to a grade 2 interest in the concrete aspects of a social concept to a grade 3 and 4 interest in more socially reflective and abstract material. The use of the word *visceral* in this context is not to be confused with Taylor's visceral information need, but rather is meant to describe a sense of association or relationship on a visceral/somatic level.[34]

The reader is reminded that the purpose of the study was to ask children about their information interests in order to improve service to the children in this library. Based on participants' responses, it appears that much of the information in which they are interested is housed in their school library media center and in most other children's libraries. However, it may not be easily accessible to children at different developmental levels. Participants at each level in this study did have unique information interests. Overall the library contains information supportive of participants' choices, but all the material is interfiled on the shelves so that access becomes more difficult for users at different levels. A kindergartener browsing for information on sharks or rainbows may have difficulty finding age-appropriate material. Kindergarten and grade 1 children most often are beginning or nonreaders who may be directed to the picture book section. Most often, information on sharks cannot be found in this area of the library. One approach might be to present the contents of the library to children in a manner that is more accessible to each developmental level and in keeping with the interests of each level. In this way, both physical and intellectual access of information for the child user might be better supported. For example, children's responses in this project can be visualized as expanding concentric circles beginning at a core that is concrete/personal/visceral, which widens to concrete/social, and widens even more to abstract/social. There are also interests that all levels share, such as an interest in animals, sports, and series books. A kindergartener, however, may want information about rabbits and *Harry the Dirty Dog*, while a child in grade 4 may look for information about pet care and *Animorphs*. One can, therefore, imagine a library that is physically configured, or perhaps virtually presented through an interface, so that the information at the core would encompass a small, personal life world. Each successive concentric circle would expand on that information in keeping with the interests of children on successive developmental levels.

An interesting notion here concerns the philosophical ramifications of a prestructured reality. Certainly any collection organized as a representation of the corpus of a culture's intellect and creativity presents a prestructured reality. This is especially true if it is formally organized, either physically or through its catalog, in such a manner as to block access to those who do not typify it in that manner. But before the organization can be addressed, the selection of that information, which will be contained in the corpus, sets a parameter on the reality available for address. In a sense, selection of information to include in the library almost validates its reality—that is, the cultural institution that is the library considers this information real and important enough to warrant address. This, in itself, sends a message to library users of all ages. Realistically, however, parameters of selection and structure are necessary. The library cannot include everything that everyone would like it to include. In addition, as discussed earlier, in order for children (and adults) to function successfully in the wider community and for the community to exchange ideas among its members, some level of intersubjectivity must be attained. It is important to also acknowledge that some level of intersubjective presentation of information is a necessity in a corpus that serves the entire community. The library, therefore, needs to support both the individual's move toward cultural intersubjectivity (children need to learn how to find information in a formally organized library) as well as satisfy the individual's information needs regardless of age, stock of knowledge, and/or perspective. It is suggested that further inquiry into the information interests of children may serve to inform the development of a means of helping children to find the information they want while moving them toward intersubjectivity with the library specifically and the larger culture in general. Given the pressures of sociocultural indoctrination that we all undergo from early childhood throughout adulthood, it may be difficult to elicit an individual's true information interests (as opposed to what that individual has been taught to respond). However, in a nonthreatening, supportive environment, in which we encourage and respect all responses, we can begin by asking the child.

NOTES

1. Susan E. Carey, *Conceptual change in childhood* (Cambridge, Massachusetts: MIT Press, 1985); Robert S. Siegler, *Children's thinking*

(Upper Saddle River, New Jersey: Prentice-Hall, 1998); Robert S. Siegler, *Emerging minds* (New York: Oxford University Press, 1996).

2. Carol C. Kuhlthau, "Meeting the information needs of children and young adults: Basing library media programs on developmental states," *Journal of Youth Services in Libraries* 2, no. 1 (1988): 51–57.

3. Jerome S. Bruner, *Beyond the information given: Studies in the psychology of knowing* (New York: W. W. Norton, 1973).

4. Bruner, *Beyond the information given*; Alfred Schutz and Thomas Luckmann, *Structures of the life world* (Evanston, Ill.: Northwestern University Press, 1973).

5. Schutz and Luckmann, *Structures of the life world*; Bruner, *Beyond the information given*; Lev S. Vygotsky, *Thought and language*, ed. Alex Kozulin (Cambridge, Mass.: MIT Press, 1986); Eviatar Zerubavel, *The fine line: Making distinctions in everyday life* (Chicago: University of Chicago Press, 1991).

6. Schutz and Luckmann, *Structures of the life world.*

7. Bruner, *Beyond the information given*, 219.

8. Schutz and Luckmann, *Structures of the life world.*

9. Eviatar Zerubavel, *Social mindscapes: An invitation to cognitive sociology* (Cambridge, Mass.: Harvard University Press, 1997).

10. Jean Piaget and Barbel Inhelder, *The psychology of the child* (New York: Basic Books, 1969).

11. Frank C. Keil, *Concepts, kinds, and cognitive development* (Cambridge, Mass.: MIT Press, 1989).

12. Keil, *Concepts, kinds, and cognitive development*, 5.

13. Vygotsky, *Thought and language.*

14. Vygotsky, *Thought and language.*

15. Ellen M. Markman, *Categorization and naming in children: Problems of induction* (Cambridge, Mass.: MIT Press, 1989).

16. Zerubavel, *Social mindscapes*, 14.

17. Claude Levi-Strauss, *The savage mind* (Chicago: University of Chicago Press, 1966), 2.

18. Eleanor Rosch, Carolyn Mervis, Wayne D. Gray, David Johnson, and Penney Boyes-Braem, "Basic objects in natural categories," *Cognitive Psychology* 8 (1976): 382.

19. George P. Lakoff, *Women, fire, and dangerous things: What cate-*

gories reveal about the mind (Chicago: University of Chicago Press, 1986), 46.

20. Carey, *Conceptual change in childhood*; Siegler, *Children's thinking*; Siegler, *Emerging minds*.

21. Paula Busey and Tom Doerr, "Kid's catalog: An information retrieval system for children," *Journal of Youth Services in Libraries* 7 (1993): 77–84; Gale E. Eaton, "What the public children's librarian needs to know about locational skills instruction in elementary schools," *Journal of Youth Services in Libraries* 2 (1989): 357–366; Leslie Edmonds, Paula Moore, and Kathleen M. Balcom, "The effectiveness of an online catalog," *School Library Journal* 36 (1990): 28–32; Kuhlthau, "Meeting the information needs of children and young adults"; Penelope A. Moore and Alison St. George, "Children as information seekers: The cognitive demands of books and library systems," *School Library Media Quarterly* 19, no. 3 (1991): 161–168; Annelise M. Pejtersen, "Design and test of a database for fiction based on an analysis of children's search behavior," in *Information technology and use: Towards a unified view of information technology*, ed. P. Ingwersen, L. Kajberg, and A. Pejtersen (London: Taylor Graham, 1986); Paul Solomon, "Children's information retrieval behavior: A case analysis of an OPAC," *Journal of the American Society for Information Science* 44 (1993): 245–264.

22. Piaget and Inhelder, *The psychology of the child*.

23. Kuhlthau, "Meeting the information needs of children and young adults."

24. Linda Z. Cooper, "Methodology for a project examining cognitive categories for library information in young children," *Journal of the American Society for Information Science and Technology* 53, no. 4 (2002): 1223–1231; Linda Z. Cooper, "A study of the relationships between categories of library information as typified by young children," in *Emerging frameworks and methods: Proceedings of the fourth international conference on conceptions of library and information science* (CoLIS4), ed. H. Bruce, R. Fidel, P. Ingwersen, and P. Vakkari (New York: Libraries Unlimited, 2002), 17–32.

25. Vygotsky, *Thought and language*.

26. Rosch et al., "Basic objects in natural categories."

27. Erik H. Erickson, *Childhood and society* (New York: W. W. Norton, 1963).

28. Vygotsky, *Thought and language;* Lev S. Vygotsky, *Mind in society: The development of higher psychological processes* (Cambridge, Mass.: Harvard University Press, 1978).

29. Rosch et al., "Basic objects in natural categories."

30. Piaget and Inhelder, *The psychology of the child*; Carey, *Conceptual change in childhood*; Paul Shepard, *Thinking animals* (Athens, Ga.: University of Georgia Press, 1978).

31. Abraham H. Maslow, *Toward a psychology of being* (3rd ed.) (New York: John Wiley and Sons, 1998).

32. Pejtersen, "Design and test of a database for fiction based on an analysis of children's search behavior."

33. Solomon, "Children's information retrieval behavior."

34. Robert S. Taylor, "Question negotiation and information-seeking in libraries," *College and Research Libraries* 29 (1968): 178–194.

EIGHT

Children's Information Seeking at School: Findings from a Qualitative Study

Melissa Gross

Until the recent development of the imposed-query model (Gross, 1995), there was limited recognition of the familiar practice of seeking information on behalf of someone else, such as an employer, teacher, friend, or family member, though it is a user behavior that information professionals have long observed. This chapter will review the findings from a qualitative study of children's questions in the school environment, and for what those findings add to understandings of the information-seeking behavior of youth, grades preschool through six, in the context of an elementary school setting.

CATEGORIZING QUESTIONS

One fundamental effect of the imposed-query model is that it dichotomizes thinking about the questions people carry and transact in their daily lives. It does this by breaking the concept of question into two types—self-generated and imposed.

A self-generated question is a question that results from the personal context and interests of a person's life and that is pursued by the person that produced it. For example, the questions that occur to a woman when she finds out she is pregnant or that develop out of the process of planning a vacation can be said to be internally derived or to result from the context of the individual's life.

In the imposed-query model, the decision to pursue a question is a key point. If an individual decides to resolve the question for him- or herself, the question is called a self-generated query. If, on the other hand, the question is turned over to someone else (their agent), then the question is called an imposed query. Imposed queries are externally generated in the sense that they do not spring from the subjective context of the person who is seeking their resolution. An imposed query is a question that is developed by one person (the imposer) and then transferred to another (the agent) who is charged with transacting the query for the imposer.

Close reading of the information-studies literature reveals some examples of imposed information seeking. Chu (1999) documents the presence of child cultural mediators who transact for their non-English–speaking parents. Metoyer-Duran (1993) describes the characteristics of ethno-linguistic gatekeepers who mediate the information needs of their communities. In the health field, it is observed that family, friends, nurses, and others often negotiate questions for the critically ill. Kuhlthau (1993) has researched and extensively described the agent's view in her studies of student experiences while working on research reports.

Research on adult reference desk use in public libraries has identified a wide variety of relationships, both formal and informal, that result in imposed information seeking (Gross and Saxton, 2001). Further, in this study, children were responsible for the largest proportion of adult-imposed reference desk use (35 percent).

METHODS

The findings reported here come from a study of imposed information seeking in elementary schools that used both quantitative and qualitative research methods. A description of the full study is reported elsewhere (Gross, 2004). The focus here is on the qualitative findings of this study, which are based on in-depth interviews with students and teachers across the elementary grades and their school library media specialist.

The subjects for this qualitative study were all recruited from the same elementary school, which was a laboratory school on the campus of a major university. Participation was sought from nine key informants (individuals who could provide insight into the children's experience) and sixteen representative subjects (the children themselves). To realize this design, participation was sought from the school library media specialist and two teachers from each grade level at the school. Grade level was conceptualized in this environment as early childhood (the equivalent of preschool and kindergarten), primary (grades 1 and 2), middle (grades 3 and 4), and upper (grades 5 and 6). For the representative subjects, four children (two boys and two girls) from each grade level were randomly chosen as subjects from the participating teachers' classrooms.

All but one of the subjects sought were recruited, as only one teacher from the early childhood level chose to participate in the study. Assent to participation in the study was sought from all children who were randomly chosen as subjects in addition to standard consent by their parents. One child declined and was replaced with another child randomly chosen from that same classroom. Subjects were interviewed individually and audiotaped. Interviews varied from about twenty minutes in length with the youngest children to about forty-five minutes in length with the older children. Adult interviews ran between one and two hours.

The general purpose of these interviews was to understand when and to what extent information seeking involves the generation of imposed queries, to look at students' perceptions of ownership versus imposition when completing school work, to get a sense of who the players in the imposed query lifecycle might be and how these roles are invoked, and to get a sense of how resource choice and use varies between self-generated and imposed queries.

The interviewer followed the general interview guide approach and kept extensive notes and an interview journal to record descriptive and reflective data to supplement the interviews in the data analysis phase. The interview guides were pretested for wording with children across the age/grade range, but who did not attend the school being studied. However, the intention here was not to address specific interview questions, but rather to gain an understanding of the imposed-query process from the point of view of those involved in it. The interview process was used to determine common themes and behaviors across the age/grade levels and to gain insight and understanding of the information-seeking behavior of these students. The perspective of teachers and the school library media specialist were important for understanding their views of the imposed-query lifecycle in the school environment, as well as their observations of the information-seeking behavior of their students. The interview guides used in this study are presented in Appendix A.

Limitations

Throughout this discussion, it is important to remember that this study investigated only one school environment and while its findings provide much food for thought, they may not be generalized to other elementary schools. In terms of accuracy, all of the data collected is dependent on self-reports, some from children as young as four years of age. Another consideration in this type of research is the degree to which the presence of the researcher might bias or affect the data that is collected. In an effort to avoid this potential, this site was chosen in part because as a lab school both students and staff are fairly accustomed to taking part in research. It is also hoped that the relative familiarity of the researcher, who spent the year before data collection as a resident fellow in the school, increased the likelihood of participation and the comfort levels of those who chose to participate.

IMPOSERS AND THE NATURE OF IMPOSITION

Early on in the conceptualization of the imposed-query model the school assignment was offered as an example of the process it describes. The three key players in the imposed-query lifecycle could be assigned as follows. The teacher was seen in the role of the imposer, the person who developed the question. The student took the role of the agent, the person responsible for transacting the query, and the school library media specialist had the role of information intermediary, a position that potentially might be assumed by any of a variety of information professionals or even an information system or resource. This scenario was easily understood and it clarified that the resolution of the query is not complete until the answer is delivered to and approved by the imposer (teacher). One of the findings of this study is an understanding that in the school environment this process is much more complex than it appears to be on the surface.

School: A Socially Constructed Environment

In general, the teachers who participated in the interviews did not like the idea that what they were doing was imposing questions on students. Although most teachers did accept the term *imposer* in a metaphorical sense and found the model useful in discussing their work, the label of imposer did not fit their self-perception of their role in the classroom. Teachers made comments like, "They're not finding it out for me."

Teachers preferred to think of themselves as "co-creators" with the children and focused on the desire to motivate, inspire, or excite their students and made little reference to grade-level curriculums and expectations for students that teachers are expected to respond to.

As the interviews progressed it became clear that a number of players contribute to the creation and continuous reproduction of the social environment at the school as well as the definition of social objects such as the classification of individuals as teacher, student, etc. Embedded within these socially constructed roles, perceptions of the function of assignments in the learning process and the appropriateness of behaviors as concerns the imposed-query lifecycle are also defined for this environment. For instance, parents, the experience of friends, family and siblings, the expectations (both public and private) that the school feeds into, and the general standards and expectations for student learning held by the community at large all help to define what school is. Within the school in its day-to-day operation students, teachers, interns, the school library media specialists, administrative staff, etc., all contribute to making the school environment what it is. Over the course of the interviews the view of the school environment that emerged was one in which imposition is an implicit force that all of the players prefer not to invoke or make explicit if they do not have to.

Children have many ways of perceiving this environment. For instance, they may believe that school is about "performing" for the teacher, that school is something they do for themselves, that they go to school in order to meet the expectations of their families, or even to represent their families in the public world. Regardless, the school environment works to elicit the compliance of children such that they will submit to a process that is intended to, in time, fashion a fully contributing member of society. To the extent that things go well, there is no reason to make the imposition explicit, and positive relationships between teachers and students work to facilitate the process. However, children who resist the imposition will find it made explicit for them in a variety of ways ranging from gentle persuasion, to notes to parents, to other types of sanctions designed to gain their participation in the process.

Teachers: Imposers or Agent Users?

The teacher is the main imposer in the school environment (Gross, 1999). However, teachers differ from other types of imposers in some important ways. For instance, although the development of questions may seem the teacher's stock and trade, on closer inspection it becomes clear that the questions they craft are didactic in nature. These questions cannot be defined as self-generated according to the models we have because they are not developed to fill a gap in the teacher's understanding. The questions that teachers fashion tend to be based on "known" knowledge and serve the dual purposes of providing a learning experience for students and a means of evaluating student progress. In practice, teachers do not always construct the questions they pose to students, but at times use the preformulated questions provided in textbooks and other materials developed by others for classroom use.

Teachers also need to be considered in terms of their place in the socially constructed environment of school. As this study progressed, it became clear that imposition at the school has many layers. Teachers are imposers for students, but teachers are also directed and imposed upon in terms of formalized curriculums, goals, and special emphasis they are expected to follow and incorporate into their teaching plans. In the case of the particular school studied here, imposition could potentially come from the research findings of the school of education that houses the lab school as well as the political hierarchy of the state as expressed in published subject frameworks adopted by the school's administration.

Imposition on teachers takes implicit, explicit, and voluntary forms. For instance, a requirement from the principal to develop student projects that can be displayed for Earth Day is not unlike an open-ended assignment a teacher might give a class that expects students to contribute their own intellectual and creative input into the process.

However, teachers also have a fair amount of autonomy in their work and enjoy wide latitude in determining how to achieve the goals of the curricular framework. They are not given specific questions to hand out and do not provide answers as such to their imposers. Teachers are subject to evaluation, but generally, their professional status allows them to operate using their best judgment. The combination of imposed context and professional judgment, however, does leave room for teachers to respond to their perception of their students' information needs. As Walter (1994) points out, adults in various roles can and do identify children's information needs and help to fill them. Thus, in response to student questions on neighborhood or world events, the teacher may decide to add or expand on certain topics. This was demonstrated in an early childhood classroom where the children happened to observe the class tortoises mating and had questions that were not part of the teacher's prepared lesson plan, but which she decided to address anyway. In such instances though, teachers are working from a basis of "known" information. Their objective is not to fill a gap in their own understanding. However, depending on the circumstances, such situations could require some personal gap-closing for the teacher and so some allowance for a view of teacher's classroom questions to be seen as self-generated should be made.

The Design of Assignments

One of the ways that imposition is downplayed at school is in the strategies teachers use in designing assignments. At all grade levels teachers made a point of providing students with assignments that allow them to either make choices about what they do or to personalize their work within a larger imposed structure. Teachers preferred assignments they felt students could "take wherever they need to." Typical assignments ran along the lines of: "We will study Native Americans—you may choose the tribe you want to learn about;" or "Our unit is on transportation—you will get to design your own vehicle;" or "We are going to be writing letters today—you may write to anyone you choose."

Teachers also revealed that sometimes there are goals imbedded in assignments that the children may not realize are there. For instance, for younger children school library media center visits are often presented as an opportunity to select materials for personal use, as a kind of fun. However, the teacher may have other unspoken goals such as encouraging reading in the home, generating a love of books, or teaching responsibility. So, as an example of implicit imposition, the borrowing and bringing back of books becomes a form of homework and not a voluntary activity. Because most children do experience going to the library and choosing books as fun, it can be a rare event for the imposition to become explicit. However, in these interviews two teachers discussed instances in which children who did not want to check out books had to be brought into compliance; they learned they had to participate by checking out and returning books whether or not the books were desired or read.

The hidden facets of assignments can make it complicated for a student to understand teacher expectations and to differentiate teacher demands from their own interests in terms of how student performance will be evaluated. Teachers report designing assignments that have a "base level" expectation, but which children can respond to in ways that are more complex. In such situations children may be evaluated on which questions they choose to answer, how many resources they use, how difficult the resources they use are, and whether they are able to stay with a topic or later opt to change to an easier one.

The Importance of Context to Questions

One of the main points made in the self-generation models of information-seeking behavior (Dervin and Dwedney, 1986; Taylor, 1962, 1968) is that questions spring from life situations and are best understood and resolved when the response to the question makes sense in terms of the context that produced it. One implication of this is that knowing only what the question is may not be sufficient for finding a useful answer. To overcome this problem, when the imposer passes the question to the agent it makes sense for the imposer to provide some context, to provide things the agent needs to know to understand the question, and perhaps even some ideas about resources where the answer might be found. Kirkelas (1983) addresses this issue by pointing out that when people go to other people for information they try to find someone who will not only understand their question, but who will understand their situation.

Teachers demonstrate that they understand that a question needs context to provide it with its sense of form. Context is used to give students a handle on the topic and as an aid to deriving questions of their "own." Time and again, teachers described this approach in the interviews. Assignments always begin with the presentation of some context, which might take the form of a presentation to the class, an experience like an experiment or field trip, or the reading of textual material. For example, children visit the local post office and then write thank-you letters, read a unit in the history textbook and then receive directions for a project, or are shown an object and then asked to identify what the object is.

Students: Issues of Question Ownership

The view of the school environment as one in which imposition tends to be an implicit structure and where an overt expression of cooperation and community are preferred to adult expressions of authority was demonstrated in students' experience of imposition at school and in their sense of ownership surrounding class work.

Although younger children tend to think of library materials as being meant for them, not the teacher, the bottom line of imposition was not completely lost on them. The early childhood students were very interested in displaying their knowledge of class rules and expected behavior, but less articulate about the substance of the direction given to them. Though weekly library visits are perceived as fun, when asked about the purpose of the visit or what happens if you do not take a book out, children responded by saying, "you keep it for a week and then bring it back," and "I think it's okay if you don't get a book because sometimes I don't find a book and we have to leave. I just don't get one," and "We don't have to, we can trick them." These children were aware of the rules meant to govern their behavior in the library; they did not talk about reading the books or being read to at home as part of the expectations for library visits and materials.

Children in the older grades have less stringent requirements for checking out books and these children easily make distinctions between materials they gather for their own use and those selected to meet teacher demands.

HOW CHILDREN FIND INFORMATION

Establishing question type, as a precursor to understanding children's information-seeking behaviors, is an important step toward understanding the processes they engage in when trying to transact information needs. In the process of finding information children face many limitations and frustrations related to developmental skill, skill level, and their dependence on adults (for instance for money, transportation, access to computers) that must be managed, compensated for, or overcome if they are to successfully locate and assimilate the information they are seeking.

How Children Look for Information

Although teachers at this school encourage students to recognize the wide range of resources that are available and work hard to maintain a classroom environment that includes a variety of materials for students, teacher-developed information packets, which contain all the information needed to complete an assignment at home, are often provided to students in this environment.

If other resources are needed, it is most common for that resource to be other people, usually family. For example, students might interview parents or grandparents as part of an introduction to a unit on immigration. Older children are the most likely to be asked to use multiple resources and have more personalized reports, but even they often receive articles and book chapters copied for them ahead of time by the teacher.

Teachers say they prepare these packets because they do not feel that they can require outside library use at the school, which many students travel long distances to attend and where the teachers are unsure of what the students' neighborhood libraries are like. They also provide materials to students because they feel that appropriate resources are hard to find across the wide range of reading and writing skills the students in their classes need.

Although teachers emphasized the value of using a variety of materials, when students were asked what resources they thought teachers liked them to use, they routinely answered, "the dictionary" and sometimes a second response was "the encyclopedia." Children also felt that teachers prefer books to electronic resources.

For their self-generated needs, students showed a strong preference for known resources whether these were books, people, or Web sites, and for sources that they owned or could easily access. When asked how they chose "fun" reading, every child but one said they would choose one of the books they owned and had at home. The other student said, "I don't do fun reading."

When asked how they solved personal needs for information, two children said their first choice was the Internet. Both children talked about going to sites they were already familiar with and had bookmarked on their home computers. The children who talked about using books for personal information needs talked about using books they already owned or were familiar with. One middle school girl steadfastly said that if she needed more information on the ghosts of Martha's Vineyard, her favorite area of interest, she would reread a book she said she had already read eight times. "Because like," she said, "after you read it once, sometimes you don't get all the information. The first time I only got the, you know, main parts of the story and I never noticed the little parts of the story."

Only three students talked about using the library to find information, and only two were public library users. One primary-level child said she would ask someone else if she needed to know something and added, "I just like people telling me." The upper-level child who said she did not read for fun said, "My favorite resource is my friends because I can talk to them about other stuff, also."

The school library media specialist was aware of the frustrations students sometimes have with school assignments, but when their information needs were imposed, she was able to take a larger view of the situation. "I'm pretty sure that they're going to be back. They will be returning. They are going to have to find that information. They are going to have to face this." In contrast, the school library media specialist felt that there was less frustration for students in solving self-generated needs. She said, "I think they are much more apt to be flexible with their own materials. If what they thought they wanted is not easily available, or found, or apparent, rather that having to really spend that time looking for one thing, I think most change what they want."

The school library media specialist also observed that children had the most difficulty answering research questions when there was nothing on a topic, or many things, but nothing specific to their needs and that, "When they have to make some decisions because their topic is subsumed in a broader topic and it's included in a book on a broader topic, what I find is there are a lot of children who want you [as librarian] to make that decision, to say, this is it. Take it. This is the right one. Take the time to evaluate it. They're not completely comfortable, they don't really like to do that."

Finding Information in the School Library Media Center

Due to extensive weeding and rearrangement of the shelves over spring break, the ability of children to find materials in the school library media center was a topic of current concern during the data collection period. Students have access to the university library catalog, which includes the holdings in their school library media center. The system does not have a special interface for these child users, but it does allow them to limit their search to their own collection, which is classified according to the Dewey system, not LC.

During their weekly visit, students were oriented to the new locations of different types of books, but in the interviews it became clear how dependent children at all grade levels were on having a stable configuration in order to find the books they wanted. The students reported they did not like to use the catalog and demonstrated little understanding of the Dewey system as a help for finding nonfiction. The students did know that nonfiction is grouped by subject, but relied most heavily on knowing the specific shelf locations for snakes, jokes, dinosaurs, etc., rather than knowing the call numbers or relating to the fact that they could use the numbers to find out where the books were now located.

In using the school library media center, children also showed a preference for known items. For the younger children, this often meant a specific book. They said, "It's easy. I find my favorite book, the truck one. I just got it double" and "I had this book I checked out practically every single time I went to the library and I knew exactly where it was, between what two books." Young children also liked to browse the books that previous users left on the tables and that had not yet been gathered up for reshelving. The third place they went was to the picture book shelves. The rule at this school is that students can only take out and use the books they can reach. These young students took pride in knowing the rules and in finding their own books, they did not report asking for help or using the catalog.

Children at the primary level also relied heavily on knowing where the books they liked were housed. In nonfiction they knew where the books on subjects that interested them were, such as insects or dinosaurs. These students, however, did seek help to find materials. They asked friends, the teacher, and the school library media specialist. They commented that they thought the good books were on shelves they could not reach and the reshelving of the library made it very difficult to use.

Middle-level children reported increased difficulty in finding what they wanted and an increased need to ask for help. These students also showed a preference for browsing tables and shelves, and relied on their memory of how the library was arranged. Like the younger children, they were most likely to look for items they had checked out previously. One boy said he used the catalog, but he also said he had two favorite subjects, and that he routinely sought them out by browsing the shelves.

Among the oldest children, known items continued to be important, although the definition of known item expanded from a particular title to books by the same author and sometimes to books in a particular genre, such as science fiction. Only one student expressed satisfaction with the catalog, but this student also mainly preferred browsing tables and shelves. All the other upper-level students interviewed expressed a lot of dissatisfaction with the catalog and said they preferred the advice of friends or the school library media specialist when they needed help.

Teachers were vague in the interviews when asked when and how students were taught to use the catalog. One teacher said she felt that the children used the catalog to play and to avoid their library responsibility, and that since the children were routinely told what shelves to go to they did not need the catalog during a class visit.

The school library media specialist was rarely involved in the development of, provision of research skills for, or the evaluation of class assignments. She did teach students to use the catalog as part of their library use one-on-one or in small groups on an as-needed basis.

Right Answers

Integral to the ability to transact a question is the capacity to recognize the right answer. The question, "How do you know when you have the right answer?" was extremely difficult for the youngest children and they could not answer it. In general, for all the children interviewed, this question made the most sense to them in terms of their study of mathematics. They said things like, "I usually add it up on the scrap paper or ask my mom for help and she might know the answer," and "Maybe I could look at my flash cards if the answer's on the top at the other side," or "Sometimes if I have a right answer I write it down and then check on my fingers." For many children this was as far as they could go with this idea.

Some children tried hard to express the process in dealing with textual material, but found it very difficult to go beyond a sense that a piece of information "sounded" or "felt" right. One primary-level child said, "You check it. You just do it over again and if it sounds funny you just do it again." When asked if there was something to check the answer against the response was, "Think! That's what I usually do because I don't want to get a whole dictionary." Upper-level students also used this strategy. For instance, one student explained, "I read the question over and over and it will be in my head. It pops in." Another upper-level student responded that you can know an answer is right when, "It doesn't sound like someone just typed it out. They thought about it for a while. It just kind of fits together with other things."

Some children were able to respond to the question, though, and many of them indicated that they would ask someone who would know, like a parent or a teacher. Some children were able to give detailed descriptions of an information-seeking situation where they knew they had the right answer. One girl told a story about helping her younger sister find a description of the type of dog their family was about to get. She said, "I found the answer. I knew because my mom told it a lot [the breed name of the dog]. She's like, 'Let's get this dog, it's so beautiful, come on let's get this dog.' So I said, 'Okay what's the name?' and she said 'well . . .' the name. So I'm like okay, I know that and then I checked and it said the same thing in the dictionary, in the encyclopedia. It said the same thing and I'm like, it's right!"

An upper-level girl said when she found a picture of Ursa Major she knew she had the answer to a teacher challenge "because it was a bear and then the picture was in the Milky Way, I mean not the Milky Way, I mean the Big Dipper and then the third one was that it said something about the bear that was what [the teacher] said would be in it."

An upper-level boy gave this advice, "After I get the question I'll think about where the place might be to find it and after I figure that out I'll go there. And to check it? If it's really important I'll go to another source and see if it has the same answer."

Another upper-level boy had to come up with thirteen causes for the American Revolution, "And I had like two here and three there, so I had gaps and then you find something that fits in between. So that leads to that."

It was only among the older children that issues about determining the relevance of documents to a particular question being transacted were expressed. The girl who identified Ursa Major did so in part because she was able to match information given in class by the teacher with what appeared in the book. Poor matches between vocabulary words and the need to use synonyms made the process very difficult. Students were frustrated by materials that did not have the exact information they needed for their assignment. They were also frustrated when they had to wade through a lot of text to find what they needed, when the terminology did not match the terms used in class, and when they had to use multiple resources because each resource provided only a little bit of the information they needed.

USING OTHERS IN THE QUEST TO KNOW

Imposed information-seeking at school is firmly grounded in teacher assignments. Parents were also shown to be imposers in this environment in that they make demands concerning what children should or shouldn't read in class and the kinds of selections they should make in the school library media center. The school library media specialists imposed sustained silent reading as part of the regular class visit time. Children are also imposers in their environment and, as will be discussed below, use friends, classmates, siblings, and caretakers in a variety of ways when seeking information.

Peer Informants in the Classroom

One of the first resources the youngest students at the school are exposed to and taught to use are other people. This strategy at the early childhood and primary levels may be related to these children's limited ability to read, but is also related to the desire to help children understand that information is available in a variety of places. One teacher gave this example, "They come to me and say, 'Can you tie my shoelaces?' I will say, 'Go and find another child who will tie your shoelaces,' for them to go to that person. So that's like a small example, but they will come to me, but I will push them out." Other teachers used similar strategies, they said things to children like, "Ask your buddy over there, he'll help you," and "I'll even say sometimes, 'Raise your hand if you're someone who can help.'"

Group work is also more commonly assigned in the earlier grade levels than in the older grade levels at this school. In classrooms set up for the younger children, the tables were typically arranged in groups so that even when students worked independently, they did so in small groups. At the upper level this changes, and students are expected to take more individual responsibility not only when they work in groups, but are more likely to receive individual assignments. This increased need to evaluate individual performance is related to teacher concerns about how their students will perform on standardized tests and their ability to transition as easily as possible to middle school when they matriculate.

One teacher describes the process this way, "At the older grades the goal is to get you started working more independently. . . . I'm making them see that there's different kinds of learning. So that not everything is done in a cooperative group, that you need to learn to do independent activities." Another teacher said, "Yes there's information you directly need, but there's, you know, this whole me/we thing . . . you know, what you're finding out for you, and what you're printing out for you, and what you're doing for the community."

Agent Users

In the interviews teachers were asked if there was a certain type of child that the others tended to go to for help, not only because they might know the answer, but because they might be able to retrieve it for them. All of the teachers said that they did observe such children in their classes and some classified them as identifiable personality types. There children were called variously "power brokers," "mother's helpers," and "nurturers." They were described as bright children who have a special skill-based expertise that their classmates recognize. Some teachers reward this behavior and in other classrooms, it has negative consequences. One teacher said, "They get in trouble for it, too. They keep others from working. Everybody knows that the teacher or the aide is there for that."

One of the primary-level teachers told this story. "They don't necessarily know, but they want to help. One day we were working on a sheet of paper and one little girl needed help writing someone's name and another child in the group, she didn't know how to write the name, but she said, 'Why don't we go over to the cubby and copy it down?' "

The students also talked about getting information from classmates they knew to have a certain skill and about learning from friends at school. Two children told stories in which another child taught them to read and another child described how a friend taught her to go down the pole on the jungle gym. They also talked about using friends for help, or helping their friends with homework. One child felt that classmates only helped their friends, that if someone else asked they would ignore the request or refuse to help.

The students had many examples of imposed information seeking. One middle-level boy said, "My brother always asks me to go and ask my mom when we're leaving for school and when's dinner." A middle-level girl was worried about keeping some exotic frogs in an aquarium with her other frogs, "So, my dad writes this letter in the computer for people to answer it and people, some people, said it wasn't a good idea, but most people said that you could" and also, "Well at home my mom always asks me to find something out on the Internet."

An upper-level boy said, "I play baseball and I'm a pitcher and so I asked my dad to find out how to throw a curve ball. Well, I mean I kind of know how to do it, except my dad knows someone who's a sports writer and so he knows how to do it, so I asked him to call him up."

One upper-level boy said that he often sought information for others. He said, "I've done lots of different work for people to find information. Like one kid wanted to know the whole schedule of the Dallas games so I had to get that for him really fast." When asked how this young man knew to go to him for information this student replied, "Everybody knows that I am a computer freak. Well, not really a freak, but I know a lot about computers. So, he asked me since he also knows that I own a lot of cards. But he asked me and I said sure and I looked it up on the Internet. I just got this new program that makes business cards, memos, calendars, everything. So I'm going to start a business."

Double-Imposed Queries

The double-imposed query describes a situation where the agent passes the question on to someone else (a second agent) for processing. In the school environment the version of the double-imposed query that gets the most attention is the one where the teacher makes the assignment and the child agent passes the query on to a parent or other caregiver who then transacts the query for the child. The teachers interviewed at this school perceived the double-imposed query as an ongoing problem. Although teachers did want and even expected parents to be involved in homework, there were also many complaints across all the grade levels about parents doing children's work for them.

Teachers said things like, "You know who did the work when the child has to get up to talk about it and they have no idea what's on the paper"; "A lot of kids, I have no idea whose work I'm grading"; "That's why I don't like to give homework, you don't know who did it"; and "I don't like grading parents' work. And you can tell you know, you're working with a kinder class and I know what he's able to do and the homework comes back perfect."

Teachers had several thoughts about why parents do their children's homework. Some felt that parents want their children to meet adult perceptions of good work and perfectionism, others see it as the parents' strong desire to see their children succeed, and still others felt the real issue was one of control in which the parents needed to direct the child's behavior even to the point of usurping the teacher's authority.

On the other hand, children talked about going to parents, babysitters, parents' work assistants and secretaries, friends, and siblings for help with their homework. Children were not asked, "Does anyone ever do your homework for you?"; rather they were asked how they went about doing homework, if they received help, when, and what kind of help. The kinds of help they described were things like checking math problems for right answers, looking up spelling words, checking grammar, and being read to. None of the children interviewed described having their work done "for them" and indicated that requests and offers for help seemed to go both ways. Some children asked for help only when they needed it, and parent or older siblings routinely asked some children if they needed help with school work.

Sharing Information

Over the course of the interviews, another variation on imposed information seeking came to light. This is the recognition that people will retrieve information for others even when they are not asked explicitly to do so. One teacher observed that when children are asked to find books for the classroom library, "They always choose books they know I like. I don't tell them to, but they do."

Another teacher said, "Some children have realized from very early on what books they can read for themselves and which books Mommy's going to want to read to them." Several teachers remarked that students "just bring in" materials related to what the class is studying without being asked to. One teacher provided this description, "A kid in the process of looking essentially for something for himself finds something and says, 'Oh that's something Marcella needs.'" These are all instances of information sharing that demonstrate how some connections between people and information are made.

This too is a familiar behavior when people are aware of each other's information interests or needs. Among these students, friends did not have to explicitly ask each other for information in order for it to be provided. Having knowledge of someone's context, tastes, and preferences can be enough for an individual to attempt to fill those needs if they come across a potential "answer" in the course of their activities. The information and/or materials are shared with the potential end-user who will determine the relevance of the information to their needs and/or the appeal of the material to their taste.

A middle-level girl gave this example. "My mom knew I liked ghost story books. So one day she came home and we were on summer vacation in our house in Martha's Vineyard, she was going, she went to the drugstore and she got me this book and I had no idea so she told me."

Twidale (1997) has also recognized this behavior between adults and calls it "serendipitous altruism." Erdelez and Rioux (2000) study similar behavior in their investigation of the use of Web site links labeled with some variation of, "E-mail this to a friend."

WHERE TO NEXT?

This investigation provides a first look at information seeking in the school environment from a perspective that differentiates between self-generated and imposed information seeking. The study is descriptive and exploratory in nature, focusing on understanding imposed queries from the point of view of those who generate, impose, carry, and/or transact them.

Some of the findings, such as children's stated preference for browsing, reinforce findings from previous study. But this work also calls attention to the need to understand the developmental process more fully, in terms of how children learn to ask and transact questions. The finding that there are children who actively seek the role of agent needs to be better understood. Who are these children? Do they have identifiable characteristics or experiences in common? How do they perform in school as compared to their classmates? How do they fare later in life in terms of attained education or choice of profession?

It is also important to explore the question of whether the desire to be an agent for others should be encouraged or discouraged in the classroom setting. Is such behavior problematic to the development of the agent's peers, or does this sharing of skills help other children to attain them? Investigation into the role that imposed queries play in the socialization of children should be of interest to educational theory.

Because the generation and transfer of questions is central to the information-seeking process, it is important to look at how question development is related to the attainment of reading, computer, and information-seeking literacies. The difficulties children have in locating information electronically and in text reflects their attainment of reading skills, but also their level of information-seeking instruction, as well as developmental factors. All of these variables may affect their ability to recognize a "right answer" when they see one.

The variations in the imposed-query model revealed in this study are also provocative. The view of the school environment as one in which various layers of imposition overlap and interact led to new views of how people use each other to find information.

Children's impositions on parents and caregivers in the double-imposed query scenario and evidence that children can choose to be agents without being asked give further insight into how information flows between people and warrant further investigation.

In other writing, the implications of the imposed query revealed in this and other studies (Gross 1998, 2000) for the performance of reference work with children and the evaluation of information programs and services have been explored. More work is needed, however, in a variety of settings such as other elementary, middle, and high schools environments, to fully understand children's information seeking in school and to what extent the findings of this study can inform teachers and school library media specialists in the performance of their professional duties.

APPENDIX A.

Interview Guidelines for Case Studies

Student Interview Guidelines

1. Do you remember going to the library this week with your class? Did you work on a class assignment there or was it free time? Please tell me about what you worked on while you were there.
Follow-up questions: Did you check out any library materials? How did you choose the materials you used? Were materials difficult to find? Did you ask anyone for help? How did you feel about your visit/assignment?
2. Do you have any homework now, or do you ever get homework assignments that you need to go to the library, bookstore, or other places or people to complete?
Follow-up questions: Are you usually pretty sure about what the teacher wants? How do you decide where to go for the answer? Does you mom or dad, brother or sister, friend, or maybe even

someone else ever help you? How do they help you? Do you ask them or do they ask you?

3. What kinds of resources, people, or places have you used for schoolwork? Which do you like best? Why?

Follow-up questions: How often do you get to use your favorite resource? What kind of resources do you think your teacher likes best?

4. If you were going to give another student advice about doing a good job on homework, what would you say is the most important thing?

Follow-up questions: What makes that part tricky? How do you handle it? Are there other parts that need special attention?

5. When you need something to read for yourself or information for something (not schoolwork), how do you go about getting it? Can you remember a time you needed to find out something? How did you handle the situation?

Follow-up questions: If you were going to do this again, would you handle it the same way?

6. When someone asks you to find something out for him or her, how do you know where to go for the answer?

Follow-up questions: How can you tell if you got the right answer?

Teacher Interview Guidelines

1. Can you tell me about an assignment your class is currently working on? Did you design the assignment yourself? How was it developed?

Follow-up questions: How was the assignment presented to your class (verbally, copied from board, part of a worksheet, other)? In this assignment, are the students meant to work alone, in pairs, or in small groups? Does this assignment require any resources outside those available in the classroom? What form is the answer to this assignment meant to take (raise hand in class, oral presentation, written answer, etc.)?

2. When your class visited the library this week, was there a plan concerning how they were to spend their time?

Follow-up questions: When do the students receive their directions concerning their library visit? What happens if they don't finish what they need to do in the allotted time? Was this week a typical library visit? What made it typical or atypical?

3. When you make assignments, to what extent are you looking for a specific answer versus evidence of some process on the part of the students? Why do you look for one or the other? Does this change at different times or under various circumstances?

Follow-up questions: How do you evaluate their process? What types of strategies might you expect of them?

4. When you give an assignment, what types of resources might you expect them to use in their work? Do you specify the resource(s) as part of the assignment?

Follow-up questions: How do you gauge the existence/availability of these resources for your students? What types of resources do you like your students to use?

5. What factors (skills, understandings, etc.) would you say most influence your students' ability to successfully complete their projects? What do you feel their biggest stumbling block?

Follow-up questions: Are there certain children the others seem to go to for help? Why do you think these children are sought out? Do you have any sense of how the involvement of parents, siblings, classmates, or others helps or hinders your students' process?

6. To what extent is your evaluation of the students' performance based on predetermined target responses (specific answers) versus evidence of process or experience?

Follow-up questions: Has a student's response ever changed your understanding of the question or assignment? Does student work ever result in changes to your evaluation of the group? Have the students' responses ever resulted in further research on your part?

School Library Media Specialist Interview Guidelines

1. Please describe a typical class visit to the library at this school.
Follow-up questions: From the point of view of the students, would you say they come to the library knowing how they are meant to spend their time? From your own point of view, do you feel you know what the teacher's expectations are concerning class visits to the library? Does your involvement in the class visit vary with grade level, by teacher, or for other reasons?
2. What are some of the assignments you are aware of that classes are currently using school library resources for?
Follow-up questions: How do you plan for these visits? Are assignments stable enough that once you see them you can anticipate their return next school year? Do you ever go into the classroom to help prepare the students for an assignment?
3. Do you have any sense of the proportion of questions brought to your library that are imposed or self-generated? Does this affect how you run your library in any way (collection development, arrangement of furniture, lesson plans, circulation rules, etc.)?
Follow-up questions: What would you say is the service mission of this library? Do you have any working relationships with other information-providing institutions the students might also be using? What is this relationship (resource sharing, referral, etc.)?
4. How does what you do differ when you are helping children with school assignments versus self-generated information needs?
Follow-up questions: To what extent are you able to plan ahead for school assignment–related queries? To what extent are you involved in the development or evaluation of student assignments? Have you noticed any particular resource as being preferred by the students or that they tend to want to consult first? Do you ever

need to consult the teacher to clarify assignments or to evaluate the appropriateness of resources?

5. What are the main stumbling blocks you see students face as they transact schoolwork in the library?

Follow-up questions: Do they have the same problems when looking for information for their own use? Do you see the same issues across age/grade levels?

6. Aside from school assignments, what kinds of information have you noticed children seeking for someone else?

Follow-up questions: Do you know whom they were getting the information for? Do you have any sense of how often this happens in your library? Why do you think these children bring these questions here?

REFERENCES

Chu, C. M. (1999). "Immigrant children mediators (ICM): Bridging the literacy gap in immigrant communities." *New Review of Children's Literature and Librarianship* 5: 85–94.

Dervin, B., and Dewdney, P. (1986). "Neutral questioning: A new approach to the reference interview." *RQ* 25 (Summer): 506–513.

Erdelez, S., and Rioux, K. (2000). "'Email this story to a friend': A study of sharing tools on newspaper websites." In *2000 Information Today, 21st National Online Meeting*. New York.

Gross, M. (1995). "The imposed query." *RQ* 35, no. 2 (Winter): 236–243.

Gross, M. (1998). "The imposed query: Implications for library service evaluation." *Reference and User Services Quarterly* 37, no. 3 (Spring): 290–299.

Gross, M. (1999). "Imposed queries in the school library media center: A descriptive study." *Library and Information Science Research* 21, no. 4 (1999): 501–521.

Gross, M. (2000). "The imposed query and information services for children." *Journal of Youth Services in Libraries* 13, no. 2 (Winter): 10–17.

Gross, M. (2004). *Children's questions: Information seeking behavior in school*. Lanham, Md.: Scarecrow Press.

Gross, M., and Saxton, M. (2001). "Who wants to know? Imposed queries in the public library." *Public Libraries* 40, no. 3 (May/June): 170–176.

Krikelas, J. (1983). "Information-seeking behavior: Patterns and concepts." *Drexel Library Quarterly* 19, no. 2 (Spring): 5–20.

Kuhlthau, Carol C. (1993). *Seeking meaning: A process approach to library and information services.* Norwood, N.J.: Ablex.

Metoyer-Duran, C. (1993). *Gatekeepers in ethnolinguistic communities.* Norwood, N.J.: Ablex.

National Online Meeting, proceedings—2000: Proceedings of the 21st National Online Meeting, New York, May 16–18, 2000. Sponsored by Information TodayInc. Edited by Martha E. Williams. Medford, N.J.: Information Today, 2000.

Taylor, R. S. (1962). "The process of asking questions." *American Documentation* 13, no. 2 (October): 391–396.

Taylor, R. S. (1968). "Question-negotiation and information seeking in libraries." *College and Research Libraries* 29, no. 3 (May): 178–194.

Twidale, M. B., Nichols, D. M., and Paice, C. D. (1997). "Browsing is a collaborative process." *Information Processing and Management* 33 no. 6: 761–783.

Walter, V. A. (1994). "The information needs of children." *Advances in Librarianship* 18: 112–115.

NINE

Domain Knowledge and Children's Search Behavior

Sandra G. Hirsh

Searching the myriad information resources available, ranging from library catalogs to Internet sites, requires a sophisticated set of search skills and knowledge. Some of the skills children have difficulty with as they attempt to navigate these resources include: typing (Eastman and Agostino, 1986; Erthal, 1985), spelling (Solomon, 1993), spacing and punctuation (Hooten, 1989; Schlagal, 1989; Taylor and Kidder, 1988), alphabetization (Edmonds, Moore and Balcom, 1990), composition of search statements using Boolean logic (Liebscher and Marchionini, 1988; Nahl and Harada, 1996; Siegler, 1991), formulation of appropriate search queries (Bilal, 2001; Large and Beheshti, 2000; Moll, 1975; Moore and St. George, 1991; Neuman, 1995; Vandergrift, 1989; White, 1990), reactive rather than planned searching (Bilal, 2000; Fidel et al., 1999; Hirsh, 1999; Schacter, Chung, and Dorr, 1998; Wallace and Kupperman, 1997), and lack of consideration of authority, accuracy, or bias of the information found (Hirsh, 1999).

Domain knowledge has been identified as a factor that influences information-retrieval task behavior among adults and cognitive task behavior, such as problem solving, among children. However, little research was found that examined how children's domain knowledge affected information retrieval. This paper explores children's domain knowledge and other factors influencing their behavior as children perform assigned searches on an information-retrieval system designed specifically for elementary school children called the Science Library Catalog.

PREVIOUS LITERATURE

Although there is a large body of research on the effect of domain knowledge on children's performance on memory, problem solving, and learning tasks, little research has examined the effect of domain knowledge on children's information-retrieval behavior. Research on domain knowledge in the psychological literature indicated that expert children in particular domains performed better than novice children on memory, problem solving, and learning tasks because their knowledge base was better defined, more complete, and structured hierarchically in a way that allowed easy access to stored information (Ceci, 1989; Chi, Hutchinson, and Robin, 1989; Gobbo and Chi, 1986). A complete and defined knowledge base enabled experts to delineate more distinctly between domain concepts and to understand the relationship between those concepts (Chi et al., 1989; Rosch, Mervis, Gray, Johnson, and Boyes-Braem, 1976). Experts were able to integrate and learn new concepts more quickly and easily than novices, particularly when information was presented to them hierarchically in ways that matched their own internal organization of the subject matter (Greene, 1989, 1991). In addition, experts were able to use alternate cognitive strategies when initial approaches were not successful.

Some research has investigated the effect of domain knowledge on adult information-retrieval behavior. Most of these studies have compared the search behavior of domain experts who were novice searchers to domain novices who were search experts. Domain knowledge, in these contexts, was measured by the number of classes taken in a particular subject, by academic status, or by job position in a particular domain (Bates, 1977; Hollands and Merikle, 1987; Hsieh-Yee, 1993; Marchionini, Dwiggins, Katz, and Lin, 1993).

The earliest study found on the role of subject area familiarity in information retrieval examined subject headings in a manual environment. In a comparison of the match rates between the subject search terms generated by novice and expert subject specialists to the actual subject headings used in a library catalog, Bates (1977) found that education in the subject area (i.e., domain knowledge) did not significantly affect the participants' ability to match their vocabulary to catalog headings in the users' first attempt at matching the catalog vocabulary.

Another study examined the role of domain knowledge and search experience on the information-retrieval process, specifically search tactics, using the ERIC online database (Hsieh-Yee, 1993). She found that subject knowledge affected the search tactics used by experienced searchers but did not seem to affect those used by inexperienced searchers. When search experts searched a topic they did not know well, they tended to prepare more carefully for the search, such as by using the thesaurus for term suggestions. When search experts searched a topic they did know well, they tended to rely more heavily on their own search terms. Novice searchers used the same types of search tactics regardless of their levels of knowledge about a particular topic.

Allen (1991) examined the effect of domain knowledge of a particular topic on people's abilities to formulate search queries and to execute them on online library catalogs. His findings indicated that people with higher knowledge used more search expressions, especially novel query terms not previously mentioned in earlier descriptions of the search topic, than people with lower knowledge.

A series of four studies examined the effect of domain knowledge and search experience on full-text hypertext systems and full-text CD-ROM systems (Marchionini et al., 1990, 1991, 1993). Some of the key findings from these studies included: subject and search experts were able to search more successfully and efficiently than novices, in terms of amount of time spent on the search and number of steps taken (1990); domain experts, on average, used more unique terms than did search experts because they possessed relevant technical knowledge (1991, 1993); domain experts took more time to conduct their searches than search experts (1991); and, domain experts scanned results to make relatively fast relevance judgments (1993). Overall, domain knowledge or subject expertise enabled searchers to understand domain concepts and relationships between concepts and to apply this knowledge to solve problems (1990, 1993).

Looking more closely at the effect of domain knowledge on the use of particular information-retrieval system features, Hollands and Merikle (1987) studied the impact of domain knowledge on the use of different menu structures (i.e., categorical, alphabetical, or random). The researchers found that performance on term-matching and definition-matching search tasks improved directly with expertise in the subject area when the categorical menu organization was used; experts completed the definition-matching task faster than novices with all three types of menu organization. Performance on the simple term-matching task was not influenced by expertise when alphabetic or random menu organizations were used. The researchers concluded that the best menu organization depended on both the user's knowledge of a topic and the search tasks they performed.

In sum, these information-retrieval studies of adult domain experts and novices suggested that domain knowledge influenced the information-retrieval process. Since most of these studies compared subject domain experts to search experts, further research in this area, which separates domain expertise from search expertise, should contribute to our understanding of the role domain knowledge plays in end-user searching of information-retrieval systems.

THE SCIENCE LIBRARY CATALOG PROJECT

The Science Library Catalog Project's goals were to design an interface for an automated library catalog that was appropriate for elementary school children and that could be used to increase understanding of children's information-retrieval behavior. The Science Library Catalog provided access to bibliographic records on science topics through a graphical interface built in HyperCard on Macintosh computers. The design of the interface, which utilized a bookshelf metaphor to correspond to children's mental model of a library catalog, was intended to minimize the known difficulties children have with existing online catalogs (e.g., spelling, typing/keyboarding, alphabetizing, Boolean logic) and to build on their skills and abilities (e.g., browsing, recognizing relevant topics, navigating hierarchical displays, using a mouse).

Four earlier experiments were performed in several elementary school libraries and public libraries to test, evaluate, and improve the Science Library Catalog interface (for a summary, see Borgman, Hirsh, Walter, and Gallagher, 1995). Each experiment tested different versions of the Science Library Catalog interface and functionality, with database sizes ranging from 250 to 8,200 records. Some of the key findings from this body of research include:

- Children were able to find science information successfully using the browsing interface without training, with success rates ranging from 60–81 percent, and average search times ranging from 1.7 to 3.1 minutes per search.
- Children were generally more successful in finding books on science topics that did not require searching deep within the hierarchy and on topics that involved more familiar vocabu-

lary (e.g., science topics were easier to find than technology topics).

- Children were persistent searchers, spending about twice as much time looking for a book record on a topic they eventually abandoned than on topics successfully completed.
- In studies comparing the Science Library Catalog with command-driven interfaces, command-driven interfaces were found to be more sensitive to age differences (i.e., older children aged twelve were more successful than younger children aged ten) and to search topics (i.e., harder to spell words were more difficult to find).
- Command-driven interfaces were more attractive to older children who liked the ability to search directly for search terms; the Science Library Catalog was more consistently liked across groups, especially among younger children who liked the graphics and the lack of required spelling and keyboarding skills.

The final version of the Science Library Catalog interface, reported in this chapter, combined a hierarchical browsing search method with a keyword search method. The browse interface utilized the Dewey decimal classification as a subject hierarchy, which was represented as a series of bookshelves that could be navigated. The opening bookcase contained ten bookshelves—each bookshelf corresponded to the Dewey classification—with only the science and technology shelves (the Dewey 500s and 600s) available as search options. Children navigated through successive levels of the science and technology hierarchies by clicking on bookshelves with a mouse. The browse approach enabled children to initiate science searches without having to generate appropriate search terms. Figure 9.1 shows a sample browse method search.

To begin a keyword search, children clicked on the bookworm (located in the lower lefthand corner of every screen) that asked

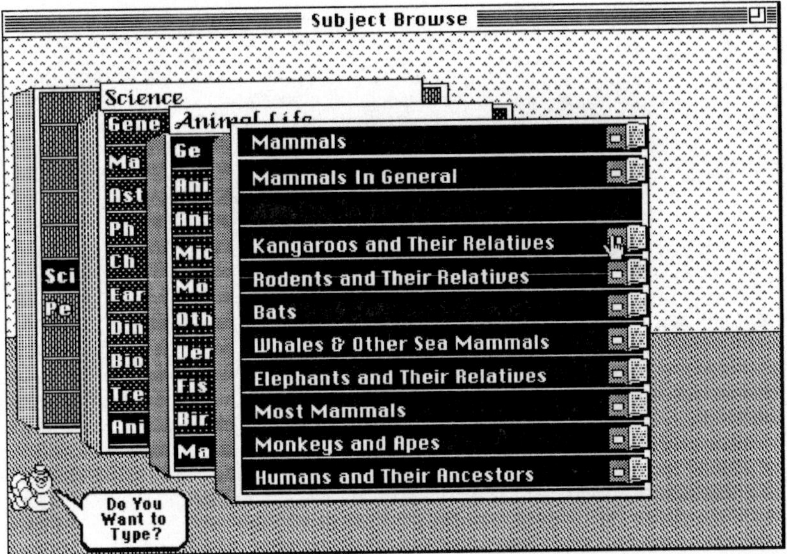

Figure 9.1 Browsing in the Science Library Catalog

"Do you want to type?" Children typed in their search query, which was automatically run through a spelling correction and stemming program. Children's search terms were matched against terms in the bibliographic record, specifically the title, subject headings, and notes fields. A rank-ordered list of shelf topic headings, containing book records matching the search request, was displayed as a result of the search. Figure 9.2 shows a sample keyword search for books on "kangaroos." When children selected one of these shelf topic headings, they were taken back into the browsing structure and the mouse pointer was automatically placed at the selected bookshelf. By embedding the keyword search method within the browsing structure, children were able to move easily between the two search methods at any point during the search process; this integration of browsing and keyword searching also provided children with useful context for their search topic. The Science Library Catalog, with its combination of

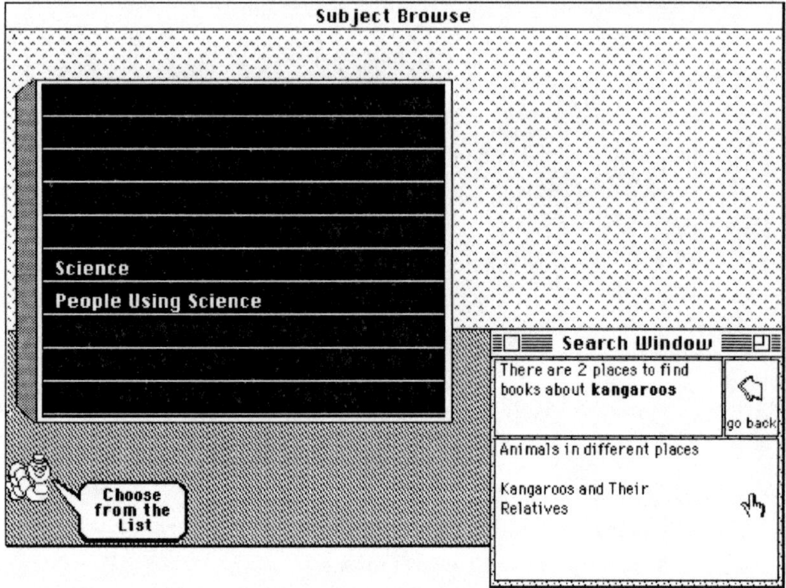

Figure 9.2 Keyword Searching for Kangaroos in the Science Library Catalog

structured browsing and embedded keyword searching, provided a unique test bed for understanding children's search behavior.

RESEARCH QUESTIONS

This study explores the effect of domain knowledge on elementary school children's search behavior on an automated library catalog. It also examines how and under what circumstances children utilized browse and keyword search methods. Specifically, the following research questions are addressed:

Does search success vary by level of domain knowledge, gender, or level of computer experience?

Does search behavior vary by level of domain knowledge, gender, or level of computer, video game, and online catalog experience?

How do the availability of keyword and browse search options influence search behavior?

RESEARCH METHOD

This study employed one-on-one interviews, online monitoring techniques, and observations to understand children's search behavior on the Science Library Catalog.

Participants

Sixty-four fifth-grade children from two public elementary schools in the Pasadena Unified School District participated in the study. The sample was balanced by sex, level of domain knowledge in science (high, low), and school (school with library, school with computers). The "school with library" provided children with a school library, but no computer resources. The "school with computers" provided children with extensive computer facilities, but no school library.

Independent Variable Measures

USER CHARACTERISTICS

User characteristics varied by sex, domain knowledge, and computer experience (i.e., school). Children were placed into high and low science domain knowledge groups, based on their science grades averaged over two quarters and teacher recommendations. Children were asked a series of questions about their experience with computers; it was found that the school they attended correlated highly with their level of computer experience and was used as a measure of computer experience.

Tasks Characteristics

Children were administered eight search tasks over two interview sessions that varied by topic (i.e., science, technology) and task complexity (i.e., browsing, keyword). Children were assigned an equal number of science topics, drawn from the Dewey 500s, and technology topics (renamed "People Using Science"), drawn from the Dewey 600s. Tasks were balanced for browsing-task complexity and topic, but not for keyword-task complexity and topic. (For more on task complexity and children's information retrieval, see Hirsh [1997].)

Dependent Variables

The independent variables were measured in terms of success and search behavior. Success in finding book records in the Science Library Catalog was operationalized by counting any book that children identified on a topic as a match, within the context of performing research for a school report. The alternative to a match was an abandoned search, which occurred when children decided they were unable to find a matching book on the topic assigned for a school report. This definition of success is consistent with all prior Science Library Catalog experiments (Borgman et al., 1995).

Search behavior was evaluated by collecting monitoring data from the built-in monitoring facility (Borgman, Hirsh, and Hiller, 1996). The monitoring program recorded every user-system interaction and provided detailed information on the sequence of children's actions, the content of those actions, and the amount of time spent on those actions. The three methods used to evaluate the monitoring log data of children's search behavior were: search method consistency and style, search path visualization, and pattern matching program. The search method consistency and style analysis is presented in this chapter; for more on search path visualization and pattern matching, see Hirsh (1996).

Search behavior was evaluated with the child as the unit of analysis by reducing monitoring data into search strategy states and characterizing search behavior across all eight search tasks. Search method consistency behavior was defined as children who consistently used the same search method (i.e., browse only, keyword only) to complete all eight tasks and children who inconsistently used search methods (i.e., mixed). Search style behavior was defined as being present in those children who demonstrated either a dominant style (i.e., used the same search method to complete at least six of eight tasks) or no dominant style (i.e., did not use the same search method to complete at least six of eight tasks). Examining use of search methods across at least six tasks (75 percent of the tasks) allowed for statistical analysis since the dominant and no dominant search style groups were dichotomous and had larger cell sizes than the search method consistency group.

PROCEDURE

One-on-one interviews were held with children on two occasions, separated by approximately one week. Each interview lasted between forty-five to sixty minutes. Children were tested on a standardized Science Library Catalog database (1500 MARC records), which was loaded on a Macintosh Powerbook 160 and used with an attached mouse.

The first interview session started with a brief automated tutorial on how to search the Science Library Catalog. When this was completed, children were asked to find book records on science topics drawn from the fifth-grade science curriculum; they were allowed to search for the topics using any search method they wanted and for as long as they wanted. Tasks were presented as story questions, similar to the way they might be asked to perform a research assignment at school. Children received the same four search tasks, but the sequencing was varied to control for order effects. Children were instructed to tell the interviewer when either: (1) they found the book(s) they would need to write a school paper on the topic, or (2) they wanted to abandon the search because they were unable to find a book on the assigned topic. During the search interviews, monitoring data (i.e., time stamps of each user and system action) were automatically collected on the Science Library Catalog.

The second interview session began by asking children to find book records on a different set of four search tasks than previously given. When they completed the search tasks, children were asked to explain their use of search methods (e.g., browse, keyword, or mixed). At the conclusion of the second session, children were asked several questions about the type and extent of their experience with computers, video games, and online catalogs.

RESULTS

Search Success Analyses

The grand mean of success for all children across all tasks was 6.4 (out of 8 possible). A factorial ANOVA was performed to test the effects of three independent variables (i.e., domain knowledge, gender, and school) on the dependent measure of success. School was included in this analysis to account for any variance attributable to this variable. As shown in table 9.1, only one significant main effect for domain knowledge was found.

The results indicate that children with high domain knowledge were significantly more successful in performing search tasks than children with low domain knowledge ($F = 4.58$; $df = 1,63$; $p = .03$). Children with high domain knowledge performed successfully on an average of 6.9 tasks of 8 tasks; while children with low

Table 9.1 Analysis of Variance of Success Scores by Domain Knowledge, Gender, and School

Source	*SS*	*DF*	*MS*	*F*	*P*
Gender	0.141	1	0.141	0.060	0.807
Domain	11.391	1	11.391	4.883	0.031*
School	1.891	1	1.891	0.811	0.372
Gender by Domain	6.891	1	6.891	2.954	0.091
Gender by School	0.141	1	0.141	0.060	0.807
Domain by School	0.141	1	0.141	0.060	0.807
Gender by Domain by School	2.641	1	2.541	1.132	0.292
Error	130.625	56	2.333		

domain knowledge completed an average of 6.0 tasks of 8 tasks. No other significant main or interaction effects were evident, indicating that the only factor significantly influencing success was level of domain knowledge.

The finding that children with high domain knowledge were more successful searchers than children with low domain knowledge is supported by studies with adult domain novices and experts (Marchionini et al., 1991, 1993).

Search Behavior Analyses

Children were allowed to select the search method (i.e., browse, keyword, or mixed) they wanted to use in searching the Science Library Catalog for each of the eight tasks presented to them. Some children chose to use the same search method to complete all of the tasks; while other children varied the search method they used by task. Search behavior data were analyzed from close examination of the monitoring logs created during children's search sessions. A very small percentage of the monitoring data (4.1 percent) were lost due to an unexpected failure in the computer-monitoring program; records of the search methods children applied during the observed experimental sessions were used to supplement the missing monitoring data.

Search Method Consistency Behavior

Few children (9 percent) used the keyword-only search method to complete all eight search tasks. About one-fifth (22 percent) of the children used the browse-only method exclusively. The majority of the children (69 percent) used mixed methods, a combination of browse and keyword methods, to complete their search tasks. Children's success using these methods varied by the individual search task. Table 9.2 shows the success rates of children who displayed search method consistency behavior by individual task topic.

Table 9.2 shows that the six children who used the keyword-only search method successfully completed all eight tasks. One of the reasons why children were so successful in finding information using the keyword-only method may be due to the spelling correction and stemming programs that were built into the keyword search method in the Science Library Catalog. Another possible explanation for the high success rates of the keyword-only searchers is that the Science Library Catalog allowed children to type in natural language queries. For example, when searching for books on "building homes," one child typed: "books about building homes" and was directed to a topic heading list that included the

Table 9.2 Success Rates on Individual Tasks by Search Method Consistency Behavior (percent)

Search Method	n	*Topic 1*	*Topic 2*	*Topic 3*	*Topic 4*	*Topic 5*	*Topic 6*	*Topic 7*	*Topic 8*
Browse only	14	71	71	100	93	93	79	79	43
Keyword only	6	100	100	100	100	100	100	100	100
Mixed	44	91	86	95	77	82	52	68	82

Search Topics
Topic 1 = Electricity
Topic 2 = Jellyfish
Topic 3 = Growing garden crops
Topic 4 = Building homes
Topic 5 = Saturn
Topic 6 = Desert environment
Topic 7 = Endangered animals
Topic 8 = Astronauts

bookshelf heading "homes." Given the limited number of children who used this method exclusively to complete all tasks, it is not possible to generalize about these findings. However, the results do suggest that all keyword-only searchers performed highly effective searches.

The fourteen children who used browse-only to complete their search tasks had varying success rates, ranging from 43 percent on Topic 8 (astronauts) to 100 percent on Topic 3 (growing garden crops). Navigating through the hierarchical structure to find book records on astronauts using the browsing method proved to be difficult for the children in this study. The browsing path required them to look under *People Using Science*, then under *Engineering*, then under *Other Branches of Engineering*, and finally under *Space Flight*. In contrast, the browsing path to find books on growing garden crops was much easier for children, mostly because the bookshelf heading corresponded well with the assigned task. These books were located under *People Using Science*, then under *Raising Plants and Animals*, then under *Garden Crops*, and finally again under *Garden Crops*.

The majority of the children ($n = 44$) used a combination of browse and keyword search methods, or mixed methods. Their success rates also varied, ranging from 52 percent on Topic 6 (desert environment) to 95 percent on Topic 3 (growing garden crops).

Search Style Behavior

Since so many children used mixed methods to complete their search tasks, search behavior was broken down in another way—in terms of dominant or no dominant search styles. The primary independent variables (i.e., level of domain knowledge, gender, school, and level of experience with electronic media) were examined to determine their influence on children's search style behavior and were analyzed using chi-square tests of association. Analysis of children's success rates by search style was also examined by performing an independent samples t-test.

Domain Knowledge

The domain knowledge variable was created by placing the children who received science grades of B + or higher in the high domain group and children who received science grades of B or lower in the low domain group. Some children, who had received science grades lower than B + were placed in the high domain group based on teacher recommendations. A chi-square test of association was performed to determine whether search style was influenced by level of domain knowledge; however, no significant differences were found. It is possible that the lack of distinct domain knowledge groups, since the domain knowledge variable was measured by both science grades and teacher estimations, minimized some of the search style differences.

A second analysis of domain knowledge allowed for more distinct domain knowledge groups by dropping the middle range of science grades to create the high and low domain knowledge groups. This analysis, based on both science grades and more distinct domain knowledge groups, was performed to make the domain knowledge measure more consonant with studies of adult behavior on information-retrieval systems. Studies with adult users measured domain knowledge according to a high level of expertise, such as the number of classes taken in a particular subject, academic status (e.g., graduate student, faculty), or job position in the domain (Bates, 1977; Hollands and Merikle, 1987; Hsieh-Yee, 1993; Marchionini et al., 1993; Shute and Smith, 1993). Thus, a subsample of children was selected for the high and low domain knowledge groups based on their science grades. The high domain knowledge group consisted of twenty-two children who received grades in the top third of the science grade distribution, and the low domain knowledge group consisted of twenty-three children who received grades in the bottom third of the grade distribution. The nineteen students in the middle third of the distribution were left out of this search style analysis.

Table 9.3 presents the frequency of children's search style for the children included in the subsample measure of domain knowledge, as well as computer experience and school. The table shows that twice as many children with low domain knowledge exhibited a dominant style than children with high domain knowledge, while twice as many children with high domain knowledge used no dominant style than children with low domain knowledge. A chi-square test of association was performed and found a significant difference in search style by domain knowledge ($X^2 = 5.021$; $df = 1$; $p = .025$).

These results can be cautiously interpreted as indicating differences in search style by domain knowledge level when the domain knowledge measure was similar to the measures applied in studies with adult users. However, since the findings were sensitive to the

Table 9.3 Frequency of Search Style by Individual Characteristic

Characteristic	*Dominant*	*No Dominant*	*Total*
Domain Knowledge*			
High	9 (41%)	13 (59%)	22 (100%)
Low	17 (74%)	6 (26%)	23 (100%)
Total	26 (58%)	19 (42%)	45 (100%)
School			
With Library	25 (78%)	7 (22%)	32 (100%)
With Computers	12 (38%)	20 (62%)	32 (100%)
Total	37 (58%)	27 (42%)	64 (100%)
Computer Experience			
Infreq./None	14 (82%)	3 (18%)	17 (100%)
Frequent	23 (49%)	24 (51%)	47 (100%)
Total	37 (58%)	27 (42%)	64 (100%)

*Forty-five children were used in the domain knowledge analysis due to the subsample measure of domain knowledge.

way domain knowledge was measured, further study is necessary to determine an appropriate measure of domain knowledge as it relates to children's search behavior and to determine the generalizability of these findings.

Other Independent Variables

No significant relationship between gender and search style was found. Children's search behavior by school was examined since this variable was found to be closely related to the level of computer experience; given this relationship, testing the school variable meant that the computer experience variable was simultaneously being tested. The chi-square test of association for search style by school was significant ($X^2 = 10.82$; $df = 1$; $p = .001$); children at the "school with library" were significantly more likely to have a dominant search style than the children at the "school with computers." Additionally, analysis of search style by level of experience with computers, video games, and online catalogs was also performed. In order to perform these analyses with large enough cell sizes, it was necessary to reduce the experience levels from three levels (i.e., frequent, infrequent, none) to two levels (i.e., frequent, infrequent/none). Due to the unbalanced distributions, three Fisher Exact tests were used to study the relationships between experience with electronic media (i.e., computer, video game, and online catalog) and search style. The only statistical relationship found using the Fisher Exact test was between level of computer experience and search style ($p = .022$). As table 9.3 shows, children who were frequent computer users were split evenly between the dominant and no dominant styles. However, the children who used computers infrequently or had no computer experience tended to exhibit dominant search styles. These results support the search style differences found by the school variable, which also identified that children with less computer experience exhibited more dominant search styles. No differences in search style were found by experience with video games or online catalogs.

Success

This analysis investigated whether search style influenced children's success in retrieving science materials from the Science Library Catalog. An independent samples *t*-test was performed to examine how the two levels of search style (i.e., dominant, no dominant style) related to search success. The results of this test were not significant; children were equally successful in finding science materials, regardless of the search style they employed.

DISCUSSION

This chapter presents search behavior findings on children's use of the Science Library Catalog to find science information, drawing on interviews, observation, and monitoring log data to evaluate children's search behavior. The discussion interprets the findings by the research questions posed earlier in the chapter; the first two research questions are discussed together: Do search success and search behavior vary by level of domain knowledge, gender, or level of computer, video game, and online catalog experience?

Level of domain knowledge was the only individual factor found to influence search success on the Science Library Catalog. Both level of domain knowledge and level of computer experience were found to influence search behavior. The remaining user characteristics studied (i.e., gender, online catalog experience, video game experience) were not found to influence search success and behavior.

Domain Knowledge

Although the influence of domain knowledge (i.e., the amount of knowledge a person has about a particular domain or subject area) on information retrieval had been investigated with adult searchers (Allen, 1991; Hollands and Merikle, 1987; Hsieh-Yee, 1993; Marchionini et al., 1990, 1991, 1993), this was the first study to examine the effect of domain knowledge on children's information-retrieval performance. Due to their well-defined and developed knowledge bases, children with high domain knowledge were more successful in performing the information-retrieval tasks than children with low domain knowledge. These findings are similar to findings with adult subject experts (Marchionini et al., 1993).

Domain knowledge was also found to influence children's search behavior when the measure was based entirely on science grades and was similar to the measures used with adult searchers. The results from this study found that children with high domain knowledge frequently did not display a dominant search style, meaning they did not use the same search method to complete at least six of eight searches. Similar to domain experts in studies with adult searchers (Shute and Smith, 1993), children with high domain knowledge were better able to refine their initial search queries based on the intermediate information-retrieval results. As a result of this refinement process, children with high domain knowledge were more flexible in applying a variety of search methods to the search tasks presented to them. In contrast, children with low domain knowledge used the same search method regardless of the search task. Similarly, the adult novice searchers in Hsieh-Yee's (1993) study applied the same search tactics (a more discrete measure than search style) no matter which topic they searched.

As this was the first study to investigate domain knowledge and children's information retrieval, further research is needed to determine the generalizability of these results and to understand more about children's subject expertise in information retrieval, especially in Web-based environments. Some research has begun to examine whether domain knowledge influences children's Internet search behavior, but so far has not found this to be the case (Bilal, 2000, 2001). Additionally, further research is needed to determine an appropriate measure of domain knowledge as it relates to children's search behavior on information-retrieval systems. In this study, different search behavior findings resulted when domain knowledge was measured by both science grades and teacher recommendations as compared to when domain knowledge was measured by science grades alone. One possible explanation is that children's attitudes toward science and motivation for learning about science can affect these findings; these measures were not addressed in this study.

Computer Experience

Children's experience with computers at school was found to influence search behavior, but not success in finding information on the Science Library Catalog. Earlier findings on the browse-only versions of the Science Library Catalog also found no success differences by children's experience with computers outside of school (Borgman et al., 1995). Taken together, these studies suggest that success with the Science Library Catalog interface (both the browsing only and advanced versions) is not sensitive to computer experience effects.

However, children with more computer experience searched differently than children with little or no computer experience. Other information-retrieval studies with adult searchers have also found a relationship between computer experience and search behavior (Elkerton and Williges, 1984; Qui, 1993). In this study, children with more computer experience used a variety of search methods, depending on the search task, suggesting that they were more comfortable in utilizing the full range of the system's search capabilities. Children with less computer experience appeared to use a single search method and typically did not explore other search methods.

Factors Not Influencing Information Retrieval

Several user characteristics were not found to influence search success or search behavior. First, no main effects for gender were found in this study, supporting earlier findings on the browse-only version of the Science Library Catalog, which found that boys and girls possessed similar abilities to conduct searches (Borgman et al., 1995). Second, video game experience was not found to influence either children's success or the search methods they employed. However, there may not have been enough variance in the measure to reliably test the effect of video games on search behavior. Third, no differences were found in search success or search behavior by level of experience with online catalogs. Since few children reported being frequent users of online catalogs, there may not have been enough experienced searchers to show any difference.

These are the findings for the final research question presented earlier in the chapter: How do the availability of keyword and browse search options influence search behavior? This version of the Science Library Catalog was unique in that it provided two subject search options—browse and keyword—on the same information-retrieval interface; the interface was designed to allow children to switch between these two search options at any point during the search process. Search-behavior data, collected through monitoring logs, interview questions about search-method choice, and observations of children's search behavior, suggested that the search options offered as part of the Science Library Catalog interface enabled children to perform information-retrieval tasks with high rates of success.

The browse method allowed children to search by using the mouse to explore successive levels of subject hierarchies. More than one-fifth of the children, mostly children with little or no computer experience, used the browse method to complete all of the search tasks and never tried the keyword search method. Children with less computer experience found the browse search option easier to use, especially since it required only a mouse to input their search selections. Many children with low domain knowledge also preferred the browse method because navigating through subject categories and relying on recognition knowledge to execute their searches required a lower cognitive load than formulating search queries with the keyword search method. Some children also used the browse method as a way to become familiar with the search system and the task domain.

However, some children found navigating through multiple levels of the science hierarchy difficult and frustrating because they often did not know what was included under each bookshelf heading without clicking on it to see. Related to this finding, many children had difficulty matching their search queries to the classification vocabulary used by the system; for example, many children did not recognize that books on the "desert environment" were classified under "ecology."

A second subject search method, the keyword method, provided keyword access to the Science Library Catalog, with built-in automatic spelling correction and stemming programs, ranked output, and integration within the browsing structure. Children with high domain knowledge and high levels of computer experience frequently reported using the keyword search method because they perceived it to be a more efficient and direct search method than using the browse method.

However, many children found keyword searching difficult because it required typing in search queries. Most children typed by hunting for letters on the keyword. For search topics with many letters, such as "desert environment," it took children a long time to find all of the letters and often they would lose their place in the word. Several children also found the keyword method difficult because it required them to formulate a searchable query. As a result of their uncertainty about what to type in with the keyword method, many of these children made extensive use of the browse method. Some children using the keyword method expressed their search queries in a natural language form rather than as expected search keys. Another problem with keyword searching, even as it was implemented in the Science Library Catalog, was spelling. Even though children were administered search tasks with correct spelling on a piece of paper they could refer to during the search and even though the Science Library Catalog had a built-in correction program, spelling issues arose when children typed in words that were not recognized by the spelling correction program (e.g., "sunlight" converted to "snails") or that were real words but not the intended search terms (e.g., "dessert" instead of "desert").

The majority of the children, particularly children with high domain knowledge or high levels of computer experience, used a combination of browse and keyword search methods to complete their searches. Many children found that the browse method was a useful starting strategy because it provided them with some context about the search topic and allowed them to explore the topic through the subject hierarchies. However, when they were unable to find what they were looking for within the browsing structure, many children switched to the keyword search option. Children appeared to view the keyword method as a backup strategy and as a more advanced search method. Other children used a combination of browse and keyword methods when they were unable to find book records with either search method; these children repeatedly switched between the search options, hoping to find a bookshelf heading or topic that matched their interests. Children who used more than one search method to complete a search task generally spent more time on their search than children who used a single search method.

CONCLUSIONS

This was the first study to examine the effect of domain knowledge on children's information-retrieval performance and search behavior. Findings from this research suggest that domain knowledge in science influences both search success and search behavior, with children with high domain knowledge more successful in completing information-retrieval tasks and varying their use of the keyword and browsing search methods on the Science Library Catalog. By considering individual differences in the design of information-retrieval interfaces, system designers can tailor information-retrieval systems to address children's specific needs, knowledge levels, and search behavior. For example, search tips and vocabulary aids based on children's level of domain knowledge could be provided in the design of information-retrieval systems. Additionally, one-on-one search assistance at the computer terminal in the library when children encounter problems during their searches could particularly benefit children conducting research in unfamiliar domains or children with little or no computer experience.

To determine the generalizability of these findings, future research is needed to examine the effect of domain knowledge on children's use of other information-retrieval systems and in other domains. In addition, alternate measures of domain knowledge should be explored, given the limitations of measuring domain knowledge by school academic grades. The present research study did not control for topic knowledge (Allen, 1991) or knowledge of an individual topic, meaning that some children classified in the low domain knowledge group could be "experts" on some of the assigned topics. Future research should take topic knowledge into consideration.

Although this research presented findings from an automated library catalog, given the nature of the hypertext interaction style and the integration of the browsing and keyword search methods in a single interface, this research has implications for other information-retrieval tools designed for children. The findings suggested that the availability of the two subject search methods—browse and keyword—enabled children to find 80 percent of their search topics successfully. Children were equally successful in performing information-retrieval searches when they predominantly used a single search method and when they switched between search methods. Other research has also suggested the importance of providing more than one search approach in the design of information-retrieval systems for adult users (Elkerton and Williges, 1984). This study found that children can be successful searchers as long as they have a variety of search tools that meet their individual preferences.

Research on children's use of Yahooligans!, which offers both browsing and keyword functionality, suggests that children are more successful when they browse, but that children often initiate their searches by typing in keyword searches (Bilal, 2000, 2001, 2002). Part of the reason that children switched from performing keyword searches to browsing was that the keyword functionality in Yahooligans!, which was implemented as a directory search rather than a search engine, did not meet the expectations of the children. This research also finds that children continue to experience many of the difficulties in the Web-based environment that they did in earlier search behavior studies, such as problems with natural language queries, spelling, and term selection. The Science Library Catalog mitigated several of these known difficulties by supporting natural language queries, implementing a spelling correction program and placing children's keyword searches in context within the browsing structure. These accommodations contributed to children's success in using the keyword search method in the Science Library Catalog. Future research needs to explore further how children use each type of search method, how children decide to switch between the two methods, and how implementing system design improvements (like spelling correction programs) in the Web-based environment can lead to better search experiences for children.

In summary, the opportunity to use multiple search options enabled most children to use the system effectively, but differences in success rates were evident based on level of domain knowledge. System designers, librarians, and teachers can all provide assistance to children as they embark on research in unfamiliar areas and can contribute to the design of information-retrieval systems that will support children's information needs and educational pursuits in an information society.

REFERENCES

Allen, B. (1991). "Topic knowledge and online catalog search formulation." *Library Quarterly*, 61: 188–213.

Bates, M. J. (1977). "Factors affecting subject catalog search success." *Journal of the American Society for Information Science* 28: 161–169.

Bilal, D. (2000). "Children's use of the Yahooligans! Web search engine: I. Cognitive, physical and affective behaviors on fact-based search tasks." *Journal of the American Society for Information Science* 51: 646–665.

Bilal, D. (2001). "Children's use of the Yahooligans! Web search engine: II. Cognitive and physical behaviors on research tasks." *Journal of the American Society for Information Science and Technology* 52: 118–136.

Bilal, D. (2002). "Children's use of the Yahooligans! Web search engine: III. Cognitive and physical behaviors on fully self-generated tasks." *Journal of the American Society for Information Science and Technology* 53: 13, 1170–1183.

Borgman, C. L., Hirsh, S. G., and Hiller, J. (1996). "Rethinking online monitoring methods for information retrieval systems: From search product to search process." *Journal of the American Society for Information Science* 47: 568–583.

Borgman, C. L., Hirsh, S. G., Walter, V. A., and Gallagher, A. L. (1995). "Children's search behavior on browsing and keyword online catalogs: The Science Library Catalog project." *Journal of the American Society for Information Science* 46: 663–684.

Ceci, S. J. (1989). "On domain specificity . . . more or less general and specific constraints on cognitive development." *Merrill-Palmer Quarterly* 35: 131–142.

Chi, M. T. H., Hutchinson, J. E., and Robin, A. F. (1989). "How inferences about novel domain-related concepts can be constrained by structured knowledge." *Merrill-Palmer Quarterly* 35: 27–62.

Eastman, S. T., and Agostino, D .E. (1986). "Commanding the computer: Functions and concepts of videotext technology for eighth-grade students." *Journal of Research and Development in Education* 19: 49–57.

Edmonds, L., Moore, P., and Balcom, K. M. (1990). "The effectiveness of an online catalog." *School Library Journal* (October): 28–32.

Elkerton, J., and Williges, R. C. (1984). "Information retrieval strategies in a file-search environment." *Human Factors* 26: 171–184.

Erthal, M. J. (1985). "The status of keyboarding." *Journal of Business Education* 60: 192–193.

Fidel, R., Davies, R. K., Douglass, M. H., Holder, J. K., Hopkins, C. J., Kushner, E. J., Miyagishima, B. K., and Toney, C. D. (1999). "A visit to the information mall: Web searching behavior of high school students." *Journal of the American Society for Information Science* 50: 24–37.

Gobbo, C., and Chi, M. (1986). "How knowledge is structured and used by expert and novice children." *Cognitive Development* 1: 221–237.

Greene, T. R. (1989). "Children's understanding of class inclusion hierarchies: The relationship between external representation and task performance." *Journal of Experimental Psychology* 48: 62–89.

Greene, T. R. (1991). "Text manipulations influence children's understanding of class inclusion hierarchies." *Journal of Experimental Child Psychology* 52: 354–374.

Hirsh, S. G. (1996). "The effect of domain knowledge on elementary school children's search behavior on an information retrieval system: The Science Library Catalog." Ph.D. diss., Department of Library and Information Science, Graduate School of Education and Information Studies, University of California, Los Angeles.

Hirsh, S. G. (1997). "How do children find information on different types of tasks? Children's use of the Science Library Catalog." *Library Trends* 45: 725–745.

Hirsh, S. (1999). "Children's relevance criteria and information seeking on electronic resources." *Journal of the American Society or Information Science* 50, 1265–1283.

Hollands, J. G., and Merikle, P. M. (1987). "Menu organization and user expertise in information search tasks." *Human Factors* 29, 577–586.

Hooten, P. A. (1989). "Online catalogs: Will they improve children's access?" *Journal of Youth Services in Libraries* 2, 267–272.

Hsieh-Yee, I. (1993). "Effects of search experience and subject knowledge on the search tactics of novice and experienced searchers." *Journal of the American Society for Information Science* 44: 161–174.

Large, A., and Beheshti, J. (2000). "The web as a classroom resource: Reactions from the users." *Journal of the American Society for Information Science* 51: 1069–1080.

Liebscher, P., and Marchionini, G. (1988). "Browse and analytical search strategies in a full-text CD-ROM encyclopedia." *School Library Media Quarterly* 16: 223–233.

Marchionini, G., Dwiggins, S., Katz, A., and Lin, X. (1993). "Information seeking in full-text end-user-oriented search systems: The roles of domain and search expertise." *Library and Information Science Research* 15: 35–69.

Marchionini, G., Lin, X., and Dwiggins, S. (1990). "Effects of search and subject expertise on information seeking in a hypertext environment." In D. Henderson, ed., *Proceedings of the 53rd American Society for Information Science annual meeting* (pp. 129–137). Medford, N.J.: Learned Information.

Marchionini, G., Meadow, C., Dwiggins, S., Lin, X., Wang, J., and Yuan, W. (1991). "A study of user interaction with information retrieval interfaces: Progress report." *Canadian Journal of Information Science* 16: 42–59.

Moll, J. K. (1975). "Children's access to information in print: An analysis of the vocabulary (reading) levels of subject headings and their application to children's books." Ph.D. diss., Rutgers University, New Jersey.

Moore, P. A., and St. George, A. (1991). "Children as information seekers: The cognitive demands of books and library systems." *School Library Media Quarterly* 19: 161–168.

Nahl, D., and Harada, V. H. (1996). "Composing Boolean search statements: Self-confidence, content analysis, search logic, and errors." *School Library Media Quarterly* 24: 199–207.

Neuman, D. (1995). "High school students' use of databases: Results of a national Delphi study." *Journal of the American Society for Information Science* 46: 284–298.

Qui, L. (1993). "Markov models of search state patterns in a hypertext information retrieval system." *Journal of the American Society for Information Science*, 44: 413–427.

Rosch, E., Mervis, C. B., Gray, W. D., Johnson, D. M., and Boyes-Braem, P. (1976). "Basic objects in natural categories." *Cognitive Psychology* 8: 382–439.

Schacter, J., Chung, G., and Dorr, A. (1998). "Children's Internet searching on complex problems: Performance and process analysis." *Journal of the American Society for Information Science* 49: 840–849.

Schlagal, R. C. (1989). "Constancy and change in spelling development." *Reading Psychology: An International Quarterly* 10: 207–232.

Shute, S. J., and Smith, P. J. (1993). "Knowledge-based search tactics." *Information Processing and Management* 29: 29–45.

Siegler, R. S. (1991). *Children's thinking*. 2nd ed. Englewood Cliffs, N.J.: Prentice-Hall.

Solomon, P. (1993). "Children's information retrieval behavior: A case analysis of an OPAC." *Journal of the American Society for Information Science* 44: 245–264.

Taylor, K. K., and Kidder, E. B. (1988). "The development of spelling skills: From the first grade through eighth grade." *Written Communication* 5: 222–244.

Vandergrift, K. E. (1989). "Are children and teenagers second-class users?" *Library Resources and Technical Services* 33: 393–399.

Wallace, R., and Kupperman, J. (1997). "On-line search in the science curriculum: Benefits and possibilities." Paper presented at the AERA, Chicago. Available at http://mydl.soe.umish.edu/papers/online_search.pdf (accessed September 5, 2002).

White, M. D. (1990). "The readability of children's reference materials." *Library Quarterly* 60: 300–319.

TEN

Research on Children's Information Seeking on the Web

Dania Bilal

Since its inception, the Web has reshaped how users access, retrieve, and use information. The escalating complexity of today's information environment and the sheer abundance of information on the Web pose challenges for all types of users. In fact, "The Web is causing educators, from preschool to graduate school, to rethink the very nature of teaching, learning, and schooling."[1] The increased use of the Web in public schools and at home, coupled with its unstructured and uncontrolled nature, raises questions about children's information-seeking behavior and success in finding information.

Web search engines have become a primary information access and retrieval tool for many users. In a recent survey, more than eight in ten American users have gone to search engines to find information on the Web. "More than one in four U.S.—about 33 million—adults present queries on search engines on a typical day."[2] Ninety-four percent of young people ages 12–17 use the Internet for school research, 78 percent believe the Internet helps them with schoolwork, and 71 percent use the Internet as the major source for their most recent major school project.[3]

Recognizing that children have cognitive developmental abilities, problem-solving skills, and information needs that vary from those of adult users,[4] acknowledging the complexity of using the Web, and finding that search engines that are specifically designed for children are far from perfect,[5] researchers have sought to examine how these young users interact with the Web to find information. This chapter focuses on this body of literature, summarizes the nature of these studies, identifies the methodologies employed, and discusses implications of these studies for future research. It focuses on research published between 1997 and 2002.

INFORMATION SEEKING

Information seeking is "a process in which humans purposefully engage in order to change their state of knowledge."[6] Typically, a user approaches an information-retrieval system with an anomalous state of knowledge,[7] and the search process begins with a problem and a need to solve the problem. The information need is one of the reasons for seeking information and approaching an information-retrieval system.[8] Information seeking is a dynamic, recursive, iterative process[9] that incorporates a user's experience of interactive thoughts, actions, and feelings in the process of construction.[10] Marchionini identifies six main factors as influencing information seeking, including the information seeker (his/her cognitive ability, experience, affective states, etc.); domain knowledge, task characteristics, system capabilities, setting or environment where information-seeking activities take place, and search outcomes.[11] Many of these factors were taken into account in studies of children's Web research.

CHILDREN'S WEB SEARCHES

Tasks, Success, and Strategies

A few researchers have investigated the structure or nature of search tasks on children's information seeking and success. In a three-part research project, Bilal studied children's behavior in using Yahooligans!, a Web search engine and directory that is specifically designed for children ages 7-12, to locate information for three tasks: one fully assigned fact-finding task, one fully assigned research-oriented task, and one fully self-generated task.[12] Fully assigned tasks have both the main topic and aspects of the topic imposed on the user. Fully self-generated tasks have both the main topic and an aspect of it selected by the user. Twenty-two middle school children participated in the project. The science teacher at the school assigned both the fact-finding and research-oriented tasks. For the former, children had to find the correct answer about "the age of alligators in the wild and in captivity." For the latter, they had to locate relevant information about "the depletion of the ozone layer and its impact on forests." Children chose topics of interest to pursue for the fully self-generated task. Children's information seeking was examined from the cognitive, physical, and affective perspectives. Factors analyzed from the cognitive perspective included search moves, browse moves and success; those from the physical perspective covered backtracking moves (use of the Netscape Back command), looping moves (revisiting previously retrieved hyperlinks and/or repeating search moves), total Web moves, and average time taken to complete each task. The author found that children's cognitive and physical behaviors varied by task and success levels. Children made more keyword searches on the fact-based task than the other two tasks. They made a higher number of natural language queries on the fact-based task (35 percent) than on the other two tasks (21 percent) combined. Using single concepts in search statements was the most common strategy followed by combined concepts and natural language. Most single- and two-concept searches that children used were appropriate to the topics sought, but not all yielded relevant information. This was mainly due to the poor structure of keyword searching employed in the engine. Misspelling was minimal on the three tasks, although errors of this type occurred more often on the fully self-generated task (by 13 percent) than on the other two tasks (4 percent) combined. Seventy-three percent succeeded on the fully self-generated task and 50 percent did so on the fact-based task. Sixty-nine percent partially succeeded on the research-oriented task (found information on one of its facets). The variation in success rate needs to be interpreted with caution. On the fully self-generated task, children selected topics of interest to them and were given the option to modify them in case they did not find information or if they decided to pursue new aspects of the topics. In addition, the researcher and the school librarian mediated the topics children selected and assisted them in formulating a focus to pursue. Subsequently, self-interest, flexibility in topic selection and modification, and topic mediation influenced children's success rate on this task. Overall, they browsed appropriate subject categories and visited appropriate sites, indicating good understanding of the topics of the three tasks. They were more successful when they browsed than when they searched by keyword mainly due to the poor structure of keyword searching in Yahooligans! Children backtracked and looped searches and hyperlinks most frequently on the fact-based task. They also took more time to complete this task (15.78 minutes) than the fully self-generated task (14.35 minutes) and the research-oriented task (10.42 minutes). Typically, research-based tasks take longer to complete than fact-based tasks due to their complexity and multifaceted nature, but this study revealed otherwise. One explanation for this finding is that on the first day of the experiment, when children performed the fact-based task, they were unfamiliar with Yahooligans! and did not have adequate skills to navigate its space. Although they gained some skills in using the search engine by the time they performed the research task, they sought specific answers to it rather than developing an understanding of the information found. The fact that most children did not go beyond the first or second page of text to locate information for this task and stopped the search process sooner than they should have influenced the amount of time they spent online. Regardless of the nature of the tasks, success levels, and time online, however, when children did not find information under specific terms, they either entered a synonym or repeated the same terms. There were instances when a few children found relevant sites, deviated from them, explored other sites, came back to the initial sites they had visited, spent little time examining content pages, and shifted back and forth between sites and content pages aimlessly. When keyword searching failed, children resorted to browsing subject categories as an alternative strategy to recover from information-retrieval problems. Schacter, Chung, and Dorr also examined the effect of task characteristics on performance in using the Web.[13] Using one open-ended task (research) and one closed task (fact-finding), they found that children were significantly more successful on the open task than the closed task. Thirty out of thirty-two children located relevant information on the former, as opposed to two out of thirty-two children who did so on the latter. Children found the closed task more difficult than the open-ended task. This finding is not surprising since closed tasks require the command of highly skilled search strategies to locate the prescribed answers. Children browsed more than searched by keyword on both tasks and employed more keyword searches on the closed task as opposed to the open task. The authors observed that, in general, children were interactive searchers, but engaged in little planning when approaching the tasks. A handful of children, for example, used multiple synonyms to refine their queries, and none of them employed sophisticated search techniques, such as Boolean logic, proximity operators, or truncation. In addition, the authors observed that most children (twenty out of thirty-two) queried search engines using natural language (i.e., used questions as search arguments). Although this finding is not surprising since this behavior is typical of children's cognitive developmental ability, it implies the need for additional training. In fact, one should not expect these young users to utilize a search engine's advanced search techniques after being exposed to basic training, especially since the interface of Infoseek is not intended for elementary school children.

Exploration of Information-Seeking Behavior

Few studies examined children's behavior on the Web without testing the effect of any variables. Large, Beheshti, and Moukdad's study of fifty-three sixth graders in using Alta Vista and Infoseek reveals that children exhibited a high level of interactivity with the interfaces but at the expense of planning searches and evaluating results.[14] Children submitted a high number of keyword searches (375 during 78 sessions), for example, and employed more searches using phrases than single concepts. The authors observed that children did not fully grasp the significance of Boolean logic. Use of the AND operator, for example, was not applied when needed (only 22 times in 324 multiterm searches). Children browsed more than searched by keyword, backtracked frequently, were not prolific at paging through retrieved hits, did not plan search steps, and spent little time scanning pages, reading them, and evaluating them. Again, this study reveals that children operate at their cognitive developmental ability level. The fact that they used search engines that had complex interfaces and advanced content knowledge may have influenced their information-seeking behavior.

Agosto investigated Simon's behavioral decision-making theories of bounded rationality and satisficing of twenty-two tenth- and ninth-grade girls in using the Web.[15] She found that participants operated under "bounded rationality" when making decisions, meaning that they dealt with information overload by using reduction and termination methods. They returned to known sites and scanned site synopses (reduction), and used the first acceptable option as the major decision-making stop rule (termination). Stopping also occurred as a result of discomfort, boredom, and time limit. The results of this study shed a new light on understanding young users' behavior on the Web as it provided an explanation of their rationale for selecting hyperlinks and terminating the search process when faced with information overload.

Bilal examined middle school students' interaction with Yahooligans! to locate information about a research task on "diet and dieting."[16] She found that children's search strategies were far from adequate. They either employed very broad or very specific terms in search arguments (e.g., education, the name of their school, respectively). Most of the activities they performed accounted for keyword searching. Children employed single concepts, two concepts, multiple concepts (up to four), and natural language in search statements. When they did not find the desired information, they either repeated keyword searches or initiated new ones. They quickly viewed the returned hit list, scrolled the display screens a third or halfway, and examined the results minimally. Based on the results they printed and submitted, the author concluded that children were most likely seeking specific answers to the task than developing understanding of the information found. Their inability to distinguish between research and fact-based tasks seemed to be related to an inadequate level of research skills, a factor that was not explored in this study. Wallace, Kupperman, and Krajcik found similar results in their study of sixth graders' use of the Web.[17] They observed that children spent most of their time conducting searches (76 percent) and examined results only 24 percent of the time. In addition, they employed Boolean incorrectly, moved too quickly from one page to another, scrolled down pages too fast, went back to searching without scrolling through the hit lists, and performed a few off-task surfing episodes. Children utilized repetitive keywords for searching, did not consider the feedback from search engines to improve their results, and had problems narrowing and broadening searches. In a few instances, they changed topics and searched using a new set of keywords. Children backtracked exclusively to navigate among the Web pages they retrieved. The fact that the Web encourages exploration and discovery at the expense of planning search steps and evaluating results may have contributed to children's behavior. It is possible that children were more interested in using the Web as an end in itself than completing the task successfully.

Hirsh explored the relevance criteria and search strategies of ten fifth graders in using electronic sources, including the Web.[18] She observed that children had little concern for the authority of textual and graphical information they found, spent most of their time finding pictures, and relied heavily on the Web for their research as opposed to other resources (print, CD-ROM). Children rarely examined the pages they retrieved and only a few questioned the accuracy of the information they found. Kafai and Bates found similar results in their study of elementary school children's interaction with the Internet.[19] They also discovered that it was difficult for younger children (grades 1-4) to evaluate Web sites and write annotations, and that they were unable to articulate their preference for specific sites. Younger children needed more guidance than older ones. Overall, children did not explore text-only sites often; preferred sites with high visual content and short, simple textual content, and liked to see more animation and interactivity on the Internet. In all cases, children were motivated to use the Internet and seeing their projects online fueled their enthusiasm.

Perceptions and Affective Dimensions

A handful of studies assessed children's perceptions of using the Web. Watson collected stories of nine eighth-grade students about their experiences with using technology, especially the Web.[20] A sense of confidence, a voice of authority with use of technology, independence, ease of access, finding current information quickly, ability to browse, joy in finding information, patience, motivation, and positive attitudes were themes that emerged from talking with the children. A few students believed in skimming text as a reading strategy to cover as much material as possible. Handling the information overload that is associated with lack of relevance was an issue for the students. Although the positive attitudes and self-confidence the students exhibited provided interesting dimensions of their perception of the Internet, they are not indicative of their information-seeking behavior or success in finding information. Children's positive and negative perceptions of using the Web were confirmed by another researcher who found that children liked using the Web, as they felt challenged and had a sense of increased self-confidence in finding information.[21] Ease of use over print sources, ability to employ keyword searching, availability of different Web sites to find the information, access to graphics, and fun were reasons for liking the Web. Negative perceptions alluded to children's inability to find relevant information easily, time to load pages, deep subject hierarchies, and information retrieval problems. In another study, Bilal assessed children's preference for the tasks they performed on the Web and asked them about reasons for their preference.[22] Of the 67 percent who articulated their preference, 47 percent mentioned the fully self-generated task, 20 percent favored the research-oriented task, and another 20 percent liked the fact-finding task. Twenty-seven percent of those who preferred the fully self-generated task mentioned the ability to find what they need and their satisfaction with the results. The researcher concluded that children's satisfaction with search results were more important to them than selecting their own topics. Large and Beheshti assessed middle school students' perception of the quality and quantity of textual and image information on the Web versus print sources.[23] They found that children had difficulty finding relevant information and encountered information overload that required sifting through a high number of hits. Children did recognize the value of the Web in terms of finding up-to-date information, information of little interest that may not be available in books, speed in locating information, and availability of color images, but found it harder to use than print sources.

The fact that children preferred print sources to using the Web is not surprising, especially since Alta Vista and Infoseek did not employ subject categories at the time of this study. This means that children were forced to use keyword searching to find the information sought. The fact that these engines employed complex interfaces and advanced vocabulary that were not designed for middle school students may have contributed to the difficulties children experienced.

Gender Effect on Search and Browse Behaviors

Little is known about the effect of gender on children's information-seeking behavior and success in using the Web. Large, Beheshti, and Rahman's investigation of middle school students' use of Alta Vista and Infoseek discovered significant differences between male and female students in relation to searching and browsing strategies.[24] They observed that groups of boys entered a lower number of keywords per search than groups of girls, and that boys used more single keywords in search statements than girls. Groups of girls employed more natural language queries than groups of boys and spent more time examining the content pages they visited. Concurrent with these findings, Schacter, Chung, and Dorr uncovered significant differences between male and female students' browsing and searching strategies on two tasks—one closed and one open-ended.[25] Boys browsed significantly more than girls on both tasks and performed more keyword searches on the closed task than girls. Girls made more keyword searches on the open-ended task than boys, a finding that is supported by Wallace and colleagues.[26] In all of these studies, male and female children worked within same-sex groups, and their preference for individual versus collaborative work was not explored. Studies that examine individual versus collaborative work preference for male and females in using the Web are needed, especially since prior research[27] reveals that boys preferred to work alone and to have control over the computer keyboard or mouse, whereas girls favored working in groups and enjoyed interacting with each other.

Children and the Design of Web Search Engines

One of the purposes of conducting user studies is to identify system design improvements that are needed to support children's information-seeking behavior and success in using the Web. A few researchers have begun to move their research to the system design stage. Bilal involved eleven middle school children in designing prototype interfaces for search engines that met their needs.[28] Using paper, pencil, and crayons, children drew good interfaces with layouts, search instructions, colors, and subject categories, and articulated functionality and visual design criteria needed to support these interfaces. Functionality referred to search, browse, and navigation features, and visual design concerned color, attractiveness, and the names of the engines. A group of researchers elicited children's design criteria for improving Yahooligans!, Ask Jeeves for Kids, KidsClick!, and Lycos Zone as a first step toward designing interfaces for them.[29] Children critiqued these engines and made nine visual design and seven information architecture criteria. Visual design included the name of the engine, color, fonts, graphics, animation, characterization, vocabulary, screen layout, and advertisements. Information architecture covered directness, keyword versus natural language searching, subject categories, metasearch links, display, help facilities, and spell-checking techniques.

METHODOLOGY

Quantitative and qualitative inquiry methods were employed in these studies. Quantitative methods provide empirical data and analyze specific variables to answer research questions; whereas qualitative methods do not depend on the measurement of any variables. When both methods are employed, data generated from qualitative methods can explain data derived from quantitative methods. Each of these methods uses specific techniques for data collection. Online capturing, Web logs, surveys, videotaping, and audiotaping have been employed in quantitative methods; whereas interviews and focus groups were used in qualitative methods. Bilal captured children's Web activities by using Lotus ScreenCam software package.[30] She gathered children's perceptions of using Yahooligans!, affective states, task preference, and experience in using the Web through a questionnaire and individual interviews. Schacter and colleagues used a URL logger to track every student's Web activities from task initiation to completion.[31] Some investigators relied on video and audio records to collect data. Wallace and colleagues captured video outputs from the computer screen for every pair of students and audio taped the students' conversations during their time online.[32] Large, Beheshti, and Moukdad utilized a similar method, but added a questionnaire instrument to elicit children's computer literacy experience and a test to gather information about their familiarity with the Web.[33] In another study, Large and Beheshti relied on structured interviews to assess middle school students' perceptions of the quality and quantity of information on the Web.[34] Watson employed a phenomenological approach to collect children's stories about their perceptions of using technology, including the Web.[35] She examined a single student story and analyzed a collection of stories to extract themes about their thoughts and feelings in using technology. Agosto used focus groups and audio taped the participants' interviews to collect data about their Web use.[36]

MEASUREMENT OF CHILDREN'S INFORMATION-SEEKING BEHAVIOR AND SUCCESS

Not all studies employed measures to assess children's information-seeking behavior and success in finding information. Bilal developed the *Web Traversal Measure*, a formula that quantified the effectiveness, efficiency, and quality of children's Web moves.[37] In addition, she used three success measures to evaluate children's performance on the three tasks they performed in Yahooligans! On the fact-finding task, children were judged to be fully successful if they located and extracted the correct answer to both facets of the task (i.e., age of alligators in the wild and age in captivity). They were judged to be partially successful if they found the answer to one of the facets (i.e., age of alligators in the wild or age in captivity). They were considered unsuccessful if they did not find the correct answer or if they submitted irrelevant information. On the research-oriented task, subject experts judged children's success based on the results they submitted.[38] Children were considered fully successful if they submitted either the whole text about "the depletion of the ozone layer," or a few pages about one facet of the topic (e.g., the impact of ozone depletion on forests). They were judged to be partially successful if they gave one of the pages about the topic; otherwise, they were deemed unsuccessful. On the fully self-generated task, children were judged to be successful if they found any relevant information about their topic of interest; otherwise, they were considered unsuccessful.[39] Schacter and colleagues collaborated with experts to judge children's performance on closed and open-ended tasks.[40] They developed an instrument for judging both students' and experts' bookmarked documents on a five-point scale that included six items: usefulness, truth, depth, practicality, helpfulness, and relevance. The authors calculated relevance scores for both students and experts in three ways: the highest single bookmark score by task, the lowest single bookmark by task, and cumulative averaged scores for all bookmarks by task.

Web Experience, Domain Knowledge, and Success

Marchionini describes experience and domain knowledge as important factors that influence information seeking.[41] However, a few researchers examined these variables. Bilal tested the effect of children's prior experience in using the Web and Yahooligans! on their success in finding information.[42] She detected a low correlation ($r = .22$; $p = .05$) between these two variables, a finding that should be used as a base for further investigation. Large, Beheshti, and Moukdad explored children's prior Web experience but did not test its effect on their information-seeking behavior or performance.[43] Bilal also tested the effect of domain knowledge, topic knowledge, and reading ability on children's success, but found no significant relationship between success and any of the three variables.[44]

Search and Browse Behavior Measures

Researchers employed a variety of measures to examine children's Web searching behavior, including use of single keywords, multiple keywords, natural language, misspelling, Boolean use, and looping or repetition of keyword.[45] Browse measures included the number of hyperlinks and content pages visited and the clicking on a browser's command features, such as Back, Forward, Stop, and so forth. A few researchers calculated the number of unique pages children visited, the number of pages children visited and looped (revisited), and the number of URL changes they made.[46] One researcher calculated the ratio of children's navigation, content pages examination, screen scrolling, and appropriateness of hyperlinks and content pages visited.[47] A few researchers calculated the time taken to complete tasks by using average time online, total minutes online, and/or time spent on each page visited.[48]

IMPLICATIONS FOR FURTHER RESEARCH

The investigation of children's information-seeking behavior and success in using the Web has advanced our knowledge of how children use this technology tool within a short period of time and indicated the level of maturity of this field of study. Compared to Web literature that has focused on adult users' information-seeking behavior,[49] however, this literature falls behind in that it lacks a model that represents children's information-seeking behavior on the Web. It is suggested that researchers consolidate their research findings to develop such a model. Testing existing models of adult users' information seeking on the Web to determine their goodness of fit may be a first step toward developing this model.

Very little is known about children's role in the design of Web search engines. Researchers should consider moving their user studies to the system-design stage so they can design effective interfaces for search engines that meet children's information needs and support their behavior. Although many factors that influence information seeking have been taken into account in children's Web research, attention should be given to additional factors, such as cognitive style, navigational style, mental models, Web experience, domain and topic knowledge, reading ability, level of research skills, and academic achievement.

Challenges to Children's Web Research

Research involving children poses many challenges. Children are information seekers with needs and development characteristics that vary from those of adults.[50] Cognitive developmental ability, memory and recall levels, emotional, social, and physical developments are factors that influence children's interaction with various information-retrieval systems, including the Web. Children are not "small adults" but an entirely different user population with their own culture, norms, complexities, curiosities, interests, abilities, and information needs. Therefore, researchers need to develop a good understanding of and sensitivity toward the needs of these young users when they involve them in research projects. When researchers test children's use of advanced search engines (e.g., Google, Alta Vista, Infoseek), they should pilot-test their studies and expose children to effective training prior to using the complex interfaces of these engines. It highly recommended that researchers examine children's behavior and success in using search engines that are specifically designed for their age group so that they provide them with positive learning experiences. Through such endeavors, researchers would be able to suggest system design improvements that would support children's use of these engines.

Adherence to federal regulations that require the review of research that involves children by an institutional review board (IRB) prior to beginning a research project can be challenging due to the amount of paperwork required and time needed for securing approval. Although regulation is important to protect children from any harm that may be inflicted upon them during their participation in research projects, its complexity may hinder many researchers from involving them in their research endeavors. Much research is still needed about children's information seeking on the Web, and it is hoped that researchers continue their contribution to this field of study.

CONCLUSION

Research of children's use of the Web began in 1997, two years after research of adult users' interaction with the Web had begun. Between 1997 and 2002, children's Web research has grown rapidly, although not at the same pace as Web research that focused on adults. Researchers drew on earlier studies of children's use of CD-ROM and online public access catalogs (OPACs) to investigate information seeking on the Web. They employed a variety of methods to gather data, including online capturing techniques, Web logs, interviews, audiotaping, videotaping, and focus groups. Measures of children's information-seeking behavior were adequately covered, but measures of their success in finding information deserve further attention. Similarly, the effect of task characteristics on children's information seeking and success was examined minimally and, therefore, requires additional study. The next step for researchers is to examine new factors such as cognitive style, mental models, and navigational style and their influence on children's information seeking and success in using the Web. In addition, they should pay more attention to children's level of research skills, academic achievement, and reading ability when investigating their information seeking and success. Research that focuses on children as designers of interfaces for Web search engines and that models children's information-seeking behavior on the Web remains a fruitful area of investigation.

NOTES

1. Ronald D. Owston, "The World Wide Web: A technology to enhance teaching and learning?," *Educational Researcher* 26, no. 2 (1997): 27–33.
2. Pew Internet Project, "Search engines are an indispensable utility for Internet users," *Pew Internet and American Life*, 2002, available at http://www.pewinternet.org/reports/reports.asp?Report=64 (accessed August 14, 2002).
3. Pew Internet Project, "The Internet and education: Findings of the Pew Internet and American Life Project," 2001, available at http://www.pewinternet.org/reports/toc.asp?Report=39 (accessed August 14, 2002).
4. Dania Bilal and Joe Kirby, "Differences and similarities in information seeking on the Web: Children and adults as Web users," *Information Processing and Management* 38, no. 5 (2002): 649–670; David F. Bjorklund, *Children's thinking: Developmental function and individual differences* (Stamford, Conn.: Wadsworth, 2000); Robert S. Siegler, *Children's thinking* (Englewood Cliffs, N.J.: Prentice-Hall, 1998); Jean Piaget and Barbel Inhelder, *The psychology of the child* (New York: Basic Books, 1969).

5. Dania Bilal, "Web search engines for children: A comparative study and performance evaluation of Yahooligans!, Ask Jeeves for Kids, and Super Snooper," *Proceedings of the 62nd ASIS annual meeting*, Washington, D.C., October 31–November 4, 1999, 70–82; Andrew Large, Jamshid Beheshti, and Tarjin Rahman, "Design criteria for children's Web portals: The users speak out," *Journal of the American Society for Information Science and Technology* 53, no. 2 (2002): 79–94.

6. Gary Marchionini, *Information seeking in electronic environments* (New York: Cambridge University Press, 1995).

7. Nicholas J. Belkin, R. N. Oddy, and H. M. Brooks, "ASK for information retrieval: Part I. Background and history," *Journal of Documentation* 38, no. 2 (1982): 61–71.

8. Tefko Saracevic and Paul Kantor, "A study of information seeking and retrieving. II. Users, questions, and effectiveness," *Journal of American Society for Information Science* 39, no. 3 (1988a): 177–196.

9. Belkin, Oddy, and Brooks, "ASK for information retrieval"; Marcia J. Bates, "The berry-picking search: User interface design," in M. Dillon, ed., *Interface for information retrieval and online systems* (New York: Greenwood, 1991), 55–61.

10. Carol C. Kuhlthau, *Seeking meaning: A process approach to library and information services* (Norwood, N.J.: Ablex, 1993); Diane Nahl, "Ethnography of novices' first use of Web search engines: Affective control in cognitive processing," *Internet Reference Services Quarterly* 3 (1998): 51–72.

11. Marchionini, *Information seeking in electronic environments*.

12. Dania Bilal, "Children's use of the Yahooligans! Web search engine. II. Cognitive and Physical Behaviors on Research Tasks," *Journal of the American Society for Information Science and Technology* 52, no. 2 (2001): 118–136; Dania Bilal, "Children's use of the Yahooligans! Web search engine. I. Cognitive, physical, and affective behaviors on fact-based search tasks," *Journal of the American Society for Information Science* 51, no. 7 (2000): 646–665; Dania Bilal, "Children's use of the Yahooligans! Web search engine, III. cognitive and physical behaviors on fully self-generated tasks," *Journal of the American Society for Information Science and Technology* 53, no. 13 (2002): 1170–1183.

13. John Schacter, Gregory K. W. K Chung, and Aimee Dorr, "Chil-

dren's Internet searching on complex problems: Performance and process analyses," *Journal of the American Society for Information Science* 49, no. 9 (1998): 840–849.

14. Andrew Large, Jamshid Beheshti, and Haidar Moukdad, "Information seeking on the Web: Navigational skills of grade-six primary school students," proceedings of the 62nd ASIS annual meeting, Washington, D.C., October 1999, 84–97.

15. Denise E. Agosto, "Bounded rationality and satisficing in young people's Web-based decision making," *Journal of the American Society for Information Science and Technology* 53, no. 1 (2002): 16–27.

16. Dania Bilal, "Children's search processes in using World Wide Web search engines: An exploratory study," proceedings of the 61st ASIS annual meeting, Pittsburgh, October 1998, 45–53.

17. Raven M. Wallace, Jeff Kupperman, and Joseph Krajcik, "Science on the Web: Students on-line in a sixth-grade classroom," *Journal of the Learning Sciences* 9, no. 1 (2000): 75–104.

18. Sandra G. Hirsh, "Children's relevance criteria and information seeking on electronic resources," *Journal of the American Society for Information Science* 50, no. 14 (1999): 1265–1283.

19. Yasmine Kafai and Marcia J. Bates, "Internet Web-searching instruction in the elementary classroom: Building a foundation for information literacy," *School Library Media Quarterly* 25, no. 2 (1998): 103–111.

20. Jinx S. Watson, "If you don't have it, you can't find it: A close look at students' perceptions of using technology," *Journal of the American Society for Information Science* 49, no. 11 (1998): 1024–1036.

21. Bilal, "Children's use of the Yahooligans! Web search engine. I."

22. Bilal, "Children's use of the Yahooligans! Web search engine, III."

23. Andrew Large and Jamshid Beheshti, "The Web as a classroom resource: Reactions from the users," *Journal of the American Society for Information Science* 51, no. 12 (2000): 1069–1080.

24. Andrew Large, Jamshid Beheshti, and Tarjin Rahman, "Design criteria for children's Web portals: The users speak out," *Journal of the American Society for Information Science and Technology* 53, no. 2 (2002): 79–94.

25. Schater, Chung, and Dorr, "Children's Internet searching on complex problems."

26. Wallace, Kupperman, and Krajcik, "Science on the Web."

27. S. Martin, "Internet use in the classroom," *Social Science Computer Review* 18, no. 4 (1998): 411–418.

28. Dania Bilal, "Children design their interfaces for Web search engines: A participatory approach," *Proceedings of the 30th annual conference of the Canadian Association for Information Science*, Toronto, Canada, May 30, 2002, 204–214; Dania Bilal, "Draw and tell: Children as designers of Web interfaces," in review, *Proceedings of the American Society for Information Science and Technology Meeting*, Long Beach, Calif., October 2003).

29. Large, Beheshti, and Rahman, "Design criteria for children's Web portals."

30. Bilal, "Children's use of the Yahooligans! Web search engine. I"; "Children's use of the Yahooligans! Web search engine. II"; "Children's use of the Yahooligans! Web search engine, III."

31. Schacter, Chung, and Dorr, "Children's Internet searching on complex problems."

32. Wallace, Kupperman, and Krajcik, "Science on the Web."

33. Large, Beheshti, and Moukdad, "Information seeking on the Web."

34. Large and Beheshti, "The Web as a classroom resource."

35. Watson, "If you don't have it, you can't find it."

36. Agosto, "Bounded rationality and satisficing."

37. Bilal, "Children's use of the Yahooligans! Web search engine. I."

38. Bilal, "Children's use of the Yahooligans! Web search engine. II."

39. Bilal, "Children's use of the Yahooligans! Web search engine. III."

40. Schacter, Chung, and Dorr, "Children's Internet searching on complex problems."

41. Marchionini, *Information seeking in electronic environments*.

42. Bilal, "Children's use of the Yahooligans! Web search engine. I."

43. Large, Beheshti, and Moukdad, "Information seeking on the Web."

44. Bilal, "Children's use of the Yahooligans! Web search engine. I."

45. Bilal, "Children's use of the Yahooligans! Web search engine. I"; "Children's use of the Yahooligans! Web search engine. II"; "Children's use of the Yahooligans! Web search engine, III." ; Large, Beheshti, and

Moukdad, "Information seeking on the Web"; Wallace, Kupperman, and Krajcik, "Science on the Web." ; Schacter, Chung, and Dorr, "Children's Internet searching on complex problems."; Andrew Large, Jamshid Beheshti, and Tarjin Rahman, "Gender differences in collaborative Web searching behavior: An elementary school study," *Information Processing and Management* 38, no. 3 (2002b): 427–443.

46. Schacter, Chung, and Dorr, "Children's Internet searching on complex problems."; Wallace, Kupperman, and Krajcik, "Science on the Web."

47. Bilal, "Children's use of the Yahooligans! Web search engine. I"; "Children's use of the Yahooligans! Web search engine. II"; "Children's use of the Yahooligans! Web search engine, III."

48. Wallace, Kupperman, and Krajcik, "Science on the Web"; Bilal, "Children's use of the Yahooligans! Web search engine. I"; "Children's use of the Yahooligans! Web search engine. II"; "Children's use of the Yahooligans! Web search engine, III" ; Large, Beheshti, and Moukdad, "Information seeking on the Web."

49. Ingrid Hsieh-Yee, "Research on Web search nehavior," *Library Information Science Research* 23 (2001): 167–185.

50. Bilal and Kirby, "Differences and similarities in information seeking"; Bjorklund, *Children's thinking*; Siegler, *Children's thinking*; Piaget and Inhelder, *The psychology of the child.*

ELEVEN

Information Seeking on the Web by Elementary School Students

Andrew Large

In a very short space of time the Web has become an important source of information for students in elementary schools just as in other academic environments. This development has been fostered by several factors. The first factor is the general societal fascination with the Web and the opportunities it offers for finding information as well as providing entertainment. Second, schools and individual classrooms in many countries are now equipped with workstations and linked to information-service providers, in some cases by high-speed connections. Third, a growing amount of information directly intended to support elementary school students in their class assignments is available on the Web. Perhaps the slowest condition to emerge has been a significant proportion of elementary school teachers who themselves are cognizant of the Web's educational potential and knowledgeable enough to exploit it, but increasingly this is also being met. There can be little doubt of students' willingness to exploit this new information resource.

Despite the intrusion of the Web into daily classroom life, it represents an information resource that cannot be effectively exploited without considerable difficulty by the students themselves.

A growing number of studies point to the multifarious obstacles strewn in the path of the young information seeker. The Web is a milieu that has evolved implicitly with adults rather than young users in mind, and attempts by elementary school students to mine its rich resources frequently are met with frustration, if not failure. This chapter focuses on these obstacles as well as the means to surmount or at least reduce them.

The focus here is on the information-seeking behavior of children in elementary schools, based on practice in North America, meaning students in grades 1 through 6 and generally between six and twelve years of age. Children at a very tender age can now be found using the Web; the daughter of a colleague, for example, was a cybernaut (with help from her parents) by the age of two, long before even starting kindergarten. Nevertheless, it seems probable that a majority of Web users in elementary schools are in grade 3 or higher, and in fact most studies of the information-seeking behavior of elementary school students have been confined to those in grades 5 and 6. They have also been conducted mainly in schools teaching through the medium of English; although my own studies in fact have been undertaken in schools that teach roughly half the curriculum in French. The majority of the students spoke English at home, and my studies were undertaken in the English segment of the school day to collect English-language information for English-language school assignments. These age and language qualifications should be borne in mind throughout the following discussion.

This restriction to elementary school students excludes a number of important studies of the information-seeking behavior of middle school students such as those by Bilal (1999, 2000, 2001, 2002a, and 2002b), Bilal and Kirby (2002) and Watson (1998), and high school students such as those studied by Fidel et al. (1999) and Lazonder, Biemans, and Wopereis (2000).

STUDIES OF INFORMATION-SEEKING IN DIGITAL ENVIRONMENTS

The emergence in the mid-1980s of digital information resources of potential use to school students prompted a growing volume of studies directed at children's information-seeking behavior in digital environments. Initially these environments comprised online public access catalogs (OPACs) (Borgman, Hirsh, and Walter, 1995; Hirsh, 1995, 1997; Solomon, 1993) and CD-ROMs (Marchionini, 1989; Perzylo and Oliver, 1992; Stevenson, 1993; Large, Beheshti, Breuleux, and Renaud, 1994; Large, Beheshti and Breuleux, 1998). But the extension of the Web into schools soon prompted a new generation of information-seeking studies that focused on the specific issues involved in searching such an enormous and nonspecialized information store.

The studies themselves can be divided into two major categories: those conducted experimentally under laboratory conditions, and those conducted operationally under field conditions (Large and Beheshti, 1999). Each category offers its own advantages and disadvantages. In the experimental approach, research problems are formed as testable hypotheses. The researchers strive to ensure as much control as possible over participants' environment and to minimize interference from external factors. They assign specific tasks to be completed. Data are collected systematically for subsequent analysis, often using statistical significance tests.

A good example of such an experimental study of children's information-seeking behavior on the Web is that conducted by Schacter, Chung, and Dorr (1998). They asked the teachers to select thirty-two grade 5 and 6 students (half male and half female) to represent a heterogeneous sample of academic ability. The students were given two search tasks—one well-defined and the other ill-defined—and both tasks were examined and validated by four experts in educational psychology. The students were allotted twenty-five minutes to complete each task. All mouse clicks and pages visited were tracked using a computer program to compile a search log. The researchers formulated five hypotheses related to information-seeking performance that would be tested in the experiment. Such an experimental approach offers control over at least some of the variables (number, gender and academic ability of students, the task, search duration, and so forth).

A potential problem when employing an experimental approach is that the subjects may lack motivation to undertake an artificially assigned task. Hirsh (1999) notes that the nature of the search assignment may impact student performance and motivation. Students who are searching for information to do a genuine class assignment may have higher motivation than those performing an artificial search established by the researchers. On the other hand, it has to be said that children perhaps are more accustomed to carrying out tasks on the instructions of others—teachers and parents principally—and lack of direct motivation cannot be assumed to affect their behavior adversely in all experimental research undertaken with them.

In contrast, operational research emphasizes the real environment, viewing the world from the actor's own frame of reference. Its techniques include interviews and participant observation. The subjects look for information they actually need for their own purposes. It gathers data on how people actually function. For example, students may be seeking information to help them complete a real class assignment designed by their teachers and not the researchers. It also facilitates longitudinal studies over a length of time that might be more realistic in terms of students' actual use of the Web.

Large, Beheshti, and Moukdad (1999) provide an example of operational research undertaken in a grade 6 classroom. Rather than select an identified sample of students, all fifty-three members of two classes participated in the study. Three computers, together with telephone jacks, were installed in the classroom, and the students used them over several weeks to find information for a class project. The teacher chose the project after discussions with the researchers. Screen activity was directly captured on video for subsequent analysis, which enabled the researchers to monitor the students as they looked for information they needed to complete their projects. At the same time, the researchers had to accept the teachers' requirement that the students would work in groups of three at the computer but hand in individual assignments. Consequently, it was hard to relate joint searches to individually produced output on the posters. The students themselves chose their group collaborators, so it was impossible for the researchers to control group makeup for gender or academic ability. In such an operational environment the researchers gain a naturalistic environment, but the price paid is some loss of control.

Bowler, Large, and Rejskind (2001) examined the information-seeking behavior of one group of these students using a case study approach. This enabled them to examine in much greater detail the activities of the group over a series of search sessions. In this case, however, the researchers must be wary of making sweeping generalizations from a specific, bounded phenomenon.

Most studies have differentiated between searching for information by means of a proprietary search engine—whether the engine has been specifically developed with children in mind—and browsing for information by means of subject categories (directories) or by following hyperlinked information trails. Each information-seeking approach poses its own challenges to Web users—adult or child—and they will be discussed here separately.

SEARCHING THE WEB

In order to search for information on the Web, the searcher must be able to encapsulate the information need into a query, which is then submitted to a search engine. Most search engines expect the query to take the form of one or more keywords that collectively express the information need in such a way that they are likely to match with the words used in potentially relevant Web pages. A few search engines, however, are designed to accept complete sentence queries rather than keywords.

In order to facilitate meaningful matches between keywords and Web pages, search engines provide an array of advanced tools and techniques that can be applied should the user so elect. These include Boolean operators to combine keywords in various relationships, phrase searching, adjacency searching, word truncation, differentiation between regular and proper nouns, media specification (sound or video clips, for example), and so on. How frequently and how successfully do young Web users employ such tools and techniques?

Kafai and Bates (1997) are unusual in that they worked with students in all grades of elementary school, including the youngest children. Students in grades 1 and 2 were not expected to enter keyword searches; instead they were shown how to enter URLs to find sites that had already been identified as relevant by their teachers. Even this proved unrealistic, however, as the children encountered difficulties in accurately typing complicated URLs. The solution was for teachers to bookmark the sites beforehand so that the students need only click on the bookmarks to access the pages. Older students in grades 3 and 4 still needed a lot of help from the teacher, who gave them a specific site to visit and evaluate, but the more "advanced" among the students were encouraged to use search engines to find additional information. By grade 5 the students were able to learn and practice a lot of search skills, and were capable of finding resources on the Web, and the grade 6 students were the most sophisticated searchers, employing techniques like Boolean term linking to improve search results.

Most studies of elementary school students have been undertaken in the fifth and sixth grades. Although students typically exhibit an enthusiasm for searching, they encounter many technical problems. Schachter, Chung, and Dorr (1998) found that children did not systematically plan or use elaborate analytic search strategies—overwhelmingly they employed browsing strategies (see below). No child in their study used Boolean operators, adjacency operators, exact term searching, or truncation. Hirsh (1999) reports similar findings from her study; the grade 5 students generally did not use any of the search refinement features offered by the search engine. They failed to keep track of previous search strategies and typically started each search anew.

In another study (Large, Beheshti, and Moukdad, 1999), also it was found that the grade 6 students did not greatly use the various search refinement features available on Alta Vista (the engine mainly employed) such as Boolean operators, and when such features were used it was often done incorrectly or inappropriately. Nevertheless, this did not encourage the students to seek online help: in the 78 sessions lasting a total of 2,041 minutes online help was requested just once! Although the students favored multiword queries by a factor of almost seven over single-word queries, they commented upon their problems in selecting suitable search terms (Large and Beheshti, 2000b). Bowler, Large, and Rejskind (2001) noted the many dead ends that the grade 6 students encountered. In some cases the students found new but irrelevant information as their searches progressed; in other cases they simply looped back to previously viewed pages. They had a tendency to enter the same query several consecutive times despite its lack of success. Search terms were entered at high speed, with very little time for thought or discussion between the group members. Little search strategy planning was in evidence.

The findings of Wallace, Kupperman, and Krajcik (2000) are similar to those of Bowler, Large, and Rejskind (2001). Most of the students used multiple rather than single keywords for each search, and they also tended to recycle these keywords in multiple search attempts. They did not assess their search as it progressed and thus could not systematically refine their strategies. The researchers often viewed students' search behaviors as random. Wallace and his colleagues (2000) also report little use of any help features provided by the search engine.

It might be assumed that children would respond more positively to a search engine that encourages complete sentence queries, thereby avoiding the need to express queries as keywords. In the study by Schacter, Chung, and Dorr (1998), twenty of the thirty-two children chose to enter full-sentence queries rather than keywords, even though the latter was expected by the search engine—for example, "What are the three most common crimes in California?" In four focus groups with children between the ages of ten and thirteen, students were asked to evaluate one search engine designed to receive queries in complete sentence form—Ask Jeeves for Kids. From their comments it would appear that the idea of being able to enter natural-language queries would be attractive to them, but its realization in Ask Jeeves for Kids generally was not greeted enthusiastically (Large, Beheshti, and Rahman, 2002a). In particular they disliked being presented with a set of questions rather than immediately receiving answers. Clearly they were not happy about engaging in a kind of "reference interview" with the portal.

Many studies have found that a major cause of search failure is misspelling of query terms by the children. Kuntz (1999), for example, reports that failed searches on one kids' portal, KidsClick, were most often attributed to this problem. For this reason, several kids' portals include either spell checking or provide an online dictionary. In fact, in our studies we have found little evidence of spelling errors, but it should be noted that we have worked with the oldest class in elementary school, and also in our research the students have normally worked in groups where there are several pairs of eyes to spot any spelling mistakes.

BROWSING THE WEB

Unlike searching, where the user must formulate a query to represent the information need, browsing relies upon recognition: here the user need only select a topic encapsulating the information need from a directory or menu of topics displayed on the screen, or follow hypertext links from place to place. Browsing, then, involves the user in less cognitive effort than searching. It also demands less subject knowledge on the user's part, as terms are recognized from a display rather than recalled from memory. It might therefore be assumed that young users in particular would be likely to favor browsing over searching. Is this the case?

Kafai and Bates (1997) found that children in all elementary grades, including the early grades, could learn to scroll through a site and use hyperlinks to other sites. In our longitudinal study of fifty-three grade 6 students seeking information from the Web to support a class assignment, the students undertook 761 browsing clicks on hypertext links and menus, compared with 375 searches. If use of the Back button is included as a browsing move, this adds a further 846 clicks—representing by far the most popular action. Browsing was clearly more utilized than searching. Wallace, Kupperman, and Krajcik (2000) also found that students used the Back button as their primary means of navigating. They were surprised, however, that students did not use hyperlinks more often. Although they made a lot of navigational moves, they did not go more than five links away from their latest list of search results. Rarely did they follow links within sites, and the researchers got the feeling that students "were tethered to the search engine on a short string."

INFORMATION ASSESSMENT

The Web constitutes such an enormous information store that even a sophisticated search is likely to retrieve for many topics a large number of sites. It is therefore important that information seekers have the ability to sort the wheat from the chaff—they must be able to make rapid, accurate relevance judgments on retrieved pages. But is this a skill that comes easily to children?

Hirsh (1999) reports that the fifth-grade students in her study developed various techniques for selecting pages from a large hit list. They relied upon summaries, followed by the opening paragraph. Wallace, Kupperman, and Krajcik (2000) found that the sixth-grade students they studied rarely read online, even when the information was relevant to their projects. The students in our focus groups (Large, Beheshti, and Rahman, 2002) made various suggestions as to how they might be aided in the task of selecting relevant hits. Some requested that the search engines restrict the number of displayed hits to no more than twenty. They asked for short but informative summaries. They also wanted relevance-ranking by the search engines, but coupled with categorization (for example, a search on "tigers" would separate pages dealing with the animal from pages dealing with the Detroit-based baseball team of that name).

Kafai and Bates (1997) found that the students could extract information for their school projects, but that selecting good sites was difficult. Titles and descriptions were sometimes misleading and difficult for children to evaluate. This problem was compounded by their reluctance to read or scan the list of results. The students observed by Wallace, Kupperman, and Krajcik (2000) most commonly evaluated hits by looking for words they expected to find in an answer to their question. They accepted the page as valuable if it contained those words. Like the students in other studies (Large, Beheshti, and Moukdad, 1999; Bowler, Large, and Rejskind, 2001), they failed to write down URLs or bookmark sites, so that they found the easiest way to go back to a page previously visited was to reproduce their search and retrace their steps. As Wallace and his colleagues comment, the students in their study treated the Web as a giant book with a table of contents and an index; they therefore tried to match the words in their initial question to the words in the text. They spent a lot of time navigating and little time on content, scrolling far too quickly to read the words on the page. Furthermore, they often did not even scroll through a list of the opening ten hits. Skimming is a useful research skill for children as much as adults, but on the Web, skimming can degenerate into such rapid movement that key information can easily be missed.

INFORMATION USE

Many students express frustration if they cannot find the precise information they are seeking. When consulting printed sources they are more familiar with, for example, an article in an encyclopedia, or a page in a book (via its index), they expect that the search will give them the kind of information they require for a class project, not only in terms of its content but also in its choice of vocabulary and literary style. The information has been processed and organized with their abilities and needs in mind. This, of course, is far from being the case on the Web. It is true that, in our research project, the students were left to roam the Web freely; they were not directed to specific sites either by their teachers or the researchers. But this was in keeping with their teacher's approach to printed material. It was not his practice to tell the students which precise pages, or even titles, to consult, but he left this information-seeking task to the students themselves. The difference is that in the case of printed materials the students, for practical purposes, were restricted to certain works by virtue of the fact that they did their research either in the school library or the children's section of the public library. Such an age categorization is not replicated on the Web; rather it is as if they had been left to browse the shelves of the Library of Congress! If children are to exploit Web resources, more attention must be devoted both to placing suitable material on the Web and offering signposts to it. It is regrettable if teachers deny students an opportunity to freely explore the information space by giving them a short list of sites to consult, but some sort of guidance other than "just look on the Web" seems necessary.

Kafai and Bates (1997), in their work with students in all grades of elementary school, found that in general many Web sites were not user-friendly for young children. The use of long words and text without pictures generated complaints from the students. The students preferred Web sites with high visual content and short, simple textual content. They also wanted to see more animation.

The various studies in which I have been involved, whether CD-ROM based (Large, Beheshti, and Breuleux, 1998) or Web based (Bowler, Large, and Rejskind, 2001; Large and Beheshti, 2000b), strongly suggest that the primary determining factor in what information the students look for and how they use that information is the assignment as specified by the teacher. Beamon (1997) reminds us that the challenge for teachers of young adolescents is to use questions to help students build new and complex learning structures as they experiment with a developing capacity for more abstract thought. Many of the research studies into elementary students' information-seeking behavior, whether experimentally or operationally founded, have presented the students with fact-finding questions that require the collection of specific, text-based information. My own observations lead me to conclude that students (not surprisingly) will take the road of least cognitive effort. If a short textual answer to the teacher's question is needed for an essay or a poster, why would the students expend time and effort to exploit the multimedia capabilities of the Web by retrieving sound or video segments that cannot be incorporated directly into their assignment? The only way to use them would be to transcribe or summarize their content in writing. Any of these actions take considerably more cognitive effort and time than using text or still images. Video and sound complicate rather than facilitate information transfer from student to teacher (or classmates). In this situation it is not surprising that students largely eschew them. The virtues of multimedia information will only be fully realized when both the content of the class projects and the way in which the students present the resulting assignments are modified to give sound and video an equal chance with text and still images. As Trilling and Hood (1999) found, "where learning through facts, drill and practice, and rules and procedures was so adaptive in the Industrial Age, now learning through projects and problems, inquiry and design, discovery and invention is more fitting for the [Knowledge Age]" (p. 10). The assignment itself suggests to the students that certain paths are worth following while others are not.

INFORMATION EVALUATION AND INTERPRETATION

The Web not only constitutes an enormous information store, but one in which quality control is absent. The good, the bad, and the ugly are all there waiting to be found. Do children have the evaluation skills, first, to appreciate this reality and, second, to separate the worthwhile from the worthless?

Hirsh (1999) found that the fifth-grade students in her study in general did not question the accuracy or validity of the information retrieved. This conclusion supports those by Kafia and Bates (1997), Schacter, Chung, and Dorr (1998), and Wallace and Kupperman (1997). She argues that children need help to evaluate the authority of Web pages. At the same time, Hirsh reports that the children were able to reach relevance judgments on retrieved information, based on topicality, novelty, and how interesting the material was considered; however, they did not include assessments of authoritativeness, accuracy, or truthfulness. Kafai and Bates (1997) report that the children were quick to assume everything they found was correct. But eventually they learned to differentiate marketing sites from neutral information sites. The students in grades 1 to 4 especially found evaluation a difficult task. Nevertheless, they were able to extract information for incorporation into their school projects

A Swedish study of children between the ages of nine and eleven found that they based their judgments as to whether a Web page was good or bad on the following criteria: content, currency, layout, usability, and interactivity (Enochsson, 2001). The author reports, however, that the children sometimes encounter difficulty in giving reasons for their choices. In their assessments of information reliability on the Web, the children were allocated to three categories: those who did not reflect at all on reliability or who thought it was illegal to put lies on the Web; those who had noticed lies but were not concerned by them; and those with a greater awareness of lies and who shared a "relativistic" view of the world.

KIDS' PORTALS

Although many children look for information on the Web using regular portals such as Google, Yahoo!, and Alta Vista, they have the opportunity alternatively to select a portal specifically designed for young users. Such portals typically offer more colorful and animated interfaces, subject categories geared toward children rather than adults, and so on. Several researchers have explored how children use and react to such portals. In a series of studies, Bilal (1999, 2000, 2001) has investigated middle school students' use of several such portals—most notably, Yahooligans!, but also Ask Jeeves for Kids and Super Snooper. More recently, she has begun to probe how grade 7 children would themselves design Web portals (Bilal, 2002a).

My colleagues and I have also investigated children's opinions on Web portal design, using focus groups to critique four such portals: Ask Jeeves for Kids, KidsClick, LycosZone, and Yahooligans! (Large, Beheshti, and Rahman, 2002a). The young focus group participants clearly indicated their interest in Web portals designed explicitly for younger users. They were attracted by the use of color, graphics, and animation, and indeed they suggested even more extensive use of all three. They had interesting and informed opinions on the importance of choosing an attention-grabbing but appropriate name for the portal, on screen layout, and the manner in which any hits should be displayed. They showed no interest in the provision of help features. Perhaps their most consistently expressed complaint was against the appearance of pop-up ads on children's portals. We concluded from this study that there certainly is a place for portals designed explicitly for young users.

REACTIONS FROM THE USERS

What do children themselves have to say about information seeking on the Web? We decided to find out by interviewing individually fifty grade 6 students at the completion of a class project for which they had sought Web-based information over several sessions (Large and Beheshti, 2000a and 2002b). On the basis of their responses we categorized the students as technophiles, traditionalists, and pragmatists. The technophiles by and large favored the Web sources in comparison with print sources for school projects. The traditionalists, and certainly such students were to be found, on balance still preferred to use the well-tried print sources. The pragmatists asserted that the relative benefits of the Web versus print depended on the kind of information being sought. They saw the Web as complementing rather than replacing printed works. A major advantage of the Web mentioned by quite a few students was its accessibility in comparison with books. It eliminated the need to visit the library for some; for others, it bypassed the problem of books not being found on the shelves. A majority thought it was faster to find information on the Web than from books.

Many of the students expressed frustration that they could not find on the Web the precise information they wanted. They were overwhelmed not only by the quantity, but also by the nature of the information—unlike the books in the school library, Web pages were seldom written explicitly for children. Content providers on the Web will rarely have this specific audience in mind, nor will they be experts at molding their information for young users even if this were the case.

The children not only in our study but in many others have expressed their impatience with poor response times. They quickly become intolerant of delays. In fact, when asked for suggestions on how the Web might be improved, their most common suggestion was to increase response rates (Large and Beheshti, 2000a and 2002b).

GENDER AND CHILDREN'S INFORMATION-SEEKING BEHAVIOR

Many published studies of children's information-seeking behavior have not discussed the specific searching differences between girls and boys. Others (for example, Borgman et al., 1995) failed to find any differences. Evidence is now accumulating, however, that some significant differences may exist. Martin (1998) reports that girls who worked together in groups during a Web-based scavenger hunt displayed more instances of cooperative work and seemed more enthusiastic about the task than did boys' groups (although both boys and girls were equally successful at completing the task). Schacter, Chung, and Dorr (1998) found that boys browsed significantly more than girls—they were either scanning the pages more quickly or were not reading the majority of information on the pages. Leong and Hawamdeh (1999) also found that girls were more cooperative in their groups and liked talking to each other, while boys preferred to do the activities alone and fought more over who controlled the mouse or the keyboard. They report that girls read more carefully online, while boys spent more time scrolling and quickly scanning text to find the answers to their questions. Boys were more impatient when pages did not include illustrations and liked more animations and colors more than the girls did.

My own research (Large, Beheshti, and Rahman, 2002b) has also revealed evidence of significant gender differences in information-seeking behavior on the Web by grade 6 students, but only in certain respects. Groups of boys used fewer words when formulating queries for search engines, often using only a single word. They spent less time viewing pages (almost one third less), suggesting they are not reading as much online. The boys were more active in clicking on hypertext links, jumping from page to page, and in general making more mouse clicks than the girls. In other respects, however, we did not identify significant differences. Neither gender, for example, demonstrated a readiness to use the various search refinement options available on the search engines.

In many elementary school classes, assignments are undertaken in groups rather than singly. Logistical limitations in numbers of available computers may only serve to emphasize this practice. My studies, as well as those of others, suggest that when given the opportunity, boys and girls in elementary school will opt to work in groups with students of the same sex. Is this a good thing? Do the differing behaviors suggest that single-sex groups at the computer are preferable, or would it be better to encourage mixed groups in an attempt to gain the best from each sex? More research is needed to answer these questions.

Interestingly, in our investigation of children's views on Web portal design (Large, Beheshti, and Rahman, 2002a), we also found evidence of a gender effect. The twelve girls in their two focus groups all chose one portal as their favorite (LycosZone), and the eleven boys all chose a different one (Yahooligans!). We intend to explore this matter further when we collaborate with teams of girls and teams of boys to design and test several prototype portals.

THE BALANCE SHEET

What can be said about children's use of the Web as an information resource to support their learning? In general, students appear to enjoy seeking information from this source, and in many cases express a preference for it over more traditional alternatives such as a visit to the school or public library. Wallace, Kupperman, and Krajcik (2000) stated that "if we had been looking primarily at student motivation or enjoyment, our results might have been entirely positive" (p. 101).

As with other computerized applications, young Web users also exhibit confidence in the technical aspects of the task. Their actions at the keyboard and mouse reveal no hesitation in the face of this technology, and, for example, they are quick to learn the techniques necessary to capture and save data.

Information seeking, especially on the Web, is by no means a straightforward task, and it should not be too surprising to discover that children do encounter problems when given the task of locating information for school projects. They find it difficult to choose search terms beyond the ones suggested by their teachers in the description of their assignment. They certainly find it challenging to modify an initial query in the light of irrelevant or no results. Much time is wasted moving forward and back again through the same sites. Bowler, Large, and Rejskind (2001) comment upon the difficulties their three-student groups encountered when searching and browsing. During the ninety minutes recorded online (over three sessions), the group followed fifty-five links but only saved ten segments of data from three pages.

Wallace, Kupperman, and Krajcik (2000) concluded from their study that students' engagement with the Web was shallow and poor, and their information-seeking behavior unplanned. Students did not engage in information seeking if that is a process defined by its inclusion of multiple stages of question asking and refining, information gathering and evaluating, and finally synthesis and use of information. Carrying out the actual searches on the Web may have become the primary goal—an end in itself. The broader task of information seeking, involving information selection, evaluation, synthesis, and application, as well as information gathering, is lost.

Following the model of the information-search process as developed by Kuhlthau (1997), when using the Web to find information, children often become fixated upon just one of the six steps she outlines—the fifth step in the process, information collection, where the task is actually to gather the needed information. Young students quickly dispense with the earlier steps of initiation (consideration of the task set by the teacher), selection (identification of a general area for investigation), exploration (exploring the information to form a focus for the research), and formulation (formation of a personal perspective or sense of meaning about the information encountered). The cursory leapfrogging of the early but crucial steps in the information-seeking process constitutes a general problem for school students, but the pressing desire to get onto the computer and immediately begin the search with little or no prior planning is especially likely when the Web is available within the classroom. Kuhlthau's sixth and final step—presentation—when the new learning is presented to the teacher, may also become an afterthought rather than the culmination of the entire process, although in my experience most children have given thought to the construction of the deliverables.

Students may be able to cope with Web technology without any great difficulty, but they seldom progress beyond the level of elementary users of search engines and Web browsers. Few of the search enhancement features available on search engines are employed, and when they are chosen they are often wrongly or inappropriately executed. This tends to result in large numbers of hits, most of which are off-target.

The tendency to retrieve large numbers of pages leads to another problem: assessing relevance. Web tools are not designed to support learning; they give almost no support for finding information based on meaning, and provide no means of using information once it has been found. Students rarely read the content online, even when it proves potentially relevant, preferring with a click of the mouse to pass quickly on to the next page. When faced with a highly navigable environment like the Web, children will exploit it to the full. As one of our studies showed (Large, Beheshti, and Moukdad, 1999), apart from pausing while an analytic search was completed or material was saved to disk, the interface seldom was stationary for more than a few seconds. We found that half the pages the grade 6 students encountered were viewed for less than thirty seconds, even though the children when they did read tended to do so slowly and aloud (Large, Beheshti, and Rahman, 2002b). This is a troublesome conclusion, suggesting as it does that the Web discourages thinking in favor of action. The children may have spent time in evaluating information after it had been downloaded, but certainly during searching, browsing, and selecting information to be saved, little contemplation was in evidence. In many computer games, points are likely to be lost if user interaction is suspended even momentarily; the same philosophy seems to be transposed to the "game" of information seeking.

Evaluating the worth (or worthlessness) of the information retrieved is yet another problem. Children, who previously were able to rely upon the selection and presentation skills of experienced authors writing specifically with elementary school students in mind, must now fight through the jungle of the Web where the valuable hardwood is swathed in worthless creepers.

How successful, then, are children in using the Web to find information for their class projects? The answer to this question is more difficult to measure in operational than laboratory environments. Schachter, Chung, and Dorr (1998), in their experiment, found that on a well-defined task only two out of thirty-two students found the required documents, but a better success rate was achieved on the ill-defined task. Wallace, Kupperman, and Krajcik

(2000) experienced similar results when comparing searches on well-defined and ill-defined tasks. This initially surprised the researchers, but in fact it is logical. On an ill-defined task there is unlikely to be just one correct answer, and there are likely to be many ways and from many different pages to find an appropriate answer. There is also a greater potential to find an answer by browsing than searching, a method favored by many students. The answer to the well-defined task, in contrast, is likely to prove more elusive as it may reside only on one or a small number of pages that can only be identified after a careful, structured search.

Several researchers, including Wallace, Kupperman, and Krajcik (2000) and myself (Large, Beheshti, and Moukdad, 1999; Large and Beheshti, 2000a and 2002b), have noted with some surprise that children remained focused on the teacher-allocated task despite the wealth of distraction available on the Web. They are not tempted to follow side trails leading from the beaten track of their assignment. To this extent their seeking is targeted.

If children encounter problems in seeking information on the Web, the same, it should be emphasized, is also true for adults. Even studies undertaken of university undergraduates have noted weaknesses in their strategies. Their elders, in fact, replicate many of the difficulties encountered by youthful information seekers. It may be that from the results of research into children's information-seeking behavior emerge lessons that can benefit all the Web's users regardless of age!

The elementary school students that have been investigated by researchers, and especially those in the higher grades, have been old enough to have been exposed systematically to print and CD-ROM sources prior to using the Web. It will be fascinating to see what research into the first totally post-Web school generation reveals concerning the students' relative evaluations of print and digital sources, and whether their enthusiasm for the latter is even stronger than that of their current counterparts.

THE NEXT STEPS

There seems no gainsaying the continued presence of the Web as a global information resource. Nor can there be little doubt that it constitutes a rich information source for students, including those in elementary schools, to be exploited in support of their class projects. At the same time, these students appear from the research studies hitherto undertaken to be encountering considerable difficulties in exploiting the Web's full potential. What might be done to improve this situation?

One approach would be to place more emphasis within even the elementary school curriculum upon information-seeking skills. The students, or at least those in the higher grades, would undoubtedly benefit from instruction in how to formulate a search query, what steps to try if an initial search fails, how to use effectively the various search refinement features offered by a typical Web search engine, when browsing might prove a better strategy than searching, and so on. My experience, at least with the older children within the elementary school system in Canada, is that they could appreciate and learn from such teaching if it were to be properly and suitably offered them. As the model formulated by Kuhlthau (1991, 1997) suggests, however, such instruction should extend beyond the narrowly defined concept of information collection to the broader aspects of seeking, organizing, and presenting the information.

A second approach is to provide younger users with more effective Web-searching tools. Web portals explicitly designed to help children search and browse the Web already exist, but my own research as well as that by others (see, for example, Bilal, 1999, 2000, 2001) suggests that these portals could be improved upon. Rather than design yet more portals for children, I am now working with small groups of elementary school children in grades 3 and 6 to help them design an intergenerational, participative design process (see Druin et al., 1999; Hanna et al., 1999): Web portals that will reflect their ideas as well as ours. Bilal (2002a and 2002b) has also begun this process with middle school students and with interesting preliminary results. The intent is to accept that children themselves have a valuable and distinct viewpoint on the world, and that we adults should not merely listen to them, but also collaborate with them closely, just as we would listen to and collaborate with (hopefully) adult user groups, before making decisions as to what is best for them.

In order to take account of actual and potential differences in the abilities and needs of children at different ages and of each gender, there seem to be good reasons to explore further the ways in which children's portals might be personalized. Large, Beheshti, and Cole (2002) have discussed ways in which a portal might be designed to adjust to various characteristics of its young users. They envisage an information architecture matrix that would assist in defining a portal's purpose so that it might mold itself into the requirements of specific user groups, thereby catering more effectively to their information-seeking requirements.

A third approach is to encourage children's information providers to make more content available on the Web, and for teachers and librarians to organize this content in such a way that it is easily found and evaluated by its seekers. This positive approach to information provision seems a far better one than resorting to the teacher having to instruct the child exactly where to look for information, perhaps by supplying URLs at the outset of an assignment. Information-seeking skills are skills for life, and it is better if we begin to acquire them from the outset. Circumscribing this process by being handed information on a plate, so to speak, will not help us gain these necessary skills. Nor will it enable students to benefit from the richness of the Web they can explore by themselves if given the necessary tools and skills.

If used well and properly, the Web can enrich the elementary school curriculum. But it is merely a tool, to be used for better or worse, to be handled competently or incompetently, to help or to hinder. It is up to teachers, librarians, designers, researchers, and, of course, the youthful users themselves, to determine to what extent it will prove a valuable educational asset in the years to come.

REFERENCES

Beamon, G. W. (1997). *Sparking the thinking of students, ages 10–14: Strategies for teachers*. Thousand Oaks, Calif.: Corwin Press.

Bilal, D. (1999). "Web search engines for children: A comparative study and performance evaluation of Yahooligans!, Ask Jeeves for Kids, and Super Snooper." *ASIS '99: Proceedings of the 62nd ASIS Annual Meeting* (pp. 70–83). Medford, N.J.: Information Today.

Bilal, D. (2000). "Children's use of the Yahooligans! Web search engine: I. Cognitive, physical and affective behaviors on fact-based search tasks." *Journal of the American Society for Information Science* 51, no. 7: 646–665.

Bilal, D. (2001). "Children's use of the Yahooligans! Web search engine: II. Cognitive and physical behaviors on research tasks." *Journal of the American Society for Information Science* 52, no. 2: 118–136.

Bilal, D. (2002a). "Children design their interfaces for Web search engines: A participatory approach." *Proceedings of the 30th annual conference of the Canadian Society for Information Science, 30 May–1 June 2002* (pp. 204–214). Toronto: Faculty of Information Studies, University of Toronto.

Bilal, D. (2002b). "Children's use of the Yahooligans! Web search engine. III. Cognitive and physical behaviors on fully self-generated search tasks." *Journal of the American Society for Information Science* 53, no. 13: 1170–1183.

Bilal, D., and Kirby, J. (2002). "Differences and similarities in information seeking: Children and adults as Web users." *Information Processing and Management* 38, no. 5: 649–670.

Borgman, C. L., Hirsh, S. G., and Walter, V. A. (1995). "Children's searching behavior on browsing and keyword online catalogs: The Science Library Catalog project." *Journal of the American Society for Information Science* 46, no. 9: 663–684.

Bowler, L., Large, A., and Rejskind, G. (2001). "Primary school students, information literacy and the Web." *Education for Information* 19, no. 3: 201–223.

Druin, A., Bederson, B., Boltman, A., Miura, A., Knotts-Callahan, D., and Platt, M. (1999). "Children as our technology design partners." In A. Druin, ed., *The design of children's technology* (pp. 51–72). San Francisco: Morgan Kaufmann.

Enochsson, A. B. (2001). "Children choosing Web pages." *New Review of Information Behaviour Research* 2, available at http://hem.passagen.se/enochfri/choosing.pdf. (accessed November 20, 2003).

Fidel, R., Davies, R. K., Douglass, M. H., Holder, J. K., Hopkins, C. J., Kushner, E. J., Miyagishima, B., and Toney, C. D. (1999). "A visit to the information mall: Web searching behavior of high school students." *Journal of the American Society for Information Science* 50, no. 1: 24–37.

Hanna, L., Risden, K., Czerwinski, M., and Alexander, K. J. (1999). "The role of usability research in designing children's computer products." In A. Druin, ed., *The design of children's technology* (pp. 3–25). San Francisco: Morgan Kaufmann.

Hirsh, S. G. (1995). "The effect of domain knowledge on elementary school children's search behavior on an information retrieval system: The Science Library Catalog. *CHI '95*: 55–56.

Hirsh, S. G. (1997). "How do children find information on different types of tasks? Children's use of the Science Library Catalog." *Library Trends* 45: 725–745.

Hirsh, S. G. (1999). "Children's relevance criteria and information seeking on electronic resources." *Journal of the American Society for Information Science* 50, no. 14: 1265–1283.

Kafai, Y., and Bates, M. J. (1997). "Internet web searching instruction in the elementary classroom: Building a foundation for information literacy." *School Library Media Quarterly* 25, no. 2: 103–111.

Kuhlthau, C. C. (1991). "Inside the search process: Information seeking from the user's perspective." *Journal of the American Society for Information Science* 42, no. 5: 361–371.

Kuhlthau, C. C. (1997). "Learning in digital libraries: An information search process approach." *Library Trends* 45, no. 4: 708–724.

Kuntz, J. (1999). "Criteria for comparing children's Web search tools." *Library Computing* 18, no. 3: 203–207.

Large, A., and Beheshti, J. (1999). "Children's information-seeking behavior: A laboratory versus an operational research environment." *Proceedings of the 27th Canadian Association for Information Science annual conference, Sherbrooke, June 1999* (pp. 134–143). Toronto: CAIS.

Large, A., and Beheshti, J. (2000a). "Primary school students' reaction to the Web as a classroom resource." *CAIS 2000: Dimensions of a global information science. Canadian Association for Information Science proceedings of the 28th annual conference*. Available at http://www.slis.ualberta.ca/cais2000/large.htm (accessed November 20, 2003).

Large, A., and Beheshti, J. (2000b). "The Web as a classroom resource: Reactions from the users." *Journal of the American Society for Information Science* 51, no. 12: 1069–1080.

Large, A., Beheshti, J., and Breuleux, A. (1998). "Information seeking in a multimedia environment by primary school students." *Library and Information Science Research* 20, no. 4: 343–376.

Large, A., Beheshti, J., Breuleux, A., and Renaud, A. (1994). "A comparison of information retrieval from print and CD-ROM versions of an encyclopedia by elementary school children." *Information Processing and Management* 30, no. 4: 499–513.

Large, A., Beheshti, J., and Cole, C. (2002). "Information architecture for the Web: The IA matrix approach to designing children's portals." *Journal of the American Society for Information Science and Technology* 53, no. 10: 831–838.

Large, A., Beheshti, J., and Moukdad, H. (1999). "Information seeking on the Web: Navigational skills of grade-six primary school students." *ASIS '99: Proceedings of the 62nd ASIS annual meeting* (pp. 84–97). Medford, N.J.: Information Today.

Large, A., Beheshti, J., and Rahman, T. (2002a). "Design criteria for children's Web portals: The users speak out." *Journal of the American Society for Information Science and Technology* 53, no. 2: 79–94.

Large, A., Beheshti, J., and Rahman, T. (2002b). "Gender differences in collaborative Web searching behavior: An elementary school study." *Information Processing and Management* 38, no. 3: 427–443.

Lazonder, A. W., Biemans, H. J. A., and Wopereis, I. G. J. H. (2000).

"Differences between novice and experienced users in searching information on the World Wide Web." *Journal of the American Society for Information Science* 51, no. 6: 576–581.

Leong, S. C., and Hawamdeh, S. (1999). "Gender and learning attitudes in using Web-based science lessons." *Information Research* 5, available at http://informationr.net/ir/5-1/paper66.html (accessed November 20, 2003).

Marchionini, G. (1989). "Information seeking strategies of novices using a full-text electronic encyclopedia." *Journal of the American Society for Information Science* 40, no. 1: 54–66.

Martin, S. (1998). "Internet use in the classroom." *Social Science Computer Review* 18, no. 4: 411–418.

Perzylo, L., and Oliver, R. (1992). "An investigation of children's use of a multimedia CD-ROM product for information retrieval." *Microcomputers for Information Management* 9: 225–239.

Schacter, J., Chung, G. K. W. K., and Dorr, A. (1998). "Children's Internet searching on complex problems: Performance and process analyses." *Journal of the American Society for Information Science* 49, no. 9: 840–849.

Solomon, P. (1993). "Children's information retrieval behavior: A case analysis of an OPAC." *Journal of the American Society for Information Science* 44, no. 5: 245–264.

Stevenson, A. (1993). "Mastery of CD-ROM encyclopedia skills by elementary students." Master's research paper, Kent State University.

Trilling, B., and Hood, P. (1999). "Learning, technology and education reform in the knowledge age or 'We're wired, webbed, and windowed, now what?'" *Education Technology* 39, no. 3: 5–18.

Wallace, R., and Kupperman, J. (1997). "On-line search in the science classroom: Benefits and possibilities." *Using on-line digital resources to support sustained inquiry learning in K–12 science*. E. Soloway, ed., available at http://www.msu.edu/~ravenmw/pubs/online_search.pdf. (accessed November 20, 2003).

Wallace, M. R., Kupperman, J., and Krajcik, J. (2000). "Science on the Web: Students online in a sixth-grade classroom." *Journal of the Learning Sciences* 9, no. 1: 75–104.

Watson, J. S. (1998). "'If you don't have it, you can't find it': A close look at students' perceptions of using technology." *Journal of the American Society for Information Science* 49, no. 11: 1024–1036.

TWELVE

Adolescent Decision Making for Careers: An Exploration of Information Behavior

Heidi Julien

A common observation of career decision making is that many people, beginning in adolescence, make career decisions on the basis of very limited information. These decisions often turn out to be unsatisfying in the long term, and Canadian employers alone lose $5 billion per year in wasted recruitment and training of workers who stay in work positions only a short while.[1] Much of this turnover is attributed to career indecisiveness[2], which can be at least partly related to a lack of appropriate career-related information. Indeed, two-thirds of American adults "would seek more information about career options if they had the chance to do it over again."[3]

The general purpose of this study was to explore adolescents' information seeking for career decision making. Although some aspects of the study are reported elsewhere,[4] this report focuses on the information behavior observable in the process of decision making. The specific research questions addressed are:

Can adolescents' approaches to career decision making be classified into categories of rational, intuitive, and dependent decision-making style?

Does adolescents' information seeking for career decision making follow an identifiable process?

Are there any apparent gender differences in the information behavior demonstrated?

A literature review on these issues suggested several useful theoretical frameworks for studying these general questions: Dervin's sense-making theory provided conceptual categories with which to analyze the views of information seekers on their information seeking.[5] Kuhlthau's information-seeking process (ISP) theory offered an example of adolescent information seeking that included consideration of affective aspects.[6] Additionally, Kuhlthau suggested that the ISP required testing in contexts outside those from which the theory was developed. Harren's decision-making theory suggested a framework for interpreting adolescent decision making.[7] Feminist theorists proposed that adolescent girls would demonstrate attitudes and behaviors that differed from those of adolescent boys.[8] These various frameworks informed the data collection and provided conceptual categories for the analysis of those data.

LITERATURE REVIEW

Literature on Career Development

Research from the fields of education and psychology that describes influences on career decision making reveals that adolescents turn to a variety of information sources when making these decisions.[9] Most notably, these include: parents, peers, guidance counselors, people working in careers of interest, and written material (books and pamphlets). The sources of information chosen, and the particular use made of those sources depend upon a variety of factors, including gender.

The Library and Information Science (LIS) literature on career development is minimal, and what exists is mostly system-centered and concerned with collection building and traditional access tools.[10] Anderson, however, provides librarians with helpful details by clearly itemizing the types of information required for rational decision making about careers that can be provided by libraries.[11]

An exception to the source-based approach of the LIS literature on career development is Durrance's work.[12] Durrance notes that information needs and information seeking in the context of career decision making will vary between individuals, and she urges librarians to attempt actively to identify those needs.[13] She suggests that these information seekers may require advice to interpret information, to become motivated, or to cope with related problems. They may require in-depth interviews to assess their needs and frequently need referrals to other agencies.

DeHart and Bleeker propose that librarians can serve career information seekers better by educating themselves and alerting their patrons about the changing labor force and about decision-making theory.[14] These researchers conclude by suggesting that LIS research could focus on many aspects of information seeking and use in problem solving and decision making.

Adolescents' Information Seeking

Although the situation of adolescents making career-related decisions has not yet been researched using the fundamental theoretical basis of this research, sense-making theory,[15] adolescents' information-seeking behavior in other contexts, has been studied. For example, Poston-Anderson and Edwards interviewed Australian adolescent girls about their information needs.[16] Interestingly, a need for information about education and work was more strongly expressed than for information about relationships. When asked what they would ask an "expert," girls indicated that they would seek "opinions, judgments, and interpretations,"[17] and strategies, rather than factual information, which was rated as easy to obtain. Most girls with educational and work concerns did not believe that their questions could be answered in their school library. A minority of girls with information needs of any kind had tried to seek information from libraries, although most girls had sought information from talking to others or reading. Poston-Anderson and Edwards point out that although libraries and indeed most formal information system providers emphasize factual information, this may not be the kind of information that most adolescents need. Some of their respondents expressed their perceptions of the school library "as a mechanism for control, as a source of only socially sanctioned material, and as dealing with subjects for curricular use only."[18]

Bernardelli and Dumont assessed occupational information-seeking behaviors in adolescents.[19] These behaviors included talking to others, making use of relevant audio-visual and print materials, and planning to or actually conducting a visit to a workplace to obtain information about particular opportunities. Males reported more information-seeking activities than did females. Studies have also shown that adolescent girls have approached their mothers and peers as information sources for general life issues more so than adolescent boys would, although these researchers note that the context of the information need affects the choice of information source.[20]

Cassie et al., through a questionnaire and structured interviews with 550 Canadian secondary school students, found that female adolescents do more career investigation than males, but that boys read more books and newspapers, used computer software career investigation tools more often, and talked to someone in their desired occupation to investigate careers more often than girls.[21] Slightly more investigation was done by girls by going to career days, writing for information, reading pamphlets, using guidance center resources, talking to guidance counselors, talking to teachers, and talking to parents. Girls also explored fewer occupations.

The variability in information-seeking behavior according to gender that is revealed by these studies was tested in the present research.

Decision Making

Insofar as career planning requires decision-making skills as well as substantive knowledge about the choices one is making,[22] an understanding of decision making is important for this research.

Jepsen summarizes decision-making theory as consisting of the following principles and process: first, the existence of a decision-maker, a situation requiring a decision, the availability of relevant information, and time in which to make a decision are assumed. Then, alternative courses of action are considered, probabilities of particular outcomes are evaluated, and commitment is made to a particular action. Individuals will use different strategies, or criteria, in making these judgments.[23]

A review of factors affecting adolescent decision making revealed that competence in making decisions is based on several factors.[24] These include cognitive development and degree of substantive knowledge, willingness to make decisions, understanding the cognitive process of decision making, degree of creativity, willingness to compromise when necessary, ability to see consequences of decisions, ability to see that some choices are superior to (more correct than) others, ability to assess the credibility of information, consistency in values, and commitment to follow through. Constraints on adolescents' decision making include:

- attitudes that suggest to adolescents that decision making is an adult-only prerogative
- peer pressures to conform to group norms
- family environment that facilitates or hinders decision making by adolescents
- legal constraints limiting the actions of minors.

Reviewing the research done on the factors affecting competence in decision-making, the authors conclude that by age fifteen, many adolescents are competent decision-makers. Therefore, it is likely that a majority of the adolescent respondents in this research should not be hindered in their career decision making by a lack of decision-making skills. However, Mann, Harmoni, and Power caution that decision-making skills should be taught to high school students who are at the stage in life when they are making decisions about their futures.[25]

Although high school students of both sexes do not receive adequate training in decision making,[26] gender has been found to influence decision-making competence. Females have been found to be more involved than males in family decision making, but males are more vigilant; that is, they report taking greater care when making decisions.[27] Males report more often that they prefer to make up their own minds about educational and vocational decisions, while females prefer to listen to others and then make decisions.[28] In light of the gender differences revealed in that research, the decision-making techniques among respondents in this study were also analyzed by gender to determine whether a relationship between gender and decision making could be confirmed.

THEORETICAL FRAMEWORKS FOR THE STUDY

Sense-Making Theory

A major theoretical approach to information-seeking that informs this research is sense-making.[29] Core assumptions and concepts of sense-making that particularly pertain to this research include: (a) perception of reality is not complete nor constant, but discontinuous and filled with gaps; (b) information is not external to humans and does not exist independently of people, but is a product of human observation; (c) information is subjective;

(d) information seeking and use are activities that people undertake to construct and create sense; (e) people use their own and others' observations to construct personal pictures of reality that guide their behavior; (f) sense-making behavior is situationally dependent and somewhat predictable on the basis of those situations; (g) sense-making focuses on discovering how people construct personal sense, rather than assuming necessary and predictable connections between information and its use.

The sense-making model centers on a relationship between *situations* or contexts in which people need to make sense of some problem, *gaps* in their understanding of how to solve problems (information needs), and *uses* of created sense (information helps, for example, the ways in which information helps people to create sense) to bridge those gaps. In this study, the situation was defined as career decision making. One aspect of any situation is how the person in it views that situation. Of specific concern in this chapter is how individuals identify their own perspective on their situations. Sense-making research has found that people's *situation-perspectives* can be clustered according to categories that Dervin has labeled as: (a) facing a *decision* (i.e., needing to choose between two or more options); (b) feeling *problematic* (i.e., being dragged down a path not of their own choosing); (c) feeling as though they are in a *spin-out* (i.e., not having a plan); (d) feeling as though they are facing a *barrier* (i.e., knowing where they want to go but feeling blocked); (e) feeling the need to be *led* (i.e., wanting to follow someone else's lead because she or he knows more and can guide); (f) feeling that they are simply *observing* (i.e., watching without feeling a need to do anything); or (g) feeling that they are *moving* (i.e., seeing themselves as moving ahead unhindered). The research data were analyzed according to this classification of situation-perspectives.[30]

Sense-making theory is incorporated into the assumptions and research questions of this work. The research respondents are assumed to be active constructors of meaning as they make sense of the world, and the study focuses on the ways in which various information sources help or do not help these information-seekers.

Information-Search Process Theory

Another theoretical model informing this research derives from library and information science. Kuhlthau has proposed a theory of information seeking grounded mainly in her research on adolescents' information seeking in the context of completing school and college assignments.[31] Kuhlthau's work is theoretically consistent with Dervin's sense-making theory: information seekers are viewed as conducting an active process of making sense, or constructing personal meaning, out of the information obtained from various formal and informal sources. As well, the affective dimension of personal construct theory,[32] Belkin's theory of anomalous states of knowledge,[33] and Taylor's theory of different levels of information need,[34] inform Kuhlthau's model. Specifically, Kuhlthau proposes a model of the information-search process (ISP) that involves six stages and identifiable feelings, thoughts, actions, and tasks specific to each stage of the process. The research data gathered in this study were analyzed for evidence of a similar pattern of feelings, thoughts, actions, and tasks.[35]

Decision-Making Theory

The decision-making theory that informs this research is provided by Harren.[36] His is a career decision-making model that, although specific to college students, is focused on late adolescents and therefore helpful when analyzing high school students decision making as well. The model also focuses on information seeking. This link to information seeking is critical, since decision making is one of the obvious outcomes of information seeking in general. The information-seeking/decision-making connection has not been explored explicitly in LIS, with a few exceptions of studies of decision making by business executives,[37] or by physicians,[38] for example. General decision-making theories, developed for the management field, recognize the role of information seeking (specifically information gathering, or analysis), but tend not to focus on that aspect of decision-making processes. Again, there are exceptions, including the field of management information systems (MIS), with some writers particularly emphasizing the importance of information.[39] All this work, however, has not focused on decision making in daily life contexts, for ordinary people, as is the case in the current study. Thus, the career-development literature, a subset of psychology, provides the most relevant decision-making theory for this research. Harren proposes that most people fit one of three basic decision-making styles: rational, intuitive, and dependent.[40] The rational decision-making style involves systematic information seeking and evaluation of information obtained. Decisions are made logically and objectively. Intuitive decision-makers conduct little information seeking and rely on self-awareness and emotional factors, rather than logic, to make their choices. Unlike the first two styles, dependent decision-makers are passive and compliant and do not take personal responsibility for their choices. They believe that the external environment and other people are responsible for their decisions. Choices made by this group often are not found to be satisfying in the long term.

Since Harren's framework emphasizes information seeking for decision making, it appeared to be an appropriate model to apply in this study, which focuses on information-seeking behavior. Thus, the data gathered in this study were analyzed to determine whether Harren's three categories of decision-makers (rational, intuitive, and dependent) fit the responses provided by these adolescents.

Feminist Theory

The feminist theory that informed this research derives from several sources. First, the objective in this study to analyze gender differences in responses was suggested by arguments that males and females may have quite different psychological identities that will influence the choices they make and the values they hold.[41] The gender differences found in preferences for particular information sources and in information-seeking behavior also provide a basis for the analysis of results by gender.

The second source of support from feminist theory focuses specifically on the suggestion that women may be particularly reliant on personal knowledge and personal experience in understanding their worlds.[42] Thus, the respondents in this study were offered the opportunity to name their experienced, inner voices (the "self") as sources of help in career decision making.

METHODS OF DATA COLLECTION

The research data were collected in a midsize Canadian city. Included in the participating schools were two large comprehensive high schools, both providing a mixture of programs for students, one within the public education system and the other in a private (Roman Catholic) education system. The third school was a comprehensive high school located in a small town a short distance from the city, attended by rural students as well as a small minority of urban students. Approval for this research was obtained from each of the three school boards involved in the study, as well as from the principal of each school. The Human Ethics Review Committee at the Graduate School of Library and Information Science, University of Western Ontario, granted ethics approval.

Quantitative data were gathered with a questionnaire surveying male and female grade 12 students in three secondary schools. Analysis of that data is reported elsewhere,[43] After the questionnaire was administered in the three settings, semistructured interviews with fifteen female and fifteen male grade 12 students were conducted. In total, ten students from each participating school were interviewed. The thirty interview participants (fifteen adolescent men and fifteen adolescent women) were recruited from among those who completed the survey. Twelve to twenty interviewees are commonly needed to achieve maximum variation, and so data from thirty interviews should provide sufficient variety in the data to reflect the general population.[44] Since it was unintentionally possible to identify students according to whether they completed the questionnaire in an academic or general level class, the interview sample was stratified according to level as well. This helped to ensure that the interview participants would present a variety of career aspirations, since students in academic English at the high school level may hold aspirations that differ from those students taking general level English. The thirty interview respondents included eighteen academic level and twelve general level students.

The interview questions included the following, and probes were used where necessary.[45] Note that this chapter does not address directly results arising from some of these questions, which are available elsewhere.[46]

What decisions have you made, are you making, or do you feel you should make about your future? (Probed for distinction between decisions that are imposed and those that are self-motivated; probed for decisions about family plans as well as career.)

What kinds of help do you need in order to make decisions about your future?

Who have you talked or listened to/where have you gone/what have you read or watched to find help? (Probed for personal experience and role models as information sources. Generated list for following questions.)

For each source mentioned (one at a time), please tell me what you found out (briefly).

For each source mentioned, please tell me if and how this helped you.
How were you feeling/what were your thoughts/what were you trying to accomplish as you sought information from each source?
How did you feel after your encounters with each of these sources (ask separately for each source)?
What concerns or questions do you still have?
How do you plan to find out more about these concerns or questions?
Can you describe the perfect source that could provide the help you want to make decisions about your future?
What would you want to find out?
What would make this source of help ideal?
What stops you from getting the help you want/what barriers have you experienced in your search for information?

The interview transcriptions were coded as soon as possible,[47] usually the same day or one day later. The transcriptions were subjected to quantitative content analysis of concepts.[48] specifically according to the theoretical foundations supporting the research. To ensure reliability, an assistant coded a sample of transcripts for each set of analyses. Following discussion of differences in assigned codes, the coefficient kappa was calculated to be .737, which reveals a high degree of agreement between coders. Thus, the reliability of the content analyses is assured.

RESULTS AND DISCUSSION

Respondents

The interview participants included fifteen females and fifteen males, ranging in age from sixteen to twenty years. The mean age of the participants was seventeen years.

Decision Making

Content analysis of the entire interview transcripts (i.e., responses to all interview questions) was done to seek evidence for Harren's categories of decision-making style. Fourteen (47 percent) of those interviewed were found to exhibit a rational decision-making style, characterized by systematic information seeking and logical and objective decision making. These respondents tended to report having approached several sources of help and having future plans to do more information seeking. Moreover, they described the decisions they needed to make as ones based on their thinking about the information they find. For these respondents, their decision making was a cerebral experience. For instance, Mary,[49] was trying to decide what area to go into when she enters university. She had discussed her options with her parents and her guidance counselor. She also had attended presentations by various universities. She expressed firm plans to seek additional information from her guidance counselor when she inquired about scholarship opportunities. She had thought about what she had learned and trusted her ability to make a good decision based on that information. Another rational decision-maker, Brenda, had been collecting information about her career decisions for several years. She eagerly sought information wherever she could find it, and said that "I'm constantly on, my ears and eyes are open, trying to find stuff."

Twelve respondents (40 percent) were closer to the intuitive decision-making style, since they conducted little purposive information seeking, relying more on self-awareness and emotional factors to make their career-related decisions. For example, although Gerald could describe several sources from which he had received help in his career decision making (e.g., his parents and an interest test taken at school), he had approached only one of these sources purposefully (he had attended a presentation by a university). Gerald said that he would prefer it "if someone was just to basically say, 'well you should go here,' and that's it, no decisions, I'll just go." Luke planned to make his career decision on the basis of his enjoyment of high school courses and university courses, thus demonstrating that self-knowledge was important to him in deciding on a career. The intuitive decision-makers preferred to use their emotions to make their choices. Kerry got her career aspiration from a suggestion made by her bus driver. Kerry said, "as soon as she said art therapy, and told me what it was about . . . it just hit me . . . that's exactly what I want to do." Only after that conversation did Kerry explore her career choice. These intuitive decision-makers reported that they spent little time actually thinking about their decisions.

Finally, four respondents (13 percent) were categorized as dependent decision-makers. These adolescents were generally passive, taking no steps to overcome the gaps they faced and did not take personal responsibility for their decisions. Holly was a typical example of this category. She said, "I haven't made much decisions . . . I haven't thought so much. I'm not a person that looks ahead . . . I've nothing that's going to be handed down to me." Although she felt that she had been helped by conversations with parents, friends, and her grandfather, in none of these instances was she deliberately seeking help for her career decision making. Her parents had pressured her into making an appointment to speak with her guidance counselor, but the initiative did not come from Holly herself, nor had this appointment actually occurred before the interview. Holly expressed a preference not to have to make a decision at all, but would have liked her guidance counselor to tell her what field to enter.

After making these categorizations, however, it became clear that Harren's categories of decision-makers are not mutually exclusive. Four (29 percent) of the rational decision-makers (three girls and one boy) exhibited elements of the intuitive decision-making style, in that they also relied to a certain extent on self-knowledge when making their career decisions. These individuals were categorized as rational decision-makers on the basis of their high degree of information seeking, but this alone was insufficient to describe their decision-making style. That a greater number of the girls than boys among the rational decision-makers suggested that self-knowledge was a significant factor in their career decision making is consistent with the argument that females may place generally more importance on self-knowledge than males.[50] However, the sample size was too small to provide strong support for that claim. Also, one of the girls and two of the boys (25 percent) identified as intuitive decision-makers exhibited traits closely tied with the dependent decision-making style, since they conducted such a minimal degree of purposive information seeking. They reported that their decision making was based on their intuitive self-knowledge, but were relatively inactive information seekers.

Therefore, perhaps Harren's decision-making styles may be more usefully considered as steps on a continuum, such as suggested by figure 12.1, rather than as mutually exclusive categories. That the data suggest a continuum of decision-making style rather

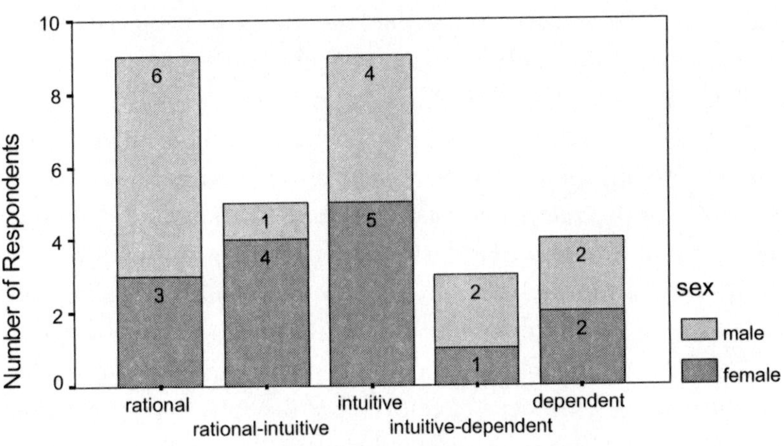

Figure 12.1 A Continuum of Decision-Making Styles

than mutually exclusive categories may result from the fact that Harren's framework is based on at least two different behavioral dimensions: locus of control and evidence of active information seeking. The first, locus of control, categorizes individuals according to whether they attribute control of their situations to external sources and conditions (other people, circumstances beyond their own control) and are therefore externally motivated, or to internal sources and conditions (i.e., themselves) and are therefore internally motivated. Harren's framework suggests that rational and intuitive decision-makers have more of an internal locus of control, so that these individuals believe they can have some control of their futures. On the other hand, dependent decision-makers have a more external locus of control, believing that they have less or even no control over the direction of their lives. The second dimension, degree of active information seeking, relates to the amount of purposeful information seeking that is apparent in the behavior of decision-makers. Another possible dimension is the degree to which decisions are made using cognitive thinking skills (rationally) or using emotions and intuition.

Thus, a mixture of decision-making styles is apparent when varying combinations of the aspects of these different dimensions are evident. Rational-intuitive decision-makers seem to have an internal locus of control like the rational decision-makers, but they conduct less information seeking and deem their self-knowledge as a factor in their decision making. Intuitive-dependent decision-makers demonstrate a more external locus of control than purely intuitive decision-makers, but they conduct more information seeking than do the dependent decision-makers. This research does not provide definitive data on this point, since it did not seek specific evidence for locus of control, but the results suggest these possibilities. Further evidence would have to be gathered to elaborate on these ideas and confirm this interpretation of Harren's framework.

The Information Search Process

The interview data were expected to extend Kuhlthau's ISP theory, which has been grounded in contexts in which information seekers were required to produce a paper or presentation of their findings.[51] The context in this research typifies a self-directed process of seeking information in order to make a life decision. The process of information seeking for career decision making differs in several ways from the ISP context. First, information seeking for career decision making is a far more heterogeneous process, in that the situations and gaps that lead to information seeking are numerous and vary considerably between individuals. The process of career decision making involves decisions regarding not only the ultimate goal of entering a particular career or job market, but a myriad of choices and decisions leading to that stage. Such decisions include determining one's interests and aptitudes, matching these with potential careers, investigating these options and the means to achieve them, and making decisions that will facilitate the achievement of the final career choice. Between individuals, these decisions appear to differ from each other in the length of time taken to reach them, the significance of each in the life of the individual, and the information sources perceived to be appropriate, available, and helpful.

As well, the sources of help to which individuals turn when making career decisions differ fundamentally from those used in the process of conducting library research to produce a paper. The adolescents in this study relied heavily on the people whom they trusted to advise and inform their decisions: themselves (self-knowledge), their families, guidance counselors, and people perceived to have personal experience, and therefore expertise, with the situations being investigated (i.e., careers, and academic institutions). The ultimate goal of this information-seeking process is also intrinsically different from that to which Kuhlthau's research participants were working. Adolescents making a career decision are very aware that this decision is intimately connected to their self-identity, which imbues each stage of this process with far more personal import than would be experienced by the typical student engaged in researching a term paper. This long-term significance of career decision-making is frightening to some adolescents who feel unprepared to make serious decisions. As well, this situation is new for most adolescents and overwhelming for some of them.

Qualitatively, then, the process of information seeking for career decision making differs from that of Kuhlthau's participants. Students engaged in library research to produce a paper have at least a minimal sense of how that process works. They know that they must glean some information from the library's resources and use it to produce an essay or presentation. Faced with a social expectation to make some decisions about what to do with their lives after high school, some of those same students have little sense of how to approach these decisions and little conception of an appropriate process of information seeking to help them overcome the gaps they face.

Thus, the feelings, thoughts, and actions, if not the tasks in the career decision-making process, differ enormously from those experienced by Kuhlthau's students, and also differ between individuals at each stage of the process. Nevertheless, some parallels can be drawn between Kuhlthau's ISP and the information seeking for particular decisions that was evident in the interview data from this study. These parallels are explored following the description of the decision-making tasks that appeared from analysis of the interview data.

Evidence of Decision Tasks in the Interview Data

Since an objectively appropriate career decision-making process has been identified,[52] and this process is reasonably generic, that framework was used to analyze the interview data. The portion of the framework appropriate to the context of adolescents making career decisions suggests that the logical progression of tasks in career decision making includes: (a) self-assessment (of personal interests, values, skills, and work styles); (b) linking this assessment with possible career areas; (c) investigating possible careers and making a selection (goal-setting); and (d) investigating possible educational institutions, or jobs, to achieve the goal.

Content analysis of the interview data was done to seek evidence for common decisions or tasks that were related to those outlined by Yost and Corbishley.[53] Three respondents (10 percent) described themselves as primarily engaged in self-assessment (abbreviated to SA). Wendy was in this category, saying that "the hardest thing right now in trying to decide what to do is what am I good at, will I find fulfillment from it." Seven respondents (23 percent) were generally investigating possible careers, while continuing to conduct some self-assessment (SA-PC). For instance, Melina was researching career possibilities, while asking herself questions such as, "Do I wanna do this for the rest of my life, do I want to work with computers?" Four respondents (13 percent) were also engaged in self-assessment while actively seeking information about a specific career (SA-SP). A good example of this group was Brenda, who was actively researching engineering as a career choice, as well as trying to understand what she enjoys: "My dad says, 'What do you have a passion for?' And . . . I don't know." Four respondents (13 percent) were conducting general searches for possible careers, with no concurrent self-assessment (PC). Connie was in this group and was researching various possible careers, assessing the choices according to "how the outlook is for the future . . . starting salaries . . . what grades you need and stuff to get into it." Two respondents (7 percent) were investigating specific careers, with no ongoing self-assessment (SP). For instance, Allan had "always" known he wanted to be a "field zoologist" and was intent upon achieving that goal, even though he did not understand what a "field zoologist" does. He had approached his guidance counselor asking "what basic stuff do you [field zoologists] do like, do you actually go out and do a bunch of studies on the field, or do 90 percent of them end up pencil pushing?" The largest group, eleven respondents (37 percent), was investigating possible postsecondary educational institutions at which they might prepare for a career (PI). Gilbert was selecting a college on the basis of course structures, potential for sports scholarships, and campus atmosphere. Included this group was the only respondent who was actively searching for a job immediately following high school graduation. Some of the respondents in this last group appeared to have conducted some previous self-assessment, while others did not comment on the degree to which they had considered their personal interests and aptitudes prior to seeking a possible educational institution. Others in this group, such as Gilbert, had not settled on a specific career, but were nevertheless selecting an institution at which to continue their education.

Thus, this analysis of the help-seeking situations described by interview respondents revealed that they were indeed conducting their information seeking within the four broad tasks noted above. However, it was also clear that these tasks were not being undertaken in the linear and logical progression suggested by Yost and Corbishley,[54] nor were the tasks always clearly distinguishable from one another. Therefore, although the respondents were not followed longitudinally, no linear "process" was apparent from the respondents' discussion of their information seeking for the tasks and decisions they were struggling with. For instance, some participants engaging in self-assessment were simultaneously thinking about possible careers or actively engaged in investigation of specific careers. Seventeen of the thirty respondents did not report any self-assessment (that is, consideration of their suitability for particular careers),[55] and many of these appeared to be seeking help to select possible careers, or even to choose a postsecondary educational institution, without having a clear notion of what their interests, values, skills, and work styles were. This finding may have been the result of a study of adolescents in Canada, who were being pressured by parents, teachers, and guidance counselors, to choose careers and educational institutions before they had been provided the opportunity to thoroughly conduct a self-assessment, perhaps even before they were developmentally ready, to determine what their interests and values were. Such a dilemma occurs primarily because of the lock-step manner in which high school courses must be scheduled, so that students as young as fourteen must selectively choose their high school courses, which largely dictate which college and university programs they can be accepted into. Thus, a student who discovers a year or two before leaving high school that he or she really enjoys physics may be forced to extend his or her years spent in high school to ensure having the required high school physics courses that will enable him or her to study physics at the university level. As well, fourteen-year-olds are too young for some of the formal standard self-assessment tools, such as interest surveys, to be used appropriately.

Information-Seeking Patterns

Table 12.1 summarizes the patterns in the data on information seeking as they were associated with the various task groups. It is important to recognize that because of the small number of respondents in this sample, the patterns discussed are indicative only and provide intriguing possible avenues for further study with larger, more generalizable samples.

Summary of Information Seeking Patterns in the Task Groups

Overall, several patterns associated with these task groups are suggested by the interview data. Figure 12.2 separates the interview respondents in these various task groups according to sex. Clearly, a greater proportion of females were in the task groups that indicated they were conducting self-assessment (ten of the

Table 12.1 Characteristics of Interview Respondents Analyzed by Task Group

*Task group**	*Sex*	*Decision Style†*	*Situation-Perspective‡*	*Sources of Help (f:i)§*	*Barriers"*	*Purposeful Help Seeking#*	*Feelings Experienced*
SA	2 F 1 M	1 I 2 I-D	1 problematic 1 spin-out 1 barrier	0.5	I 3.00 E 1.00	6/3 (2.00)	Anxiety, confusion
SA-PC	6 F 1 M	2 R-I 3 I 2 D	4 spin-out 1 decision 2 moving	0.51	I 1.14 E 1.57 (3 no I, 3 no E)	12/7 (1.71)	Anxiety, pressure to make a decision
PC	1 F 2 M	1 R 2 I	1 spin-out 2 decision	1.00	I 3.00 E 1.33 (1 no E)	10/3 (3.33)	Anxiety, overwhelmed
SA-SP	2 F 1 M	3 R	1 decision 2 moving	1.67	I 1.33 E 1.33 (1 no I, 1 no E)	8/3 (2.67)	Some uncertainty, cautious optimism
SP	1 F 2 M	1 R 1 R-I 1 I	2 decision 1 barrier	1.50	I 0.67 E 2.00 (2 no I, 2 no E)	9/3 (3.00)	Mixed: discouragement, excitement
PI	3 F 8 M	5 R 2 R-I 2 I 2 D	5 decision 4 moving 1 problematic 1 barrier	1.30	I 0.36 E 0.73 (9 I no, 7 no E)	24/11 (2.18)	Optimism, excitement, confidence

* SA = self-assessment; PC = generally investigating possible careers; SP = investigating a specific career; PI = selecting possible institution

° R = rational; RI = rational-intuitive; I = intuitive; ID = intuitive-dependent; D = dependent

‡ These labels for the respondents' views of their situations are from Dervin, "Will information bury us?".

§ Ratio of formal (F) to informal (I) sources

" I= internal barriers; E = external barriers. The figure given is the number of barriers mentioned per respondent in that task group. Note that some respondents claimed to experience no internal (I) or no external (E) barriers.

Mentions of purposeful help seeking/respondents (ratio).

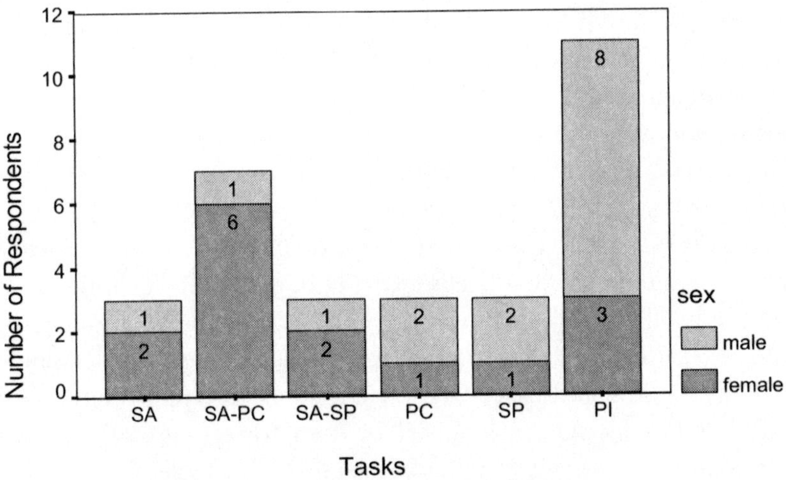

SA=self-assessment; PC=generally investigating possible careers;
SP=investigating a specific career; PI=selecting possible institution

Figure 12.2 Task Groups, Analyzed by Sex of Respondent

fifteen females), sometimes along with general or specific investigation of possible careers. On the other hand, a greater proportion of the males were deciding on a possible postsecondary educational institution, regardless of whether they had done any serious self-assessment. Perhaps the boys wished to convey that they were well along in their career decision making; or perhaps there is greater social acceptance for females to self-reflect or to admit to conducting self-assessment.

The rational decision-making style also seems to be associated with those respondents who were investigating a specific career or selecting an educational institution. Perhaps it is easier to demonstrate a rational decision-making style when one is faced with these particular tasks. Information or help to approach these tasks may be more accessible than that available for those conducting self-assessment or generally investigating multiple career possibilities. Certainly external help is relatively more plentiful for students at the stage of investigating specific careers and choosing educational institutions. There is much internal effort involved in conducting self-assessment and apparently less emphasis on this in the school setting. One implication of this finding is that apparent decision-making style may change depending on the task faced by the decision-maker. Since information seeking also shifts according to decision-making style; this would certainly fit with Dervin's claim that information seeking is contextually dependent. Thus, the assumptions of Harren's framework, based to a large extent on personality factors, and Dervin's emphasis on the context of decision making are difficult to reconcile from a theoretical perspective.

Related to decision-making style is the finding that the types of information sources to which adolescents turn can shift, depending on the task faced. This shift seems appropriate to the needs of each task, since those conducting self-assessment have fewer formal sources of help to turn to and naturally seek the advice of those who know them best, such as family members and friends. Adolescents investigating specific careers or selecting educational institutions have more formal sources of help at their disposal. Those selecting educational institutions also seem to experience the fewest barriers to their information seeking and view their situations as relatively unproblematic, findings that are logical considering the relative abundance and availability of these formal sources of help for that task. Viewing one's situation as a "decision" or as "moving" may relate to the experience of facing fewer barriers, having access to more information, and gaining increasing confidence as one comes closer to the socially acceptable position of having selected a career and a path to reach it.

The final patterns evident from these analyses show that the respondents who are conducting self-assessment and have not yet apparently selected a career express feelings of general uncertainty and anxiety about the future. Those respondents investigating specific careers or educational institutions report more confidence and optimism. Once again, the reasons for this may include easier access to information and more social acceptance related to having made some concrete and visible career decisions.

It is the final pattern apparent in the data, the shifts in feelings across the tasks of career decision making as discussed by the respondents, that corresponds most closely with Kuhlthau's ISP.[56] If Yost and Corbishley's four stages of the career decision-making process[57] are characterized as tasks to be achieved, then a continuum of the tasks facing the interview respondents can be envisaged. This continuum begins with those conducting self-assessment and ends with those selecting educational institutions. It must be remembered, however, that this study was not longitudinal, so respondents were not observed moving along any continuum of tasks. As well, the data clearly show that the respondents did not approach their career decision making in the ideal fashion proposed by Yost and Corbishley.[58] Nevertheless, describing the tasks as positions along a career decision-making process allows a parallel to be drawn with Kuhlthau's six-stage ISP. Further longitudinal study might provide further evidence in support of a process very similar to the ISP. Clearly, the tasks and goals to be achieved differ from those described by Kuhlthau, but these data do provide evidence that the shift in feelings from uncertainty and anxiety to optimism and confidence apparent in Kuhlthau's theory of information seeking are indeed apparent in the pattern of feelings expressed by the task groups that emerged from the data. A fuller description of a career decision-making process as suggested by the data would require longitudinal analysis of career decision making. Each task group suggested by the analysis of the interview transcripts would require detailed investigation, such as that conducted by Kuhlthau, in order to characterize the aspects of thought, feeling, and behavior associated with each task. This study took each act of information seeking as the unit of analysis, rather than the task of career decision making, since these stages were not initially apparent but emerged from analysis of the interview data. Therefore, a more careful analysis of Kuhlthau's taxonomy of thought, feeling, and behavior would have to be based on longitudinal analysis of the information seeking occurring for each task.

CONCLUSION

This research has both theoretical and practical significance. Sense-making theory was tested for its adaptability to a new context (adolescents seeking help with their career decisions); Kuhlthau's ISP was tested in a context very different from the one from which it was developed; and Harren's decision-making theory was tested to determine its usefulness for assessing adolescent career decision making. Furthermore, adolescents are an understudied group with regard to information behavior. The degree to which adolescent information seeking is comparable with evidence from studies of adult information seeking is only beginning to be explored. Thus, adolescents have been marginalized in information-seeking research and, therefore, have a claim on researchers to recognize their unique information needs and to start to characterize their information behavior.

From a practical point of view, this research was undertaken to shed some light on ways in which adolescents prefer to get the help they need to make career decisions. Greater understanding of adolescents' perspectives on this process can assist information providers to deliver their services in a more effective manner. In the long term, greater awareness of the types of help that adolescents need, and of the importance of career decision making for female adolescents in particular, can help to ameliorate difficulties faced by youth as they seek information—both for career decisions and in other contexts in which adolescents require access to helpful information.

In addition to enriching theoretical understanding of information-seeking behavior, particularly in this context, there may be practical implications that can be drawn from this analysis. For example, information-service providers can be aware of the experiences of these decision makers as they face various tasks. These experiences include a particular perception of the situation or context in which they find themselves, feelings about that situation, and the barriers to help seeking they perceive. As well, help providers can be aware of the relative formality of help sources likely to be approached and the decision-making style likely to be manifested. As is the case in all instances in which greater understanding of the perspective of the help seeker can be provided, improved delivery of useful and timely help to information seekers may result.

ACKNOWLEDGMENT

Warmest thanks to Dr. Gillian Michell, formerly at the University of Western Ontario, for her superb supervision of my Ph.D. thesis. I also wish to thank the research participants who shared their time and thoughts so generously.

NOTES

1. Brian Balcombe, "The importance of career education in the 1990s," *Guidance and Counselling* 10 (Winter 1995): 19–26.

2. Balcombe, "The importance of career education."

3. Joan C. Durrance, "Developing need-based job and career information services in public libraries," *Collection Building* 12, no. 3/4 (1993): 105–112, quote on p. 105.

4. Heidi Julien, "Adolescent career decision-making and the potential role of the public library," *Public Libraries* (Nov./Dec. 1998): 2–7; Heidi Julien, "Barriers to adolescents' information seeking for career decision-making," *Journal of the American Society for Information Science* 50, no. 1 (1999): 38–48; Heidi Julien, "How does information help? The

search for career-related information by adolescents," Ph.D. thesis, University of Western Ontario, 1997.

5. Brenda Dervin, *An overview of sense-making research: Concepts, methods, and results to date* (Seattle: University of Washington School of Communications, 1983); Brenda Dervin, "From the mind's eye of the user: The sense-making qualitative-quantitative methodology," in ed. Jack D. Glazier and Ronald R. Powell, *Qualitative research in information management* (pp. 61–84) (Englewood, Colo.: Libraries Unlimited, 1992).

6. Carol C. Kuhlthau, "Inside the search process: Information seeking from the user's perspective," *Journal of the American Society for Information Science* 42 (June 1991): 361–371.

7. Vincent A. Harren, "A model of career decision making for college students," *Journal of Vocational Behavior* 14 (April 1979): 119–133.

8. Carol Gilligan, Nona P. Lyons, and Trudy J. Hanmer, *Making connections: The relational worlds of adolescent girls at Emma Willard School* (Cambridge: Harvard University Press, 1990); Carol Gilligan, Janie Victoria Ward, and Jill McLean Taylor, eds., *Mapping the moral domain* (Cambridge: Harvard University Press, 1988); Mary Field Belenky, Blythe McVicker Clinchy, Nancy Rule Goldberger, and Jill Mattuck Tarule, *Women's ways of knowing: The development of self, voice and mind* (n.p.: Basic Books, 1986).

9. Thomas Abernathy and William Davis, "Student perceptions of influences on career and educational decision-making," *Canadian Counsellor* 12, no. 3 (1978): 162–166; Maureen Baker, *What will tomorrow bring? A study of the aspirations of adolescent women* (Ottawa: Canadian Advisory Council on the Status of Women, 1985); Donald Posterski and Reginald Bibby, *Canada's youth: Ready for today: A comprehensive survey of 15–24 year olds* (Ottawa: Canadian Youth Foundation, 1988); Richard Young, John D. Friesen, and Jo-Anne M. Dillabough, "Personal constructions of parental influence related to career development," *Canadian Journal of Counselling* 25 (April 1991): 183–190; Catherine A. Loughlin, "Part-time employment and adolescents' work-related attitudes, beliefs, and aspirations," Master's thesis, Queen's University, 1993; Brenda A. Tomini and Stewart Page, "Vocational bias and gender: Evaluations of high school counsellors by Canadian University undergradu-

ates," *Canadian Journal of Counselling* 26 (April 1992): 100–106; A. J. C. King, *The adolescent experience* (Toronto: Ontario Secondary School Teachers' Federation, 1986).

10. Byron Anderson, "Introduction: Expansion of career and job information services," *Reference Librarian* 36 (1992): 1–6; Nancy L. Larson and Carole Minor, "Information empowers people to build careers," *Reference Librarian* 36 (1992): 7–16 Alan J. Farber, "Evaluating occupational information for use in libraries and career resource centers," *Reference Librarian* 36 (1992): 105–119; Diane Tuccillo, "Looking ahead: Developing and promoting a career information center for teens," *Emergency Librarian* 16 (Sept./Oct. 1988): 29–31.

11. Byron Anderson, "Delivering career and job information: A place for libraries," *Reference Librarian* 36 (1992): 17–32.

12. Durrance, "Developing need-based job and career information services"; Joan C. Durrance, Kathleen M. Savage, Mary Jo Ryan, and Stephen M. Mallinger, *Serving job seekers and career changers: A planning manual for public libraries* (Chicago: American Library Association, 1993).

13. Durrance, "Developing need-based job and career information services."

14. Florence DeHart and Gerrit W. Bleeker, "Helping young adults use information in problem solving," *Journal of Youth Services in Libraries* 1 (Spring 1988): 305–309.

15. Dervin, *An overview of sense-making research*; and "From the mind's eye of the user."

16. Barbara Poston-Anderson and Susan Edwards, "The role of information in helping adolescent girls with their life concerns," *School Library Media Quarterly* 22 (Fall 1993): 25–30.

17. Poston-Anderson and Edwards, "The role of information," 27.

18. Poston-Anderson and Edwards, "The role of information," 30.

19. Jack de Stefano Bernardelli and Florent Dumont, "Occupational information-seeking as a function of perception of locus of control and other personality variables," *Canadian Counsellor* 17 (January 1983): 75–81.

20. Albert W. Gould and John Mazzco, "Age and sex differences in early adolescents' information sources," *Journal of Early Adolescence* 2 (Fall 1982): 283–292.

21. J. R. Bruce Cassie, R. G. Ragsdale, G. E. Burns, and M. Robinson, *Sex role stereotyping: Incidence and implications for guidance and counselling of students* (Toronto: Ontario Institute for Studies in Education, 1980).

22. David A. Jepsen, "Antecedent events to adolescent career decision processes," *Guidance and Counselling* 4, no. 5 (1989): 5–14.

23. Jepsen, "Antecedent events to adolescent career decision processes."

24. Leon Mann, Ros Harmoni, and Colin Power, "Adolescent decision-making: The development of competence," *Journal of Adolescence* 12 (September 1989): 265–278.

25. Mann, Harmoni, and Power, "Adolescent decision-making."

26. Cassie, Ragsdale, Burns, and Robinson, *Sex role stereotyping*.

27. Jacob E. Brown and Leon Mann, "The relationship between family structure and process variables and adolescent decision making," *Journal of Adolescence* 13 (March 1990): 25–37.

28. Cassie, Ragsdale, Burns, and Robinson, *Sex role stereotyping*.

29. Dervin, *An overview of sense-making research*; and "From the mind's eye of the user."

30. This list of situations, gaps, and uses are from Dervin, *An overview of sense-making research*, as summarized by Dervin in "Will information bury us?," lecture at the Graduate School of Library and Information Science, University of Western Ontario, London, June 7, 1989.

31. Kuhlthau, "Inside the search process."

32. G. A. Kelly, *A theory of personality: The psychology of personal constructs* (New York: Norton, 1963).

33. N. J. Belkin, H. M. Brooks, and R. N. Oddy, "ASK for Information Retrieval," *Journal of Documentation* 38 (1982): 61–71.

34. R. S. Taylor, "Question-negotiation and information seeking in libraries," *College and Research Libraries* 29 (1968): 178–194.

35. Kuhlthau, "Inside the search process."

36. Harren, "A model of career decision making for college students."

37. Ethel Auster and Chun-Wei Choo, "CEOs, information, and decision making: Scanning the environment for strategic advantage," *Library Trends* 43 (1994): 206–225.

38. Paul N. Gorman, "Information seeking of primary care physicians:

Conceptual models and empirical studies," in T. D. Wilson and D. K. Allen, eds., *Exploring the contexts of information behavior: Proceedings of the second International Conference on Research in Information Needs, Seeking and Use in Different Contexts,* 13–15 August 1998, Sheffield, UK (London: Taylor Graham, 1998), 226–240.

39. Thomas H. Davenport, *Information ecology: Mastering the information and knowledge environment* (New York: Oxford University Press, 1997).

40. Harren, "A model of career decision making for college students."

41. Gilligan, Lyons, and Hanmer, *Making connections*; Gilligan, Ward, and McLean Taylor, *Mapping the moral domain*; Belenky, McVicker Clinchy, Goldberger, and Mattuck Tarule, *Women's ways of knowing.*

42. Belenky, McVicker Clinchy, Goldberger, and Mattuck Tarule, *Women's ways of knowing.*

43. Julien, "Adolescent career decision-making"; "Barriers to adolescents' information seeking"; "How does information help?"

44. Anton J. Kuzel, "Sampling in qualitative inquiry" in Benjamin F. Crabtree, and William L. Miller, eds., *Doing qualitative research* (pp. 31–44). (Newbury Park, Calif.: Sage, 1992).

45. Michael Brenner, "Survey interviewing" in Michael Brenner, Jennifer Brown, and David Canter, eds., *The research interview: Uses and approaches* (pp. 9–36) (Toronto: Academic Press, 1985).

46. Julien, "Adolescent career decision-making"; "Barriers to adolescents' information seeking"; "How does information help?"

47. Matthew B. Miles and A. Michael Huberman, *Qualitative data analysis*, 2nd ed. (Thousand Oaks, Calif.: Sage, 1994).

48. Barbara Mostyn, "The content analysis of qualitative research data: A dynamic approach," in Michael Brenner, Jennifer Brown, and David Canter, eds., *The research interview: Uses and approaches* (pp. 115–146) (Toronto: Academic Press, 1985).

49. All participants have been assigned fictitious names.

50. Field Belenky, McVicker Clinchy, Rule Goldberger, and Mattuck Tarule, *Women's ways of knowing.*

51. Kuhlthau, "Inside the search process."

52. Elizabeth B. Yost and M. Anne Corbishley, *Career counseling: A psychological approach* (San Francisco: Jossey-Bass, 1987).

53. Yost and Corbishley, *Career counseling*.

54. Yost and Corbishley, *Career counseling*.

55. Interestingly, nor did any interview participants mention turning to themselves as sources of help in their career decision-making. The reasons for this are unknown, and it is puzzling in light of the questionnaire data that showed that the self was one of the two most used sources and one of the most helpful sources.

56. Kuhlthau, "Inside the search process."

57. Durrance, Savage, Ryan, and Mallinger, *Serving job seekers and career changers*.

58. Yost and Corbishley, *Career counseling*.

THIRTEEN

Adolescents' Information Seeking and Utilization in Relation to Drugs

Ross J. Todd and Susan Edwards

The study of human information behavior is built on the widely accepted assumption that information has the potential to change what people already know and the belief that understanding more about how it changes people can contribute to more effective provision of information services and products. Considerable attention has been given in recent years to understanding the behavioral, affective, and cognitive dimensions of human information behavior, and some attention has been given to identifying patterns in the scope and nature of this inquiry. The purpose of this chapter is to further explore the concept of information utilization by looking at adolescents in the context of life concerns, particularly that of drugs. It reports findings derived from the ongoing analysis of data from Australian research undertaken by Edwards and Poston Anderson (1993–1996) and Todd (1999a, b). Using an analytical framework based on the propositional statements of Chatman's Theory of Information Poverty (Chatman, 1996), the interplay of several factors, particularly notions of insiders and outsiders; judgments about risks, costs, and benefits; and social norms appear to have created an information world rich in potential sources but in reality for these adolescents a world that is devoid of sources of information they can utilize in relation to their needs about drugs.

BACKGROUND

The notion of information utilization has been identified as an important concept in the study of people's information-seeking behavior, albeit a seldom-studied area (Vakkari, 1997, p. 460). In recent years, there has been considerably more focus on this dimension, and Todd (1999b) presents an extensive review of this literature . It is characterized by a diverse range of definitions built on different concepts of what information is, ranging from notions of applications of specific social science research programs to decisions in ways to make a difference, to consumption of information, helps, and active strategies of adoption. As a whole, the literature conveys the sense that information utilization is all about people and information coming together; it is about people "doing something" with information they have sought and gathered themselves, or that was provided by someone else. Historically, the study of information utilization centers on organizational or systems contexts where it has been largely conceptualized as "acting"—a "behavioral doing"—with particular attention given to the types of organizational change, end-states, external behaviors, actions and outcomes of the impact of science, and social science-based expertise and research by groups of people in public policy, organizations, and professional practice. Such end-states are concrete, overt, tangible, perceptible to the people involved, and open to direct and objective observation and measurement by others. Information utilization is seen to begin after the information is produced or created, and information is said to be utilized when it is implemented as part of a program or directly leads to some specific decision or specific course of action. The end-states are the evidence of information utilization.

The shift to a user-oriented paradigm in information science in the past two decades has also seen emphasis being placed on the study of information utilization in a wider social context of the information needs and information-seeking behaviors of individuals and from the perspective of the individuals. It is conceptualized more holistically as a complex interactive change process, with attention given to the process of "thinking"—a cognitive "doing"—as well as "acting"—the behavioral outcomes and end-states. This more holistic view of information utilization firmly embeds the notion of cognitive and behavioral changes as central concepts and makes the distinction between "utilization" as doing something with information and making a difference to the thoughts and actions of people; with "impact," seen as modifications in a program or policy, and "utility," referring to the relevance of the information (primarily research findings) to an area of policy or program. The focus is on the complex dynamic of information needs, context, information seeking, interaction with information sources, and cognitive and behavioral outcomes. The sense-making theory developed by Dervin (1989) has contributed substantially to this perspective. As a set of assumptions about the nature of information and human communicating and how people utilize information, sense-making is portrayed as a constructive process, and sense is the product of that process. Information utilization is posited as a "constructing" activity, that is, "the successive modifications of internal pictures of reality, a series of constructings and reconstructings (Dervin, 1983, p. 5). Consistent with the constructing activity, Dervin's uses/helps, conceptualized in terms of how the individual is helped, facilitated, or sometimes impeded by the information, are presented as verbs, rather than nouns, such as: got encouraged; got new/altered specified pix; got new/altered general pix; could see the road ahead; identified possibilities; found direction/planned; got away from bad feelings; and avoided pitfalls (Dervin, Harlock, Atwood, and Garzona, 1986); arrived/ made progress; creating ideas, finding directions or ways to move, acquiring skills, getting support or confirmation, getting motivated, getting connected to others, calming down or relaxing, getting pleasure or happiness, and reaching goals (Dervin, 1992).

ADOLESCENTS' INFORMATION SEEKING AND UTILIZATION

To date considerable attention has been given to understanding the information behavior of adolescents, particularly in school contexts and in relation to learning curriculum content. These studies examine various aspects of the relationship between student learning and their engagement with the information environment, particularly school libraries and the World Wide Web. Characteristically, they seek to understand more precisely and specifically how targeted groups of students, across a wide range of age groups, curriculum settings, and instructional designs, seek and utilize different information sources. How this can best be enabled, the specific impacts of the development of information scaffolds, and the range of behavioral, affective, and cognitive dimensions that shape the information behaviors of students are also examined.

Kuhlthau's (1991, 1993, 1994, 1999) research centering on the information search process (ISP) has played an important part in shaping subsequent research that has explored the cognitive, behavioral, and affective dimensions of adolescent information seeking and utilization. Three major generalizations can be identified from this body of research. First, a process approach, focusing on the systematic and explicit development of students' abilities to connect with, interact with, and utilize information to construct personal understanding, results in improved performance in terms of personal mastery of content. This is shown in examination and assignment grades and through the mastery of a wide range of particular information skills (Gordon, 2000; Grant, 1998; Hawkes, 1997; Jones, 1996; Lance, Rodney, and Hamilton-Pennell, 2000;

Lewis, 1999; Maxwell, 2000; Moore, 1996; Todd, 1995; Todd, Lamb, and McNicholas, 1993). Second, the systematic and explicit development of students' abilities to connect with, interact with, and utilize information to construct personal understanding, results in: more positive attitudes to learning; increased active engagement in the learning environment; and more positive perceptions of students themselves as active, constructive learners (Moore and Poulopoulos, 1999; Rich, 1999; Todd, 1995; Todd, Lamb, and McNicholas, 1993). Third, there is clear evidence that active reading programs encouraged by the school library can foster higher levels of reading, comprehension, vocabulary development, and language skills. Indeed, research spanning many decades highlights that when there is access to diverse reading materials, more reading is done, and literacy development is fostered (Digiovanna, 1994; Halliwell, 1995; Krashen, 1993; Lipscomb, 1993; McQuillan, 1997).

A second stream of research focuses on the characteristics of adolescents' information-seeking behavior on the World Wide Web. Although primarily exploratory in nature, this research highlights a number of aspects: the structure of the task impacts Web searching performance (Schacter, Chung, and Dorr, 1998); lack of systematic planning of search strategies (Schacter, Chung, and Dorr, 1998); inefficiency in navigating and using the Web (Large, Beheshti and Moukdad, 1999; Wallace and Kupperman, 1997); superficial browsing (Fidel, R., R. K. Davies, M. H. Douglass, J. K. Holder, C. J. Hopkins, E. J. Kushner, B. K. Miyagishima, et al. 1999; Hirsh, 1999); high levels of information overload and inability to manage and reduce large volumes of information (Atkin, 1998; McNicholas and Todd, 1996); and difficulties in making relevance and authority judgments (Hirsh, 1999; McNicholas and Todd, 1996; Wallace and Kuperman, 1997). This research, in contrast to the commonly held view that adolescents are gurus in this vast digital world, suggests that the intuitiveness, ease, certainty, and success as input and outcome attributes of adolescents' searching the World Wide Web are highly questionable.

Against this backdrop, considerably less attention has been given to adolescents' information-seeking behavior in daily life contexts, and even less in relation to their life concerns. Although there is considerable research relating to leisure reading and mass media use, there are fewer studies that deal with information about concerns such as drug usage, health, careers, and unemployment, as well as evaluating the impact of information provision programs on behaviors related to these. (Buysse, 1996; Edwards and Poston-Anderson, 1993, 1996; Julien, 1999; Makkai and McAllister, 1990; Mayton, Nagel, and Parker, 1990; Mirzaee, Kingery, and Puitt, 1991; Newell-Withrow, 1989; Poston Anderson and Edwards, 1993). With some exceptions, these studies have not been from the perspective of adolescents themselves and have tended to use quantitative structured data collection methods. One of the key assumptions underpinning this research is the notion that school and public libraries can be powerful catalysts in a young person's life, providing both an environment and access to sources to information that can shape choices and decisions about life and lifestyle matters.

Poston-Anderson and Edwards's (1993) study of thirteen- and fourteen-year-old girls, using structured interviews, found that although adolescents have no difficulty expressing their information needs, very few actively sought information from libraries and other information agencies. The school library was perceived as a mechanism for control, as a source of only socially sanctioned material, and as dealing with subjects for curricular use only. In a later study focusing on concerns about future jobs and future education, Edwards and Poston-Anderson (1996) found that adolescents engaged in little or no formal information seeking and tended not to approach friends, teachers, career advisers, and librarians. Julien's (1999) analysis of adolescents' information seeking for career decision making, using both a written questionnaire and semistructured interviews, found that despite the apparent lack of barriers, 40 percent of the adolescents did not know where to go to get help to make their decisions, and a similar number found that there were too many places to go for help in their information seeking. The study also showed that the lack of clarity of appropriate processes for career decision making led many to feel anxious and overwhelmed, and when offered assistance, they did not know what questions to ask. Todd's (1999a) study of how adolescents utilize information about heroin identified five types of cognitive information utilization: get a complete picture, get a verified picture, get a changed picture, get a clearer picture, and get a position in a picture. These types of cognitive information utilization can be conceptualized as information intents, that is, information, deliberately and intentionally selected from what is available, and its utilization, that enable people to adapt and create pictures of their world. In the process of doing something cognitively with this information, people are able to move on—get complete, changed, verified, or clearer pictures, and form opinions and state viewpoints. These intents represent cognitive goals that shape the process of information utilization. The study showed that adolescents in this study were not passive, robot-like processors of information; rather they were active creators of new knowledge, manipulating information selectively, intentionally, and creatively to build opinions, viewpoints, arguments, explanations, and to change and/or verify facts.

THE RESEARCH STUDIES

This chapter seeks to present some further insights derived from the continued analysis of data collected by Edwards and Poston-Anderson from 1992 to 1998 and Todd from 1995 to 1997 with the aim of further concept and theory generation in relation to adolescents' evolving information processes in relation to their life concerns, and in particular some of the factors that influence their information seeking and utilization. Edwards and Poston-Anderson's work centers on girls in grades 7, 8, and 9, in public and private schools from different socioeconomic areas in Sydney, Australia, selected on the basis of purposeful and convenience sampling and collecting qualitative data through a series of extended structured and semistructured interviews. This work focuses on the role of information in helping adolescent girls with their life concerns: how they express their information needs relating to life concerns, the extent to which they perceive school and public libraries as sources for meeting those information needs, and how they conceptualize those information needs when they interact with formal information systems. Todd's (1999a, b, c) work has centered on understanding the cognitive dynamics of how adolescents build their knowledge about one particular life concern, that of the drug heroin. It centers on seventeen-year-old girls in grade 12 in a private school in Sydney and from different cultural backgrounds who were nonrandomly selected to work with in-depth to gather detailed "thick" data on how they build their understanding about this drug. The data were collected by employing a quasi-experimental methodology, free generation written discourse, and question answering protocols through a semistructured interview, together with an extended debriefing interview. The lengthy debriefing interview focused on identifying the enabling effects of the exposures, as well as discussing their perceptions of the knowledge-building process and the factors that have shaped or hindered this.

The framework for the analysis reported here is comprised of the six propositional statements posed by Chatman (1996) describing an impoverished information world:

> People who are defined as information poor perceive themselves to be devoid of any sources that might help them.
>
> Information poverty is partially associated with class distinction.

That is, the condition of information poverty is influenced by outsiders who withhold privileged access to information.

Information poverty is determined by self-protective behaviors that are used in response to social norms.

Both secrecy and deception are self-protecting mechanisms due to a sense of mistrust regarding the interest or ability of others to provide useful information.

A decision to risk exposure about our true problems is often not taken due to a perception that negative consequences outweigh benefits.

New knowledge will be selectively introduced into the information world of poor people. A condition that influences this process is the relevance of that information in response to everyday problems and concerns.

Chatman's "Theory of Information Poverty" (Chatman, 1996, p. 197) as expressed through these propositions has been derived from a number of empirical studies of "ordinary people" and their searching for information undertaken by Chatman. These are studies of adults: janitors, single mothers, and aging women. Intuitively these propositions seemed to explain and help us make sense of some of the empirical observations in the interviews with the adolescent girls in the studies reported here. Rather than taking Chatman's propositions and testing them against the data, our purpose was to identify aspects of adolescents' information seeking and utilization in relation to drugs, which might be similar and different to Chatman's propositions, in order to draw some further understandings about the information world of adolescent girls. In order to conceptualize similar patterns or characteristics, the constant comparative method of Glaser and Strauss (1967) was used. This is an interactive process of comparing and aggregating pairs of ideas on the basis of look-alike characteristics guided by Chatman's propositions and formulating some findings accordingly. The findings here thus represent some tentative understandings about adolescents and information poverty, in the light of Chatman's Theory of Information Poverty. (Transcript extracts used throughout this study are retained in the Department of Media Arts, Communication, and Information at the University of Technology, Sydney, Australia.)

FINDINGS

The Emergence of the Concern

The girls in these studies identified drugs as one of their major current life concerns, and there was a definite starting point among all the girls. There were a number of reasons for this. Interestingly, all the girls saw the concern beginning around the same point—the time of their transition from primary school (grade 6) to secondary school (grade 7) in Australia, and continuing throughout their high school years. This transition for all girls meant a change of school, new teachers, new patterns of learning, more and new students in the same grade, and more important, exposure to older students and new ideas:

> Well I s'pose it would've started when we hit high school, because like in primary school everything's, I s'pose you're really sheltered from life in general but when you hit high school it's like you're exposed to everything . . . and like the drugs were introduced because we had like I s'pose new people who were into it and everything and like a lot of us weren't and so we all try it. I didn't personally but a lot of friends did.

Several things appear to happen at this transition point that made drugs suddenly become a major concern. First, they reported hearing others talk about drugs when no one talked about drugs in primary school: "they talk more freely about drinking and smoking and about their friends doing all sorts of drugs." Drugs seemed to become a noticeable part of life with the move to high school. The girls also observed that some of their friends began to change with this transition. They saw their friends associating with students who were involved in drugs and beginning to experiment with drugs. Along with this experimentation, the girls consistently indicated that they observed the behaviors and personalities of their friends undergoing some changes. The perceived changes most often mentioned were that their friends were becoming more aggressive in their interactions with others, they had decreased academic performance, they withdrew from their established friendship groups, and they experienced a change in their physical appearance, for example, they claimed they looked sick, or unhealthy, or withdrawn:

> You just kind of look at them and they're all like, like really sick and really stupid I s'pose . . . emotionally they go like really weird and upset and everything . . . they fight with friends and their parents and everything and they end up just hating everyone and everyone hates them and they get all worried . . . it's just hopeless. . . . . Like with smoking or something you can see the people and their hands are different colors and their teeth are different colors and they're coughing. They go all moody.

It was clear that the girls' preexisting knowledge about drugs and their effects, learned before going to high school, was drawn on to help them understand and explain the behaviors of their friends. They knew of, for example, the addictive nature of drugs, that "once you start you can't stop"; and of the bad health effects, for example, smoking: "it's bad and you get lung cancer and stuff." The most common expression was "I know it's bad." This preexisting knowledge was derived in particular from the antismoking and antidrug campaigns on television: "you see a lot on television and it gradually sinks in"; from some parents: "my mum keeps telling me how bad drugs are"; and from some of the older students: "you learn a lot by listening to the older kids talking about what they do, and bragging about it." The drug education classes as part of the school curriculum were also an important source: "we get it non-stop at school in our health classes, year after year." However, the girls' perceptions of these classes were almost entirely negative, as these classes were characterized in many cases by "the boys mucking around" and "everyone laughing at the teacher." In addition to these sources of existing knowledge, there was knowledge constructed through their own observations of parents as well as those in their peer group and thinking and reflecting on what they were seeing: "you see and hear things that trigger your curiosity, and you go away and think about them a bit." Interestingly, very few girls mentioned friends or peers as sources of preexisting information.

Against this environmental background and their preexisting knowledge, it was apparent that the girls knew a lot of the standard things about drugs that adults particularly want them to know, for example: "smoking causes lung cancer"; and that "peer pressure is one reason for getting into drugs." This knowledge was also linked to what they were seeing their friends do at high school. However, what appears to stand out in the data is the girls' perceptions that this knowledge did not provide them with what they needed to make sense of what was going on around them—to make sense of drugs and high school life—and even more important, to be able to help their friends who had entered, or were planning to enter, the drug culture. For many girls, it was this instrumental use of knowledge—putting it to effective use—that was so crucially important. Although the girls were accepting of this knowledge, they indicated clearly that it did not satisfy them in terms of answering some of the deep questions that were confronting them. For instance, they saw people change when they took drugs, and they wanted to know what makes them act that way; why does their behavior change; why do they become so aggressive: "they look bad, they smell bad . . . why?" It was apparent that although the girls accepted these things, they were not satisfied in their understanding of why this was happening to them. The standard information about drugs that adults particularly wanted them to know was "surface" information to the girls. It did not satisfy their deep questions, their "deep" information needs.

Deep Questioning

Within this context, this leads to the phenomena emerging from these studies that can be labeled "deep questioning." Deep questions are those information needs—the need to know, find out, and understand—that actually on the surface sound like commonplace or everyday standard questions, like "why do people get into drugs" and "what are the effects of taking drugs," but that take the girls beyond the commonly provided and accepted answers—the type of questions that media, schooling, and adults typically answer—to in-depth probing levels of "why," "how," and "what" beyond the everyday response. The girls mentioned several types of deep questions, which we have categorized in the following way:

Deep Questioning about Motives

These questions related to why people, particularly the girls' friends and peers, take drugs:

> "I know her life is bad, but why does she take drugs?"
> "I know she has a hard life but why does she do it?"

For these girls, just saying they had a "hard" or "bad" life was not a satisfactory answer; what they were interested in knowing was why some people who have hard lives or bad lives do not take drugs, while some who have hard or bad lives do take drugs.

> "I know it's peer pressure, but why do boys pressure each other? They all do"

One girl, talking about her friends' smoking, said: "friends say it is just fun, gives you a high for a second. I thought, well, that's not a very good answer because that doesn't explain anything. It just doesn't seem true, the real reason."

Deep Questioning about the Drug Experience

For girls who had not tried drugs, their questions centered on understanding what it was actually like to take drugs. Although they knew the long-term effects, for example, that smoking can cause lung cancer, they wanted more explicit information that gave them a clear and intimate sense of the effect of drugs:

"What does it really really feel like on drugs?"
"What actually makes it feel so good to them?"
"I want to know like why they get high on it and the long-term effects. It's very hard to explain, like the guys, they get high. How? And why? What is actually happening?"
"I want to know what it really feels like to take drugs . . . what it does to my body and mind in a very detailed way, as if by knowing about it I can almost actually feel it."
"It's wanting to know what it actually does to you—so I'm able to look at heroin from different sides rather than having a narrow fixed view."

Deep Questioning about the Processes and Effects of Taking Drugs

These questions related to what drugs specifically do to the body and how this actually happens:

> With smoking you get lung cancer like that's a known thing you're basically taught now from when you're little. But like from drugs like, like the only side effect I could even think of would be . . . you

go like kind of stupid and you can lose your head. . . . [later] what's actually, I s'pose what's in it that like makes them go all, all silly and do funny things . . . if they give me some technical name I wouldn't really understand but like why does it actually affect them, like what is it, does it attack the brain or something. And like that it sets off a reaction or something and does it like get into your blood and that goes through your brain . . . you look for something and no one ever actually says . . . there has to be some little thing in them that does it to them.

"What are the specific effects of different drugs—not just like drugs make you go brain dead, like this drug does this to you?"
"What goes on in your brain? I want to know what is happening inside a person's head."
"We're told smoking causes heart attacks . . . but how does it cause a heart attack?"

Deep Questioning about Addiction

These questions related to why people can't stop taking drugs:

"I know that it is addictive, but what is it that can't make them stop?"
"I know that you can overdose, but how much does it take?"
"What is it like to overdose? What does it do?"
"I know that you get high on drugs, but I don't know what 'high' is—how do you really know?"

Deep Questioning about the Drugs and Drug Culture

These questions focused on understanding some of the processes and mechanisms used by people in obtaining drugs:

"Where do they get these drugs from?"
"What are the drugs like?"
"How do you buy it?"
"Where do they get the money from to buy it?"
"Like I know they get it from dealers, but dealers have to get it from somewhere . . . do they grow them in their backyards or something, not like in an exact backyards as such, but like little backyards they blend in with other plants I suppose?"
"I know like marijuana it's a plant but like so what, like I know you just can't pick a leaf off it—bang—you've got a drug. What do they do to it to get it to the drug and, you know, what do they add in it that's so bad for you?"
"Where does she get the money?"

Deep Questioning about Social Aspects

These questions related to broader historical, legal, and economic aspects of drug culture outside the girls' immediate experience:

"I want to know how on earth it could have wound up here, and how they could have got people to start buying it."
"Who made the first one and why did they do it? Why didn't they stop them?"
"I know it is addictive but how hard is it to quit? Will they ever quit? How did it start? Who did the first cigarette?"

Deep Questioning about Tactics

These questions related particularly to how to help their friends:

"How can I help my friends stop?"
"What is the convincing argument I can provide for my brother?"

"I want to know where I stand—to develop my own view to be able to speak to others."
"I want to be able to present a more accurate argument."
"How can I build a stronger case? . . . help me express an opinion based on fact."
"What shall I tell them when they want to do something bad to themselves, like commit suicide?"

SOURCES OF INFORMATION

It was quite easy for the girls to generate these questions—they had no trouble doing this quickly, and they clearly considered these concerns and questions as important—that there was a need and urgency to find answers to their questions in order to understand what was going around them:

"Should I do something about smoking drugs? Should I try to help them?"
"What can I say when they call me when I am on drugs and they want me to help them?"

However, there was the clear perception that the easily accessible sources, such as books in the school library and interpersonal sources including significant others and friends, did not provide the specific information they needed to answer these questions, and that the girls did little to actively search for answers. Siblings as information sources were rarely mentioned, and when they were, they were not portrayed in a helpful light: "we never talk"; "I'm not close"; and "we always fight." What stands out in this analysis is that there was almost no information seeking outside of themselves, primarily because of the perceived barriers and costs to getting the information. The girls conveyed the impression that answers to these deep questions are privileged information. Four interrelated aspects appear to contribute to this, and these focus on Chatman's notions of (1) insider-outsider; (2) cost and benefits; (3) unwillingness to disclose and share personal information; and (4) social norms. These four aspects are elaborated by examining the interrelationships between the girls and the potential sources of information they identified in the interviews.

Girls: Norm Group

The evidence from this study shows that impersonal sources of information, including friends, and in particular the girls' norm group, are not useful sources of relevant information. This is a picture not dissimilar to that described by Chatman. There are several reasons for this. First, there was evidence from the studies to indicate that if girls do not smoke, drink, or take drugs, they are somehow different from groups of girls who do smoke, drink, or take drugs, and that there is a great deal of distrust and animosity between these two types of norm groups. Most of the girls in the samples did not smoke, drink, or take drugs, nor did they have any intention to do so on an ongoing basis. Their norm group was composed of girls who were like them, and they perceived that it was not appropriate to raise drug-related issues or ask important questions to their friends in their norm group:

"We just don't discuss smoking. They just think it is kind of uncool, so we don't talk about it at all. They don't like the people who do."

"There's not many people that I can really talk to, but there are friends, but you know they do not care about it . . . because they don't do it and they have no concern about it. . . . I'm sort of in two different groups, and one of the groups don't smoke at all and the other group smokes. So they don't really know of other people from the other group so they don't really care."

When they were asked if they ever tried to discuss it with friends who don't smoke their replies were:

> "They sort of change the subject. . . . Whenever I try to talk to them they are always ignoring me. . . . they are probably thinking in their heads 'oh I know what she is going to say. I can't be bothered to listen.'"
>
> "My friends are so against it that they can't open up. They would go all funny on me."

The fact that they have an interest in these drug activities and want to ask deep questions to their norm group indicates that they may have perceived themselves as outsiders, thinking and behaving somehow differently from their norm group, and thereby excluded in terms of engaging in seeking answers to these questions.

The second reason why the norm group was "devoid of any sources which might help them" was that they perceived that the answers to so many of the deep questions demanded firsthand knowledge derived from real experiences to provide satisfactory answers, and that the norm group did not have the experiences from which these answers could be derived. Friends with no experience were not perceived to be able to provide any useful information:

> "Friends don't know more than I do about the facts of drugs."
>
> "They've never experienced it, so they just wouldn't know about what I want to know."

The third reason related to the nature of the conversations within the norm group is the way friends talk to each other. One rule mentioned repeatedly was that in finding out, learning, or understanding, "you don't ask questions"; rather, "you have to wait for a topic to arise naturally in the group conversations." Given that this group rarely talks about drugs, as it is not an important part of their lives, these chances for naturally arising conversation do not often occur:

> "We talk about it, drugs and what they do to you. But you know, you don't like to ask any questions about it or anything, it's like oh, don't you think this person's really stupid because they do this?"
>
> "Unless they are a close friend, you wouldn't really ask any questions."

When asked what that would be, they responded:

> "I don't really know, it's just something you don't talk about. You don't ask friends questions unless you're in a discussion about it."
>
> "Once I thought about asking a friend and I thought about maybe bringing it up sometime on the bus, but the opportunity didn't come and I just sort of shied away from it."

What emerges from this analysis is that social norms are important in determining which topics are acceptable for pursuing and discussing and which methods are appropriate for pursuing this information.

Drug Users

In contrast to the girls' norm group, the drug users, "druggers," those who actually engaged in smoking, taking drugs, and drinking alcohol, were thought to be potentially the most important source of answers to their deep questions, based on their presumed experience with the drugs and knowing their impact firsthand. However, the cost of disclosing their information needs with this group and particularly asking questions were substantial. First, as mentioned previously, the girls were well aware that drug use changed the personality, particularly toward the more aggressive and antisocial behaviors; therefore, offending druggers could carry both psychological/social and physical risks. At a physical level, there was a fear of personal harm, for example violence:

> "I'm not really going to go out and ask anyone because you don't know what they are like."

And later in the interview:

> "I'm too scared to ask, afraid of what is going to happen, what they are going to do."

At the less physical level, the girls expressed status concerns:

> "They'll think I'm a dork."
> "It isn't cool to ask questions."

There was also a perception by the girls that if they offend those taking drugs, they would fear more social ostracism and physical abuse because those using drugs would think they were going to report them to various authorities—"dob them in"—or talk because of the erratic behaviors the girls observed in drug taking. It is quite obvious in some of these schools the power relationships affected the information seeking. For example, if the druggers were part of the "in group," the risk of offending them became even greater, with fear of physical repercussions. Information need and information seeking to satisfy that need are potentially dangerous things:

> "They make life so miserable for you that you have to leave the school."
> "They might hit me, or cause some kind bodily or property harm."

> They ask you "why do you want to know? Are you dobbing on use?" You ask some questions and they like kind of think that you are going to go dob on them or something. . . . I suppose they feel guilty or something, then they kind of think that you are going to dob on them . . . people get so upset . . . I've got one friend who has left, has left already because everyone turned against her. I've got two friends this year who are leaving because everyone's turned against them just because they did one thing and someone else didn't agree or they offended one of the cooler people of the grade and everyone else turned against her so they just leave.

The drug users group was clearly perceived to have potentially relevant stories—the specific details of their experiences and stories, given in the narrative below, provides a look at the vicarious experience of taking drugs:

> We can know a lot about drugs by hearing the intimate stories of their lives—what got them on to drugs, what it was like, what happens to their minds and bodies and how they fit into society. When you hear that, it's like you almost can feel it is happening to you, and can know it through their experience. It makes it like a real thing for you.

Teachers and Parents

If the girls' own peer groups were problematic in information disclosure about drugs, the sharing of their deep questions was even more risky where parents and teachers were concerned. As mentioned earlier, people with experience were perceived to be sources of more credible information. Teachers were perceived to have no experience, especially with illicit drugs, and this was compounded by a perception that they could not be trusted if the girls disclosed information, including confidential information, to them. They perceived that teachers talked a lot, and they felt that teachers "spilled" on them if they went to confide in them, and therefore were not to be trusted:

> "Oh yes, it's private and confidential, but like the whole staff room will know about it before lunchtime. Like they think that we're stupid, oh yes, it's private and confidential, but the whole, they'll all know before the day's out."
>
> "Mr. X says he's never takes drugs or smoked and it just makes him seem like even stupider to us. . . . oh, not stupid but like, why is he teaching it if he's never been in the situation? . . . The boys would listen to someone who has been in a bad situation."

The girls were also reluctant to disclose an information need to an adult because they believed that in discussing personal situations and problems, they are perceived to only have the information need because they are having a problem centered firmly on taking drugs.

> "You can't ask the teachers. There's nowhere to get information, and if you asked one of the teachers they think 'Oh my God, she's a drugger.'"
>
> "I'd never ask a teacher or a librarian for information. Like, how stupid is that! You know they are going to straight away think that I'm doing drugs, because they think that is the only reason I would want to know about them."

For the girls, this was even more of an apprehension where parents were concerned. Almost universally they saw that sharing information would be perceived by the parents as a drug problem—if not their own problem, then that of one of their friends:

> "They'll think I am a druggie and they'll 'kill' me, they will ground me for years. They would send me to another school."

Some of the girls had experience with parents getting upset when they raised questions about drugs:

> "They would get so angry, straight away believing I'm on to drugs, and wouldn't believe me if I tried to explain that I just wanted to know more."

The girls didn't perceive that answers to their deep questions would automatically come from their parents without prompting, or as one girl described: "further interrogation." The likelihood of opportunities for discussion that would provide an environment for deep questions did not seem to happen. The girls believed that such information was believed by their parents to be dangerous to know, and if any attempt were made to discuss some of these deep questions, the discussion often led to a focus on providing regulatory frameworks for girls' behaviors:

> "Whenever I used to try and discuss these things, even if we are all watching TV and the topic comes up, inevitably I get the 'don't do it' lecture."

The girls appear to perceive their parents as information sources who, without the experience with drugs, were only able to provide the surface sanitized factual information, usually given with the ulterior motive to warn them off drugs and unlikely to actually provide the answers to their deep questions. In the few references to interpersonal sources, these tended to be older people: young adults or adults—uncles, girlfriends of their older brothers who they could talk to—who most often had direct experience with drugs and were perceived as trustworthy, someone who would respect their confidentiality and who they felt would give the information without perceiving there was an underlying problem.

The analysis of the interviews suggests that the girls did not ask about their information needs because they clearly saw the risks involved in asking their deep questions. In some contexts, as shown above, there was the perception that physical harm could result; there were risks also related to recriminations and restrictive punishments, as well as to identity conceptions and indeed misconceptions. Signs of weighing information seeking against potential consequences are clearly evident. Consistent with Chatman's (1996, 1999) analysis, the girls might have gained from seeking and using the information they needed, but after weighing the potential consequences, they chose not to take these risks. They acknowledged that they knew where they might go to get these answers, but there were barriers to and costs involved in getting them contributed to their perception that the negative consequences of attempting to get the information outweighed the benefits they would receive from it. On the basis of this analysis, there is some evidence to suggest that the girls perceived themselves as "devoid of any sources that might help them" (Chatman, 1996, p. 197).

What is also clear from this analysis is that to have an information need about drugs is not to have a cover for a drug problem. The girls in these studies perceive that adults think they are covering a drug problem if they were to express any sort of deep question about drug information needs. The girls, however, made references to wanting to help people close to them, such as friends and family members whom they perceived were in drug-related situations, or to guide them in their own life decisions:

> "I know my brother is on heroin, so I really do want to know."
> "This is something I will be thinking about in the near future—you know, getting married and having kids."

The analysis did not provide any strong evidence of secrecy and/or deception as self-protective behaviors. Chatman (1996, p. 199) defines secrecy as the "deliberate attempt not to inform others about one's true state of affairs"; the deliberate withholding of information. Although it was clear that the girls made decisions not to seek information and that they realized the risks and consequences of seeking information about their deep questions, there was only one reported instance that centered on deception. In this particular instance, a girl went to the school library with her mother. While she was there, she looked for information in books on drugs. Her mother asked her what she was doing, and the girl said she was actually looking for history information. Her mother said "stupid goose."

SUMMARY AND DISCUSSION

Transition to high school marks a critical time in the development of adolescents' concerns about drugs. It is a time when adolescents more readily hear other students talk about drugs and they are able to observe the impact of students' experimenting with drugs, including behavioral, cognitive, and affective changes. Although it is evident that the adolescents brought to this new environment some clearly established and developed ideas and attitudes about drugs, this preexisting knowledge was insufficient to answer their deep questions, answers that would help them make sense of what was going on around them, to make sense of drugs and high school life, and even more important, to be able to help their friends who had entered or were planning to enter the drug culture. These deep questions, which they seemed able to formulate quite readily, concerned: motives—why their friends and peers take drugs; the drug experience—understanding what it was actually like to take drugs; the processes and effects of taking drugs—what drugs specifically do to the body and how this actually happens; addiction—why people can't stop taking drugs; the drugs and drug culture—the processes and mechanisms used by people in obtaining drugs; the social aspects of drugs—the broader historical, legal, and economic aspects of drug culture outside the girls' immediate experience; and tactics—particularly how to help their friends.

The interplay of several factors, particularly notions of insiders and outsiders, judgments about risks, costs and benefits, and social norms, appears to have created an information world rich in potential sources, but in reality for them a world that is devoid of sources of information that can help them in relation to their needs about drugs.

The girls identified themselves as belonging to a social group of friends who were like them—they did not smoke, drink, or take drugs—and they perceived that it was not appropriate to raise drug-related issues or ask important questions of their friends in this norm group, despite their strong desire to ask some of these deep questions. This was because of the risk of being perceived differently by their group and thereby possibly being excluded from it, as well as perceiving that the group conversation rules did not foster this. Their circle of friends was also considered not to possess the information they needed to answer their deep questions, in that they did not appear to have firsthand knowledge derived from real experiences with drugs from which to provide satisfactory answers.

Consequently, the girls did not share their information needs, expressed as deep questions with their norm group. They perceived that there is only one group—the drug users—who has the stories and experiences that would really help, yet that group was largely inaccessible to them because of the risks involved and the cost of disclosing their information needs with this group. The fear of offending the group, personal harm and abuse, social ostracism, being labeled as "dobbers" made information seeking from this group potentially dangerous, and they chose the path cogently expressed in Mooers Law: "An information source or system will tend not to be used whenever it is more painful and troublesome for the user to have the information than it is not to have it."

This analysis shows that the sharing of their deep questions was even more risky where parents and teachers were concerned. Teachers were perceived to have neither the experience with drugs, nor could they be trusted to provide confidentiality if the girls were to ask their deep questions. As with their parents, they perceived that asking such questions would be misconstrued as being derived from their own drug problem or that of their close friends. The girls also saw that in disclosing their information needs to parents, they would be subject to regulatory and/or restrictive behaviors, sometimes harshly. The few examples of sources actually utilized by the girls were people with experience, and people whom they felt they could talk to confidentially and with trust.

Is this an information-poor world for these adolescents and their drug concerns? Adolescents seem to be devoid of sources that can help them. They were unwilling to share information about their information needs. There was no evidence in the interviews that they wanted the information to deal with using drugs themselves; they primarily sought this information to build their own understanding of perplexing questions arising because of the context they were in, and because of a desire to help their friends. The girls are in situations where information about drugs is not discussed freely. The parents are the ones who have the means to help them get these stories and experiences either from drug users or other adults, but the girls do not perceive the parents as thinking that they should actually have this information as it is presented. Because of the interplay of group dynamics and relationships to significant others, such as parents and teachers, judgments about risks, costs and benefits, and social norms, for these girls, it appears to be an information-poor world that has many characteristics in common with Chatman's propositions. The girls shielded themselves from needed resources, and the importance of their needs took second place to the circumstances they found themselves in.

Although further targeted research is needed that focuses on the issues raised here to confirm these findings, this analysis suggests some important implications. Information provision needs to be based on identifying information needs that go beyond the surface questions and for providing a trusting and safe environment for young people to seek and access the answers to these deep questions without fear or threat and without assumptions made as to why the information is needed. In the construction of understanding, adolescents do not always require the collection of facts typically provided for them through school libraries and other information services and deemed suitable, sufficient, and safe to meet their information needs. Although specific facts play an important role in constructing knowledge, this information does not have universal and constant applicability. Adolescents want more than facts when accessing information about drugs. They are looking for contextualized and personal information that is also viewed by them as credible, rather than lists of salient facts presented in a bland and objective way that answer their probing, inquiring questions that enable them to build an intimate and shareable knowledge about drugs. Too often presenting the facts conveys the idea that simply making the information available, sometimes with graphic portrayal of serious consequences of drug abuse, will convert the existing drug problems of young people into nonproblems. This conveys the idea that without any special effort on behalf of these young people, truth and positive personal and social action will prevail. Underpinning this is the assumption that the very existence of information presses it toward effective use and change. The study shows that no matter how compelling or authoritative information might be in the minds of others, no matter how useful someone else might think the information is, these qualities do not guarantee its receptivity and utilization by particular groups of people.

One of the essential challenges is the provision of access to information that centers on the real experiences of real people in ways that go beyond the provision of sanitized, even censored details. Parents and teachers do not provide the opportunity for young people to get information through access to real life experience; drug users are one identified group who does have such information through experience, and parents and teachers, possibly believing that such access would contribute to increased uptake of drugs, are unlikely to endorse such a strategy. This raises complex moral and social dilemmas. Social norms and the social landscape help define and shape information seeking. If society decides such information is to be provided, then how to present the stories and experiences of real people and in real time is the key challenge. The answer to access does not necessarily lie in school and public libraries being the focal point. Rather the challenge is for providers to think beyond these traditional and underutilized access points and to explore new opportunities. The World Wide Web as a virtual space to offer anonymous, confidential, safe, real time, and personalized information services that address the deep questions of adolescents in relation to drug concerns is beginning to be explored. At a broader level there is also an information challenge to parenting and teaching—establishing a safe, trusting, and open environment where children and adolescents grow up, able to ask the deep questions that perplex them, able to discuss them without blame or suspicion.

REFERENCES

Buysse, A. (1996). "Adolescents, young adults and AIDS: A study of actual knowledge vs. perceived need for additional information." *Journal of Youth and Adolescence* 25, no. 2: 259–271.

Chatman, E. (1996). "The impoverished life-world of outsiders." *Journal of the American Society for Information Science* 47, no. 3: 193–206.

Dervin, B. (1983). "An overview of sense-making research: Concepts, methods and results to date." Paper presented at the International Communication Association annual general meeting, Dallas.

Dervin, B. (1989). "Users as research inventions: How research categories perpetuate inequities." *Journal of Communication* 39, no. 3: 216–232.

Dervin, B. (1992). "From the mind's eye of the user: The sense-making qualitative-quantitative methodology." In J. Glazier and R. Powell, eds., *Qualitative research in information management* (pp. 61–84). Englewood, Colo.: Libraries Unlimited.

Dervin, B., Harlock, S., Atwood, R., and Garzona, C. (1986). "The human side of information: An exploration in a health communication context." *Communication Yearbook* 4: 591–608.

Digiovanna, L. (1994). "The importance of recreational reading and its impact on children's motivation, attitude toward reading, as well as reading achievement." Unpublished master's thesis, Grand Valley State University.

Edwards, S., and Poston-Anderson, B. (1993). "The Dinkum Oil: Information needs and life concerns of Australian adolescent girls." *Youth Studies Australia* 12, no. 2: 34–37.

Edwards, S., and Poston-Anderson, B. (1996). "Information, future time perspectives, and young adolescent girls: Concerns about education and jobs. *LISR* 18: 207–223.

Fidel: R., Davies, R.K., Douglass, M.H., Holder, J. K., Hopkins, C. J., Kushner, E. J., Miyagishima, B. K., and Toney, C. D. (1999). "A visit to the information mall: Web searching behavior of high school students." *Journal of the American Society for Information Science* 50, no. 1: 24–37.

Glaser, B., and Strauss, A. (1967). *The discovery of grounded theory: Strategies for qualitative research.* Chicago: Aldine.

Gordon, C. (2000). "Putting the learner in charge: Are information literacy skills enough?" *Scan* 19, no. 1: 32–39.

Grant, V. (1998). "Information skills and their impact on learning: A New Zealand study." *Scan* 17, no. 2: 50–54.

Halliwell, C. (1995). "Relationships between free voluntary reading and eighth grade Missouri writing assessment." Unpublished master's thesis, Central Missouri State University.

Hawkes, J. (1997). "Views from the top: The information skills process and senior students." *Scan* 16, no. 3: 47–52.

Hirsh, S. (1999). "Children's relevance criteria and information seeking on electronic resources." *Journal of the American Society for Information Science* 50, no. 14: 1265–1283.

Jones, E. (1996). "The value of research assignments." *Scan* 15, no. 3: 45–48.

Julien, H. (1999). "Barriers to adolescents' information seeking for career decision making." *Journal of the American Society for Information Science* 50, no. 1: 38–48.

Krashen, S. (1993). *The power of reading: Insights from the research*. Englewood, Colo.: Libraries Unlimited.

Kuhlthau, C. C. (1991). "Inside the search process: Information seeking from the user's perspective." *Journal of the American Society of Information Science* 42, no. 5: 361–371.

Kuhlthau, C. C. (1993). *Seeking meaning: A process approach to library and information services*. Norwood, N.J.: Ablex.

Kuhlthau, C. C. (1994). *Teaching the library research process*. Lanham, Md.: Scarecrow Press.

Kuhlthau, C. C. (1999). "Student learning in the library: What library power librarians say." *School Libraries World Wide* 5, no. 2: 80–96.

Lance, K., Rodney, M., and Hamilton-Pennell, C. (2000). *How school librarians help kids achieve standards.* San Jose, Calif.: Hi Willow Research.

Large, A., Beheshti, J., and Moukdad, H. (1999). "Information seeking on the Web: Navigational skills of grade six primary school students." In *Proceedings of the 62nd ASIS annual meeting. Washington, D.C., October 31–November 4, 1999* (pp. 84–97). Medford, N.J.: Information Today.

Lewis, E. (1993). "Science instruction and information literacy: Information is power." *Scan* 18, no. 1: 49–53.

Lipscomb, L. (1993). "Recreational reading and its effects on the reading achievement of first through third graders." Unpublished doctoral dissertation, University of Texas at Austin.

Makkai, T. and McAllister, I. (1990). "Knowledge and information about drugs in Australia." *Journal of Drug Education* 20: 337–352.

Maxwell, E. (2000). "Integrating information skills and exposition texts into the year 7 science program." *Scan* 19, no. 2: 27–31.

Mayton, D., Nagel, E., and Parker, R. (1990). "The perceived effects of drug messages on use patterns in adolescents." *Journal of Drug Education* 20, no. 4: 305–318.

McNicholas, C., and Todd, R. (1996). "New kids on the box: Is it worth the investment?" *Scan* 15, no. 4: 40–42.

McQuillan, J. (1997). "Access to print and formal instruction in reading acquisition." Ph.D. diss., University of Southern California.

Mirzaee, E., Kingery, P., and Puitt, B. (1991). "Sources of drug information among adolescent students." *Journal of Drug Education* 21: 95–106.

Moore, P. (1996). "Information literacy: The importance of questions." *Scan* 15, no. 1: 43–46.

Moore, P., and Poulopoulos, N. (1999). "Butterflies and elephants in the classroom: Teachers researching information literacy." *Scan* 18, no. 4: 49–53.

Newell-Withrow, C. (1989). "Identifying health-seeking behaviors: A study of adolescents." *Adolescence* 21: 641–658.

Poston-Anderson, B., and Edwards, S. (1993). "The role of information in helping adolescent girls with their life concerns." *School Library Media Quarterly* 22, no. 1: 1–6.

Rich, W. (1999). "Enhancing the participation and achievement of girls in school science." *Scan* 18, no. 2: 46–50.

Schacter, J., Chung, G., and Dorr, A. (1998). "Children's Internet searching on complex problems: performance and process analysis." *Journal of the American Society for Information Science* 49: 840–849.

Todd, R. (1991a). "Utilization of heroin information by adolescent girls in Australia: A cognitive analysis." *Journal of the American Society for Information Science* 50, no 1: 10–23.

Todd, R. (1999b). "Back to our beginnings: Information utilization, Bertram Brookes and the fundamental equation of information science." *Information Processing and Management* 35: 851–870.

Todd, R. (1999c). "Adolescents and drugs: Responsive information services in schools and libraries." *Orana* 35, no. 3: 32–42.

Todd, R. J. (1995). "Integrated information skills instruction: Does it make a difference?" *School Library Media Quarterly* 23, no. 2: 133–139.

Todd, R. J., Lamb, L., and McNicholas, C. (1993). "Information skills and learning: Some research findings." *Access* 7, no. 1: 14–16.

Vakkari, P. (1997). "Information seeking in context: A challenging meta-theory" In P. Vakkari, R. Savolainen, and B. Dervin, eds., *Information seeking in context. Proceedings of an international conference on research in information needs, seeking and use in different contexts*. August 14–16, 1996, Tampere, Finland. London: Taylor Graham.

Wallace, R., and Kuperman, J. (1997). "On-line search in the science classroom. Benefits and possibilities." Paper presented at AERA, Chicago.

FOURTEEN

Future Direction and Bibliography

Mary K. Chelton

FUTURE ISSUES

This last chapter covers pressing problems for researchers of youth information-seeking behavior, beyond those already raised by the other chapters' authors. These questions relate both to the chapters included here as well as to authors included in the selected bibliography. By providing a roadmap to paths that have been taken, directions that have been followed, and findings that have been discovered, this bibliography should be viewed as a work in progress, a fluid, rather than static, representation of the research in this area.

INFORMATION SYSTEM DESIGN

Although there has been research into how children and young adults use existing systems, and in particular, Delia Neuman's observations about design fallacies for both young people and novice users, there has been little work on newer systems, either studies of their success in simplifying searching, increasing visual cues, and so forth, or how new features have been incorporated into them, with the exception of Sandlian's article. There is still a tendency to define "information literacy" as the ability to find, use, evaluate, synthesize, and present information on existing, admittedly inadequate, systems.

INTERNET VERSUS OTHER RESOURCES

Although the Web has become an important information resource, it has supplanted the use of older, more traditional information sources that still remain viable. A problem facing us now is that young people do not learn how to use, nor do they value information resources other than the Internet. Furthermore, many of our youth do not know how to evaluate the information they retrieve on the Web. Many believe that as long as it is published on the Web, it is "true." This is a serious problem, especially given research that suggests that the Internet is a major resource for adolescents' sexual health information needs.

Even within Internet resources, youthful use of instant messaging (IM), e-mail, chat rooms, and blogs needs more attention in terms of personal information use. IM has replaced phones among many adolescents for keeping in touch with friends, but it also offers an opportunity for dispensing information to youth.

There is also increasing research suggesting that literacy among boys is enhanced by access to and use of computers. The relationships between "literacy" as understood in its traditional sense, and "information literacy" as enumerated in *Information Power*, are worthy of examination, especially in relation to gender.

SOCIAL RESPONSIBILITY AND INFORMATION USE

Also related to the Web, many people—adults as well as youth—do not understand copyright restrictions on Web materials. In fact, some research has found that Web users have no idea how to locate the copyright holder of Web materials, nor do they have an incentive to try when plagiarism is made easy through technology. The downloading of music by youth has blurred the entire notion of "intellectual property." Whether the recording industry's efforts to halt this practice succeed has implications for other contexts in which the same young people function.

PORNOGRAPHY AND ILLEGAL CONTENT

While there has been a huge policy and legal debate over unrestricted Internet access by youth, Sandvig's study is the only one that has attempted to observe how children behave in an unrestricted context. Many school librarians report anecdotally that Internet filters impede legitimate school-based information seeking, but few scholars within the library and information science (LIS) field have examined this issue from the perspective of how children and youth actually seek information in a filtered Internet environment.

The category of "child" or "youth" is a social construction. What are the boundaries of "youth"? We have discussed developmental stages, but there are legal and regulatory issues involved here as well. In the United States, youth are believed to need "protection" from potentially harmful information materials. Attempts have been made to regulate access to such harmful materials; however, the Web poses new challenges to these protections. One of the most controversial issues at this time, given First Amendment rights, concerns the right of adults to prohibit access to any type of information that youth may seek.

PERSONAL INFORMATION SEEKING

Although it is harder than researching the captive audience in schools, there needs to be much more attention to personal information seeking among different kinds of young people and at different developmental levels. For example, what difference does it make, if any, for young people who have had access to electronic toys and games their entire childhood and adolescence when they attempt to search for information, as opposed to those who have not had such access? The sexual health education field has studied youth information seeking for years with little collaboration with LIS researchers.

SELECTED BIBLIOGRAPHY

Akin, L., "Information Overload and Children: A Survey of Texas Elementary School Students." *School Library Media Research* 1 (1998), available at www.ala.org/aasl/SLMQ/overload.html (accessed December 7, 2003).

American Association of School Librarians and Association for Educational Communications and Technology. *Information Power: Building Partnerships for Learning*. Chicago: American Library Association, 1998.

Barclay, D. A. *Teaching Electronic Information Literacy: A How-to-Do-It Manual*. New York: Neal-Schuman, 1995.

Bilal, D. "Children Design Their Interfaces for Web Search Engines: A Participatory Approach." *Proceedings of the 30th Annual Conference of the Canadian Society for Information Science, 30 May–1 June 2002*. Toronto: Faculty of Information Studies, University of Toronto, 2002, pp. 204–214.

Bilal, D. "Children's Use of the Yahooligans! Web Search Engine II: Cognitive and Physical Behaviors on Research Tasks." *Journal of the American Society for Information Science* 52 (2001): 118–137.

Bilal, D. "Children's Use of the Yahooligans! Web Search Engine I: Cognitive, Physical and Affective Behaviors on Fact-Based Search Tasks." *Journal of the American Society for Information Science* 51 (2000): 646–665.

Bilal, D. "Web Search Engines for Children: A Comparative Study and Performance Evaluation of Yahooligans!, Ask Jeeves for Kids, and

Super Snooper." *ASIS '99: Proceedings of the 62nd ASIS Annual Meeting*. Medford, N.J.: Information Today, 1999, pp. 70–83.

Borgman, C. L., Hirsh, S. G., and Walter, V. A. "Children's Searching Behavior on Browsing and Keyword Online Catalogs: The Science Library Catalog Project." *Journal of the American Society for Information Science* 46, no. 9 (1995): 663–684.

Booth, D. *Even Hockey Players Read: Boys, Literacy and Learning*. Markham, Ont.: Pembroke, 2002.

Borzekowsi, D., and Rickert, V. "Adolescent Cybersurfing for Health Information." *Archives of Pediatric and Adolescent Medicine* 155 (July 2001): 813–817.

Bowler, L., Large, A., and Rejskind, G. "Primary School Students, Information Literacy and the Web." *Education for Information* 19, no. 3 (2001): 201–223.

Broch, E. "Children's Search Engines from an Information Search Process Perspective." *School Library Media Research* 3 (2000), available at www.ala.org/Content/NavigationMenu/AASL/Publications_and_Journals/School_eLibrary_Media_Research/Contents1/Volume_3_(2000)/Volume_3_(2000).htm (accessed December 7, 2003).

Burdick, T. A. "Success and Diversity in Information Seeking: Gender and the Information Search Styles Model." *School Library Media Quarterly* 25 no. 1 (Fall 1996): 19–26.

Busey, P., and Doerr, T. Kids' Catalog: "An Information Retrieval System for Children." *Youth Services in Libraries* (Fall 1993): 77–84.

CMLEA. *From Library Skills to Information Literacy: A Handbook for the 21st Century*. Castle Rock, Colo.: Hi Willow, 1994.

Cooper, L. Z. "A Case Study of Information-Seeking Behavior in 7-Year-Old Children in a Semistructured Situation." *JASIST* 53, no. 11: 904–922.

DeBell, M., *Computer and Internet Use by Children and Adolescents in 2001*. Washington, D.C.: National Center for Educational Statistics, 2003.

Dresang, E. T. "More Research Needed: Informal Information-Seeking Behavior of Youth on the Internet." *Journal of the American Society for Information Science* 50 (1999): 1123–1124.

Dresang, E. T., Gross, M., and Holt, L. E. "Project CATE: Using Outcome Measures to Assess School-Age Children's Use of Technology in Urban Public Libraries, A Collaborative Research Process," *Library & Information Science Research* 25 (2003): 19–42.

Druin, A., Bederson, B., Boltman, A., Miura, A., Knotts-Callahan, D., and Platt, M. "Children as Our Technology Design Partners." In *The Design of Children's Technology*, edited by Allison Druin (pp. 51–72). San Francisco: Morgan Kaufmann, 1999.

Eaton, G. "Lost in the Library: Are Spatial Skills Important in Shelf Searches?" *Journal of Youth Services in Libraries* 5, no. 1 (1991): 77–86.

Edmonds, L., Moore, P., and Balcom, K. M. "Effectiveness of an Online Catalog." *School Library Journal* 36, no. 10 (October 1990): 28–32

Eisenberg, M. B., and Berkowitz, R. E. *Information Problem-Solving: The Big Six Skills Approach to Library and Information Skills Instruction*. Norwood, N.J.: Ablex, 1966.

Fasick, A. M. "What Research Tells Us About Children's Use of Information Media." *Canadian Library Journal* 49, no. 1 (February 1992): 51–54.

Fidel, R., Davies, R. K., Douglass, M. H., Holder, J. K., Hopkins, C. J., Kushner, E. J., Miyagishima, B. K., and Toney, C. D. "Visit to the Information Mall: Web Searching Behavior of High School Students." *Journal of the American Society for Information Science* 50 (1999): 24–37.

Fitzgerald, M. A. "Evaluating Information: An Information Literacy Challenge." *School Library Media Research* 2 (1999), available at www.ala.org/Content/NavigationMenu/AASL/Publications_and_Journals/School_eLibrary_Media_Research/Contents1/Volume_2_(1999)/vol2_fitzgerald.htm (accessed December 13, 2003).

Gordon, C. A. "Effects of Concept Mapping on the Searching Behavior of Tenth-Grade Students." *School Library Media Research* 3 (2000), available at www.ala.org/Content/NavigationMenu/AASL/Publications_and_Journals/School_Library_Media_Research/Contents1/Volume_3_(2000)/mapping.htm (accessed December 10, 2003).

Gross, M. "Imposed Information-Seeking in Public Libraries and School Library Media Centers: A Common Behavior?" *Information Research* 6 Vol. 6, No. 2 (January 2001), available at http://informationr.net/ir/6-2/paper100.html (accessed December 10, 2003).

Gross, M. "Imposed Query and Information Services for Children." *Journal of Youth Services in Libraries* (Winter 2000): 10–17.

Gross, M. "Imposed Queries in the School Library Media Center: A Descriptive Study." *Library and Information Science Research* 21 (1999): 501–521.

Gross, M. "Imposed Query." *RQ* 35, no 1 (1995): 236–243.

Gross, M. "Pilot Study on the Prevalence of Imposed Queries in a School Library Media Center." *School Library Media Quarterly* (1997): 157–165

Hanna, L., Risden, K., Czerwinski, M., and Alexander, K. J. "The Role of Usability Research in Designing Children's Computer Products." In *The Design of Children's Technology*, edited by Allison Druin (pp. 3–25). San Francisco: Morgan Kaufmann, 1999.

Hirsch, S. "The Effect of Domain Knowledge on Elementary School Children's Search Behavior on an Information Retrieval System: the Science Library Catalog." *CHI '95*: 55–56.

Hirsch, S. "Children's Relevance Criteria and Information Seeking on Electronic Resources." *Journal of the American Society for Information Science* 50 (1999): 1265–1283.

Hirsch, S. "How Do Children Find Information on Different Types of Tasks? Children's Use of the Science Library Catalog." *Library Trends* 45 (Spring 1997): 725–745.

Hirsh, S. G., and Borgman, C. L. "Comparing Children's Use of Browsing and Keyword Searching on the Science Library Catalog." *International Conference on Research and Development in Information Retrieval, ACM Special Interest Group on Information Retrieval* (SIGIR), Seattle, July 1995.

Jacobson, F. F. "Information Retrieval Systems and Youth: A Review of Recent Literature." *Journal of Youth Services in Libraries* 5, no. 1 (1991): 109–113.

Jacobson, F. F., and E, Ignacio, N. "Teaching Reflection: Information Seeking and Evaluation in a Digital Library Environment." *Library Trends* 45 (1997): 771–802.

Julien, H. "Adolescent Career Decision Making and the Potential Role of the Public Library." *Public Libraries* (November/December 1998): 376–381.

Julien, H. "Adolescents' Information Seeking for Career Decision Making." *Journal of the American Society for Information Science* 50 (1999): 38–48.

Kafai, Y., and Bates, M. J. "Internet Web-Searching Instruction in the Elementary Classroom: Building a Foundation for Information Literacy." *School Library Media Quarterly* 25 no. 2 (1997): 103–111.

Kuhlthau, C. C. "Inside the Search Process: Information Seeking from the User's Perspective." *Journal of the American Society for Information Science* 42 (1991): 361–371.

Kuhlthau, C. C. "Student Learning in the Library: What Library Power Librarians Say." *School Libraries Worldwide* 5 (1999): 80–96.

Kuhlthau, C. C. *Seeking Meaning: A Process Approach to Library and Information Services*. Norwood, N.J.: Ablex, 1993.

Kuhlthau, C. C. *Teaching the Library Research Process*. 2nd ed. Lanham, Md.: Scarecrow Press, 1994.

Kuhlthau, C. C. "Learning in Digital Libraries: An Information Search Process Approach." *Library Trends* 45, no. 4 (1997): 708–724.

Large, A., and Beheshti, J. "The Web as a Classroom Resource: Reactions from the Users." *Journal of the American Society for Information Science* 51, no. 12 (2000): 1069–1080.

Large, A., Beheshti, J., and Breuleux, A. "Information Seeking in a Multimedia Environment by Primary School Students." *Library and Information Science Research* 20 (1998): 342–376.

Large, A., Beheshti, J., and Breuleux, A., and Renaud. , A. "A Comparison of Information Retrieval from Print and CD-ROM Versions of an Encyclopedia by Elementary School Children." *Information Processing and Management* 30, no. 4 (1994): 499–512.

Large, A., Beheshti, J., and Cole, C. "Information Architecture for the Web: The IA Matrix Approach to Designing Children's Portals." *Journal of the American Society for Information Science* 53, no. 10 (August 2002): 831–8.

Large, A., Beheshti, J. and Rahman, T. "Design Criteria for Children's Web Portals: The Users Speak Out." *Journal of the American Society for Information Science* 53, no. 2 (2002): 79–94.

Large, A., Beheshti, J., and Rahman, T. "Gender Differences in Collaborative Web Searching Behavior: An Elementary School Study." *Information Processing and Management* 38, no. 3 (2002): 427–443.

Latrobe, K., and Havener, W. M. "Information-Seeking Behavior of High School Honors Students: An Exploratory Study." *Journal of Youth Services in Libraries* 10 no. 2 (1997): 188–200.

Lazonder, A W., Biemans, J. A., and Wopereis, I. G. J. H. "Differences Between Novice and Experienced Users in Searching Information on the World Wide Web." *Journal of the American Society for Information Science* 51, no. 6 (2000): 576–581.

Leong, S. C., and Hawamdeh, S. "Gender and Learning Attitudes in Using Web-Based Science Lessons." *Information Research* 5 (1999). Available from: informationr.net/ir/5-1/paper66.html (accessed on December 7, 2003).

Loertscher, D. V., and Wools, B. *Information Literacy, A Review of the Research: A Guide for Practitioners and Researchers*. San Jose, Calif. Hi Willow Research and Publishing, 2002.

Marchionini, G. "Information Seeking Strategies of Novices Using a Full-Text Electronic Encyclopedia." *Journal of the American Society for Information Science* 40, no. 1 (1989): 54–66.

Martin, S. "Internet Use in the Classroom." *Social Science Computer Review* 18, no. 4 (1998): 411–418.

Miller, Matthew. "Instant Messaging as a Therapy Tool." *Newsday. Section D: Health and Discovery* (May 14, 2002): D9.

Moore, P. A., and St. George, A. "Children as Information Seekers: The Cognitive Demands of Books and Library Systems." *School Library Media Quarterly* (Spring 1991): 161–168

Nahl, D. "Learning the Internet and the Structure of Information Behavior." *Journal of the American Society for Information Science* 49 (1998): 1017–1023.

Nahl, D., and Harada, V. H. "Composing Boolean Search Statements: Self-confidence, Concept Analysis, Search Logic, and Errors." *School Library Media Quarterly* 24 no. 4 (1996): 199–207.

Neuman, D. "Designing Databases as Tools for Higher-level Learning: Insights from Instructional Systems Design." *Educational Technology Research and Development* 41, no. 4 (1993): 25–46.

Neuman, D. "High School Students' Use of Databases: Results of a National Delphi Study." *Journal of the American Society for Information Science* 46 (1995): 284–298.

Neuman, D. Learning and the Digital Library. *Library Trends* 45, no. 4 (1997): 687–707.

Oliver, R., and Oliver, H. "Using Context to Promote Learning from Information-Seeking Tasks." *Journal of the American Society for Information Science* 48, no. 6 (June 1997): 519–526.

Perzylo, L., and Oliver, R. "An Investigation of Children's Use of a Multimedia CD-ROM Product for Information Retrieval." *Microcomputers for Information Management* 9 (1992): 225–239.

Pitts, J. M. "Mental Models of Information: The 1993–94 AASL/Highsmith Research Study Award." Edited by Joy H. McGregor and Barbara K. Stripling. *School Library Media Quarterly* (1995): 177–184.

Rosenberg, J. B., and Borgman, C. L. "Extending the Dewey Decimal Classification via Keyword Clustering: The Science Library Catalog Project." Proceedings of the 54th American Society for Information Science Annual Meeting, 29. October 26–29, 1992, Pittsburgh. Medford, NJ: Learned Information, 171–184.

San Jose Mercury News/Kaiser Family Foundation. *Growing Up Wired: Youth and the Internet in the Silicon Valley.* May 18, 2003, available at www.kff.org/content/2003/20030518a/ (accessed July 31, 2003).

Sandlian, P. "Rethinking the Rules." *School Library Journal* (July 1995): 22–25.

Sandvig, C. "Unexpected Outcomes in Digital Divide Policy: What Children Really Do in the Public Library." In B. M. Compaine and S. Greenstein, eds., *Communications Policy in Transition: The Internet and Beyond* (pp. 265–293). Cambridge: MIT Press, 2001.

Schacter, J., Chung, C., Chung, K. W. K., and Dorr, A. "Children's Internet Searching on Complex Problems: Performance and Process Analysis." *Journal of the American Society for Information Science* 49 (1998): 840–849.

Schneider, B., and Stevenson, D. *Ambitious Generation: America's Teenagers, Motivated but Directionless*. New Haven, Conn.: Yale University Press, 1999.

Shenton, A. K. and Dixon, Pat. "Just What Do They *Want*? What Do They *Need*?: A Study of the Informational Needs of Children," *Children & Libraries*, Vol. 1, No. 2 (Summer/Fall, 2003): 36–42.

Small, R. V. "An Exploration of Motivational Strategies Used by Library

Media Specialists During Library and Information Skills Instruction," *School Library Media Research* 2 (1999) available at www.ala.org/Content/NavigationMenu/AASL/Publications_and_Journals/School_Library_Media_Research/Contents1/Volume_2_(1999)/vol2_small.htm (accessed December 10, 2003).

Smith, M. W., and Wilhelm, J. D. *"Reading Don't Fix No Chevys": Literacy in the Lives of Young Men*. Portsmouth, N.H.: Heineman, 2002.

Solomon, P. "Children's Information Retrieval Behavior: A Case Analysis of an OPAC." *Journal of the American Society for Information Science* 44 (1993): 245–264.

Stripling, B. K., ed. *Learning and Libraries in an Information Age: Principles and Practices*. Westport, Conn.: Libraries Unlimited, 1999.

Thornburgh, D. and Lin, H. S., eds., "Committee to Study Tools and Strategies for Protecting Kids from Pornography and Their Applicability to Other Inappropriate Internet Content," National Research Council. *Youth, Pornography, and the Internet: Can We Provide Sound Choices in a Safe Environment?* Washington, D.C.: National Academies Press, 2002.

Wallace, M. R., Jupperman, J., and Krajcik, J. "Science on the Web: Students Online in a Sixth-Grade Classroom." *Journal of the Learning Sciences* 9, no. 1 (2000): 75–104.

Walter, V. A., Borgman, C. L., and Hirsh, S. G. "The Science Library Catalog: A Springboard for Information Literacy." *School Library Media Quarterly* 24 (Winter 1996): 105–112.

Watson, J. S. "'If you don't have it, you can't find it': A Close Look at Students' Perceptions of Using Technology." *Journal of the American Society for Information Science* 49 (1998): 1024–1036.

Watson, J. S. "Students and the World Wide Web: Issues of Confidence." *Teacher Librarian* 29, no. 1 (October 2001): 15–19.

Wozny, L. A. "Online Bibliographic Searching and Student Use of Information: An Innovative Teaching Approach." *School Library Media Quarterly* (Fall 1982): 35–42.

About the Authors

Dania Bilal is associate professor in the School of Information Sciences at the University of Tennessee, Knoxville. Dr. Bilal's research interests center on children's use of Web search engines; in particular, how they understand and use the various features available to them in this new information environment. Dr. Bilal is also interested in ways to involve children in the design of Web search engines in order to make them more effective for this population.

Mary K. Chelton is professor in the Graduate School of Library and Information Studies, Queens College, City University of New York. She received her doctorate from the Graduate School of Communication, Information and Library Studies at Rutgers University. Her dissertation was titled "Adult-Adolescent Service Encounters: The Library Context." Chelton's primary research focus is on marginalized users and services in library contexts. In this regard, she is particularly interested in the information seeking of adolescents, adoption searchers, readers' advisory services for adults, and popular culture genres. In 1985, she received ALA's Grolier award for outstanding work with children and young adults.

Colleen Cool is associate professor in the Graduate School of Library and Information Studies, Queens College, City University of New York. She received her doctorate from the Graduate School of Communication, Information and Library Studies at Rutgers University. Her primary research area concerns the relationship between people of all ages and computers, particularly information-retrieval systems. The theoretical framework employed by Cool is one that treats computers as social actors and looks at the human-computer interaction process as one that can be understood from social interaction theory. This focus has guided both her dissertation research and publications thereafter.

Linda Cooper is assistant professor at the Pratt Institute School of Information and Library Science, in New York City, where she is the lead faculty member of the library media specialist program. Dr. Cooper's research and publications focus on information-seeking behavior in children and organization of information with a user focus.

Susan Edwards is an honorary research associate in the Department of Media Arts, Communication and Information at the University of Technology, Sydney, Australia. Her research focuses on information seeking and utilization, "everyday" information needs, the information behavior of adolescents, and the conceptualization and measurement of "information poverty."

Melissa Gross is assistant professor in the School of Information Studies at Florida State University, Tallahassee, Florida. Her general research interest is in the area of information-seeking behavior, with a particular focus on the interaction between children and adult information providers. Her model of the imposed query has received extensive attention in the scholarly literature.

Violet Harada is an associate professor at the University of Hawaii. Her specialties include information literacy, school library management, and multiethnic collection development. Her current research interests include intervention and assessment strategies in teaching information-searching processes, grades K–12; content analysis and curriculum uses of Asian American resources for children and youth; and professional development strategies and alternatives for adult learners.

Sandra Hirsh is an information research consultant in the Global Library and Information Services organization at Hewlett Packard Corp. Her primary research interests are in information seeking, information retrieval, and the use and evaluation of information by children and other user groups. Additional research areas center on the usability of library portal sites.

Carol Collier Kuhlthau is professor and coordinator, School Library Media Specialization, at the School of Communication, Information and Library Studies at Rutgers University, New Brunswick, N.J. Since 1981, her research has centered on understanding the information search process (ISP), which attempts to reveal the users' perspective of information seeking and use. Dr. Kuhlthau is internationally known for her work in this area and her scholarly work includes numerous articles and several books.

Heidi Julien is an assistant professor at the School of Library and Information Studies, University of Alberta, Canada. Her research interests include information behavior, information literacy, and information policy.

Andrew Large is a professor at the Graduate School of Library and Information Studies, McGill University, Montreal, Canada. His primary research areas are information retrieval, multimedia, and human-computer interaction. Professor Large has published numerous articles on youth information seeking on the World Wide Web.

Joy McGregor is a senior lecturer and discipline leader in teacher librarianship in the School of Information Studies at Charles Sturt University, Wagga Wagga, NSW, Australia. Her research interests include how students think as they use information, effective tools for implementing effective information, and how information use for personal interest is different from school use. Dr. McGregor was the 1998 recipient of the Mary Mason Lyon Award for Junior Faculty for excellence in scholarship, teaching, and service at Texas Woman's University and is a member of Phi Kappa Phi and Beta Phi Mu Honor Societies.

Diane Nahl is an associate professor and the LIS program chair in the Library and Information Science Program, Information and Computer Sciences Department, University of Hawaii at Manoa. Her specialties include information technology literacy and human system interaction. She is a frequent presenter at ASIST, and her current research interests are human-system interaction; information problem solving; information behavior; and affective and cognitive information processing.

Delia Neuman is an associate professor at the College of Information Studies at the University of Maryland, where she is also the coordinator of the school library media program. Her research interests include instructional systems design, qualitative research, learning in information-rich environments, and school library media programs. She has written numerous articles and book chapters and was the writer for "Information Power: Building Partnerships for Learning," the national standards for school library media programs developed by the American Association of School Librarians (AASL) and the Association for Educational Communications and Technology (AECT). She edited the "Current Research" Column of *School Library Media Quarterly* for four years and has served on various editorial boards. She is currently the chair of the editorial board of the *Journal of Education for Library and Information Science* and a member of the board of directors of the Association for Educational Communications and Technology. She has received AECT's Qualitative Research Award

(1993) and Best Journal Article Award (1995) and ALA's Carroll Preston Baber Research Award (1991). In 1995, she was a visiting scholar at the University of Technology, Sydney.

Denise Cantrell Streitenberger earned her doctorate degree from Texas Woman's University in 1997 and is currently a teacher-librarian at Clark Elementary in Issaquah, WA. She collaborates with teachers in a flexible schedule and teaches information literacy as well as a love of literature. She continues her investigation into how students use information from both print and non-print sources. Her research agenda includes: primary student's reading skills of nonprint text; students' use of information during self-directed inquiry; and expository writing with young children.

Ross Todd is associate professor and Director of the undergraduate major in information technology and informatics at the School of Communication, Information and Library Studies at Rutgers University, New Brunswick, N.J. He is also co-director of CISSL, Center for International Studies in School Libraries. His research focuses on the interaction between people and their information environments, with particular emphases on the study of adolescent information seeking and use; knowledge management; and professional education for librarians.

Jinx Stapleton Watson is an associate professor at the University of Tennessee's School of Information Sciences, part of the College of Communication and Information. Her research interests include children's literature and services and youth information-seeking behavior.